SALLY STUART'S GUIDE TO GETTING PUBLISHED

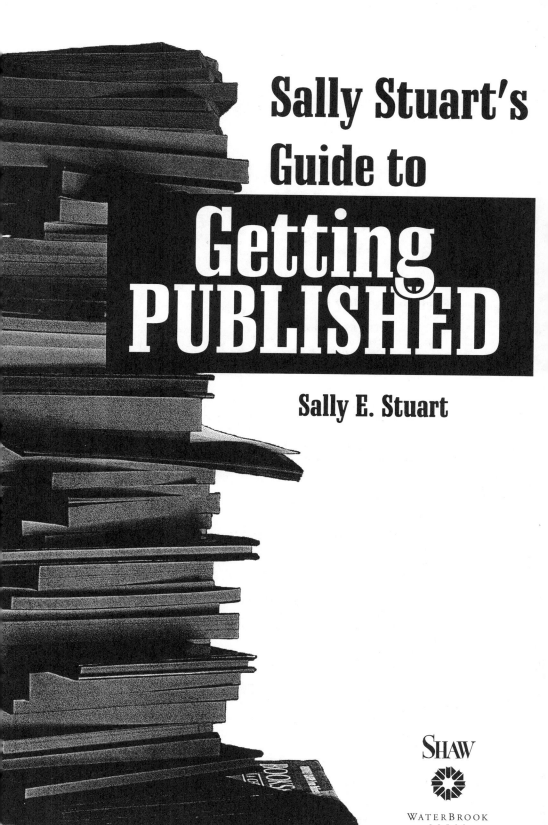

Sally Stuart's Guide to Getting PUBLISHED

Sally E. Stuart

SHAW

WATERBROOK PRESS

Sally Stuart's Guide to Getting Published
A SHAW BOOK
PUBLISHED BY WATERBROOK PRESS
2375 Telstar Drive, Suite 160
Colorado Springs, Colorado 80920
A division of Random House, Inc.

ISBN 0-87788-331-9

Cover and interior design by Thomas Leo

Library of Congress Cataloging-in-Publication Data

Stuart, Sally E.
Sally Stuart's guide to getting published / by Sally E. Stuart.
p. cm.
Includes bibliographical references and index.
ISBN 0-87788-331-9 (pbk.)
1. Authorship—Marketing. 2. Authors and publishers. I. Title. II. Title: Guide to getting published.
PN161.S78 1999
808'.02—dc21 99-34875
CIP

Printed in the United States of America
2003

10 9 8 7 6 5 4 3 2

Contents

List of Figures

Introduction

The process of writing this book started about twenty years ago when I stood by the book table at one of my first writers' conferences. I looked over the selections, searching for a book that would teach me the basics of writing and that would guide me through this new publishing field. I never found what I was looking for.

Fifteen years ago, writers started asking me if I could recommend a writing/publishing book to buy that would be their guide—the one that would *tell all*. Still there was no selection.

Ten years ago, a new crop of writers asked why someone didn't write such a book. I directed them to what was available. Not exactly what they needed, but it was helpful.

Five years ago, the writers started asking me why *I* didn't write the book that would take them from neophyte to published writer. I laughed nervously.

During the last five years I have moved closer and closer to answering their question, realizing how desperately we need such a book. Yes, there are a lot of writers' books, but not *one* book that *tells all* and *shows all*. But now the time is right to put together the book, a companion volume to the *Christian Writers' Market Guide* (the one-stop guide to the market).

Through the last twenty years of refining ideas and suggestions, I have been made ready to tackle such a book. I have done a lot of writing myself. I have done the *Market Guide* for the last eighteen years. And perhaps most important, I have worked with hundreds of writers at writers' conferences and via phone, fax, email, or letter for many of those years. I have answered their questions, struggled with their problems, critiqued their manuscripts, evaluated their contracts, taught their workshops, and given a ton of advice.

Now I'm ready!

How to Use This Book

This book has been set up with a dual purpose. As with most writing books, it is divided into chapters on various topics associated with writing or the writing business—such as how to get started, set up an office, or write a book. However, in an effort to help you easily find the specific information you want, each chapter is actually a grouping of the specific elements that make up that particular topic, each with its own subhead to help you identify and find what you need. Therefore, there are two ways to approach this book.

The Chapter Approach

If you are interested in the general topic of a chapter, you can read and study all of the sections within the chapter, or skip over those that don't apply to or interest you right now. Each chapter could also be used as a lesson guide for individuals or writing groups. Use the table of contents to locate the right chapter.

The Topic Approach

On a second level, you can use this as a quick reference book and simply look up the answer to a specific question or information on the topic of your choice. Use the topical index on page 279 to locate the appropriate page. The subhead on that page should help you easily find what you are looking for and allow you to read just that portion of the chapter that will tell you what you need to know. Each of those subsections will usually stand on its own even if you have not read the rest of that chapter.

A Plan of Action

If you are a beginning writer, start at the beginning of the book, reading everything to give yourself a good overview of the writing/publishing process. Then go back and reread or study those sections that apply to you right now. Although the suggested activities throughout are optional, beginners should try to do as many as possible. If you have been at this writing business a little longer, but are having difficulties in specific areas—such as marketing or time management—reviewing those sections and doing any suggested activities may be helpful. If you need answers to specific questions immediately, use the index to find those answers before moving on to more general questions or areas of interest. The chapters have been arranged in a logical order but they do not necessarily have to be studied or even read in that order. Feel free to jump around within the book to areas of prime interest or personal concern. I trust this will be a book you will keep next to your *Christian Writers' Market Guide* and refer to on a regular basis.

Chapter 1

On Getting Started

So You Want to Be a Writer?

I have met all kinds of would-be writers—those who have always wanted to write (and may have been closet writers for years), those who never wanted to write (but have had an experience that must be written), those who are looking for a creative outlet (and think writing might be it), and those who don't have a clue what they are doing, but feel God is leading them in this direction. Most of us have arrived here through one of those doors.

But whatever got us to this place, we all share the same desire: to learn more about the craft of writing. The problem we often have is knowing exactly where to start in this whole process. Since there are many different aspects of the writing business—many of them equally important—it's hard to identify a first step. For that reason, this book begins with general background information that will lead you into the specifics later on.

We all have different beginning places, different levels of experience, and different backgrounds in writing. This book is written to answer questions at all writing levels, but begins on the ground floor, so even the beginning writer can keep up.

But no matter where we start, at some point we all ask the same questions: How do I know if I really am a writer? How can I tell if my writing is any good? Will people laugh at me if I tell them I'm a writer? Such doubts are common.

Be encouraged: The fact that you have come this far in pursuit of a dream gives it validity. If you care enough about this desire to write to start learning more about it, pursue the possibility until the doors close—or until you decide this writing business is not for you. By the time you've worked your way through this book, you will likely have a strong sense of whether or not you are pursuing the right dream at the right time.

Not only do we begin with doubts about whether the writing life is for us, we all start with doubts about our writing ability as well. As you get involved in the writing/publishing process, seek opportunities to get feedback from experienced writers. This can be done through writers' groups and organizations, through mail or email round robins (where you critique each other's material), or by paying a professional for a critique. (These different options will be discussed throughout the book.)

For now, put aside your doubts and move on to learning all you can about the business of writing. At some point you will need to decide where you would like to go with that information. Being a writer does not take a special degree or formal training, but it does take commitment.

Many years ago when I first started writing, I complained about deadlines and editors—or simply about having to write. It was then that my daughter asked why I did it. Why didn't I quit? she asked. It was then that I began asking myself that same question.

About that time I read one of my favorite columns by Leslie Conger in *The Writer* magazine. She made me face the question head on. She asked, "If you suddenly came into a million dollars, could you walk away from the typewriter (computer) of yours without a backward look, sail around the world, live it up, and not care a moldy fig if you ever write another word? Think about it. And think about libraries, bookstores and stationery shops—think about the smell of a new book, reams of blank paper, freshly-sharpened pencils." The images have changed somewhat over the years, but she suggests that you are ready to quit only when these things lose their magic—when both the *dream* and the *dreamer* within you are stone-cold dead.

I realized then that I was a writer, because there was no way I *couldn't* be a writer. Over the years I've discovered that most people fail not for lack of talent, but for lack of commitment. Once you know you won't quit—no matter what—that's the point you start becoming a professional—the point when you know you are a writer.

Work Habits

The key to becoming a successful writer is learning all there is to know about the craft and continually honing your skills. Since there is no college degree or course of study required in becoming a writer, individuals must pursue their own course of learning. Those who succeed in the business are usually those who develop an ongoing program of self-education, those who work and work hard.

What's the first step? *Make time in your life for writing.* (See the "Time Management" section for specific suggestions.) Trying to squeeze writing into an already too-full schedule does not work. You must give up some things you are currently doing in order to make room for writing. Writing takes time.

Initially you will want to set aside time on your calendar to read about writing, study your market guide, and write as much as you possibly can. Don't just talk about writing—write. It is by the act of writing that you hone your skills, recognize areas of need, and explore questions of craft and format and presentation—questions this book can answer for you.

Set a schedule that works for you. The ideal goal is to write every day. But, truthfully, I know few writers who do this. Look at your weekly schedule with a realistic eye and set a schedule you can keep. Get away from the notions that you can't write unless you have hours at a time, or that you must get away by yourself to write, or that you need to accomplish some other task first (like setting up an office, moving to a new house, raising a child, or sharpening your pencils). *Writers write.* If you are not writing, you are not a writer and never will be. If you are waiting for the perfect circumstances in which to write, you will end up being a *waiter,* not a writer.

With more than thirty years' experience as a writer, I have

learned that I can write under any circumstances. It has little or nothing to do with the location, how much interference I encounter, how tired I am, or what else is happening in my life. I simply plan my work and then work my plan, refining and changing it as needed to keep my work and me moving forward.

It is important for every writer to give time to all the activities necessary for the writing life. You may find it helpful to divide your available times during the week into segments, using certain times for distinct tasks: writing, reading, research, or marketing. Most of your time, at first, will be spent writing, but once you reach the place where you are ready to market your writing, plan on giving time to the other aspects of the writing business.

Goal Setting

As with any endeavor, *setting specific goals* will help you achieve success at a perceivable and measured rate. Set your goals based on your level of writing expertise, on any areas you know need work (such as grammar, plotting, research, etc.), on the type of writing that interests you, and on any other factors that are unique to your situation, to where you are in the various stages of writing. You may want to set specific goals in the following areas: hours of creative writing per day/week/month; time reading/analyzing target markets; time researching in the library or on the Internet; time sending out submissions; time reading how-to materials.

Write your goals in a journal or on a wall chart if it's easier to follow them that way. Then track the time actually spent in each area.

You won't have time to do *everything* you'd like to do, so concentrate on those areas that are most important to where you are right now. And if you want to succeed, don't shortchange yourself in time spent writing and marketing your work. The length of time set for each task is not as important as actually following through on it. You will be surprised how much you can accomplish in even ten to thirty minutes a day of consistent writing time.

Journal Writing

You may have heard that daily journal writing is good discipline for the writer. If you've never done it, give it a try. Now, I say *try* it out, because people are either journal writers or they are not. I happen to be one of the *are not*s. If forced, I'm sure I could keep a journal, but I cannot do so naturally or comfortably. I used to beat myself up over that, believing I couldn't be a "real" writer unless I kept a journal. Now I know that is not true and have given myself permission *not* to keep a journal. I extend the same permission to you.

If, on the other hand, you would like to give it a try, here are a few suggestions for getting started. Find a paper source that seems right for you—blank book, steno pad, or notebook—to use exclusively for your journal writing. (Though some people might want to keep their journals directly on the computer.) It requires discipline—especially when developing the habit—but it's worth it. Most people set a specific time and place to write in their journals: the first or last thing each day or before or after reading or having personal devotions. Use an established time of the day that works best for you.

Don't think you have to write several pages to make it worthwhile. Even a short entry each day, if it reflects your true thoughts and feelings, will have great value. Some days you will only write a sentence or two, while others may naturally produce a few pages. Avoid routine entries like: "Cleaned the house today" or "Met Mary for lunch." A personal journal is not a calendar of events, but a tracking of the events of your life as you see them through your heart and mind. It is an intensely personal experience. For the writer, it is good practice in expressing oneself on paper and clarifying one's thinking. Keep your journal private—or you won't be honest. Never tear out pages or edit it once it is written; those original words are usually the closest to your real feelings.

Date your entries and number the pages, but avoid printed journals that give you a dated page for each day. If you don't write every day, those blank pages will make you feel like you've failed. Keeping a journal needs to be a "want to" not a "have to" experience.

There are several ways to keep a journal. One writer friend of mine types intimate letters to friends and family and simply keeps copies of those letters as a kind of personal record. Rather than a personal journal, you may prefer to keep a "people notebook," which some fiction writers use. In it they describe the way people look, talk, and behave. This is similar to the "literary journal." In this kind of journal-keeping, you jot down notes that might later be used in an article or poem, such as overheard dialogue or speech patterns, news items, unusual phrases, descriptions. These notes, in turn, may be useful in your writing. Even a personal journal can be used in your writing. Another friend of mine kept a detailed journal through the experience of losing a child. Later, she was able to use that journal to write a book to help other parents experiencing the same thing.

Reading

Writers must be readers—or so they say. I have met a lot of writers or would-be writers who were not voracious readers. Still, the most successful writers I know *do* read a lot. Most of them have *always* read a lot. If you aren't a reader, reconsider. It is one of the best new habits you can develop as a writer. One editor I know suggests that, in order to become a better writer, one should read five hours for every one hour spent writing.

The writers I know who don't read much complain that there simply isn't enough time to keep up with the Ought-to-Read list. That's true for most of us. But, with some effort, we can "redeem" some time for reading. The writers who read a lot don't watch much television or spend much time surfing the World Wide Web for entertainment or sending their friends email jokes. They often carry books with them everywhere they go and read every spare moment they can squeeze out of the day.

Never be guilty of giving up on reading because you "don't have time." If you are going to be a successful writer, you must be dedicated to reading.

"What should I be reading?" Read a wide range of things. Begin with books and periodicals on how to write. As a new writer, I subscribed to *The Writer* and *Writer's Digest* (before there were Christian writers' magazines). I read every issue, cover to cover—even topics I wasn't interested in. I was intent on filling my reservoir of knowledge about writing.

Then begin reading the periodicals you'd like to write for. I subscribe to a different one each year so I have a year's worth of samples to study.

Also read the type of books you want to write. If it is Christian fiction, read the best Christian authors, as well as authors in the general (or "secular") market who write in your genre of interest.

If you want to write for the general market, read the best and most popular books available in that market. Unless you are keeping up with what is currently being written in the general market, you can't hope to compete in that marketplace.

In addition to your regular readings of the Bible—for direction, inspiration, and education—read it as literature. And read the classics.

If you want to write for children or young people, then before you start writing, read at least one hundred books written for your intended audience's age group. Also read books on child development to get an understanding of the different stages and interests of children and young people.

If you are moving into a new genre or area of writing, read as much preparatory material as you can before writing.

Honing Your Craft

The primary concern for most writers is how to improve their writing skills—how to hone their craft. I was fortunate to sell the first things I ever wrote, but I realize now it was probably God's way of keeping me interested until I discovered writing was my calling. It wasn't long, however, before I realized that I didn't know what I was doing right *or* wrong. It was not until a veteran writer sat down with me and went over a manuscript line by line that I began to recognize my areas of strength and weakness, what I needed to do to improve, and where I could cut. It was my first lesson in honing my craft.

How can you hone your skills? Reading this book is a good start. And as I said before, reading and writing as much as possible is essential. But for the basic tools of the craft—usage, composition, form, and style—I suggest you read Strunk and White's *The Elements of Style.* This book provides you with all the honing information you will need in a very few words and a very few pages. And though it's considered a basic writing starter kit by some, many great writers keep it as a companion volume on their desks and return to it again and again.

Finding Ideas

"How do I find ideas for writing?" This question is often asked—but only by beginning writers. Most writers who have been at it a while have more ideas than time to develop them. It is not that you *find* more ideas once you get into the writing life, but that you learn to *recognize* them. Good ideas are everywhere; the trick is in learning to acknowledge and evaluate them effectively.

Here's the acid test to evaluate an idea: When you come up with an idea for a piece, work with that idea. Refine and define it until you can sum it up in one sentence, a sentence that captures the essence of your piece. (This is sometimes called a précis or a thesis.) If you are not able to get that idea summarized into a clear and helpful description, it is probably not a workable idea.

The world around you—in concert with your brain—is an incredible Idea Factory. That factory needs to be in the business of constantly generating ideas in a conscious, deliberate, and intelligent way. However, like any new factory, you may need to "prime the pump" to get the ideas flowing. Here are a few activities that may help:

1. Make a list of five things you know well enough to teach others (look at your job history, personal life, hobbies, and interests for list ideas). Take the answer to the question "What do you know?" and you now have an idea for an article. The answer to "Who would want to learn it?" provides you with a target audience for the article.

2. Read the newspaper every day, looking for potential story ideas. (TV news is not a good substitute for the paper: Ideas are sparked from the details provided in the newspaper accounts.) Use your own interests as a guide for the types of stories to look for. Find at least one article idea in the newspaper every day to keep your idea-generation in full production.

3. Look at every magazine as a potential market. When you pick up a new magazine, determine at least one article you might write for that magazine. Learn to look beyond the obvious. So you don't think you have a lot to offer this specialized magazine? Keep in mind that most specialty magazines also carry some articles on general topics of interest to their readers. Read the magazine's table-of-contents page to identify such articles, and ask yourself if you could have written any of the articles listed there.

4. When you find yourself strongly disagreeing with something you see or hear, turn that passion into an article—or at least a letter to the editor.

5. Talk to people every chance you get. Listen to their experiences. Write articles based on their needs or concerns.

6. Fill your life with *unreproducible experiences*. Be open to those

things you have never done before and will likely never do again. Most of us spend the majority of our time doing and seeing the same things over and over again. We see the same people, eat at or go to the same places, attend the same church and civic functions, and volunteer for the same jobs. As a writer, constantly challenge yourself to step out of those comfortable places into less comfortable ones. These are the places that we learn and grow—the places where ideas are born.

7. Skim the classified ads, personal ads, news sections of favorite magazines, and even the yellow pages for ideas.

❖

Every time you have what you think might be a good idea, test it out. See if it is "big" enough—can be fleshed out enough—to develop into a full-blown article. If the article does not have enough angles, then abandon it.

I know this is an unusual approach, but it helps me to compare a potential idea to the general three-point sermon outline: Does the idea have more than two aspects? If so, pursue that idea. Few ideas come fully developed; your job is to nurture them.

The last piece of advice I have about ideas is to always write them down. Most people would be rich if they remembered all the great ideas that "got away." Carry a small notebook with you in your pocket or purse, and keep extra notebooks in every room of your house and at work. Never assume that you'll remember the idea later. Write it down now, because if you are generating a lot of ideas, one idea can bump the previous idea from your mind—never to be seen again.

Resources for Writers

Many types of resources are available to the writer. (Specific resources will be addressed in appendix B.)

Magazines. Read both general-market and Christian periodicals for writers. Many are available at your public library. Keep in mind that the techniques of writing are the same for any market. The differences lie in the purpose or presentation of the content. A Christian publication will help you better understand the unique needs of the Christian market. These publications are important tools of your trade.

College or Adult Education Classes. Feel like you've been away from the classroom too long? You might want to take a refresher course or a creative writing class to get your writing dream going.

As you select a class, keep the following in mind. "Creative writing" courses are not the same as "writing for publication" courses. Creative writing classes often focus more on the literary aspects of writing, rather than on what most publishers are looking for. Find out what the curriculum will cover and what you can expect to learn in the class.

Also, find out something about the instructor, because even with good curriculum, a class with a poor instructor is not worth your while. Talk to one of the teacher's former students, or call the school ahead of time and ask for information about the teacher. If the instructors have not been published, they will probably not be able to give you the kind of help you need. Keep exploring all the possibilities until you find the best teacher and the best curriculum.

Correspondence Courses. For those who are unable to attend a regular class or a writers' conference, correspondence courses are good options. All kinds of correspondence courses are available, both general and Christian. Some of the more popular ones are listed under the resources section in the *Christian Writers' Market Guide.** For those of you who are interested, some general-market courses, such as those offered by *Writer's Digest,* have Christian instructors. But no matter what course you choose, be sure that the instructor you work with has experience in writing for publication and understands the industry.

*The resources section of the *Christian Writers' Market Guide* contains additional resources, many on the Internet, which will provide invaluable help and instruction at little or no cost.

Writers' Groups

Writing can be an isolated and lonely business. But writers' groups often can bring the writer out of isolation and help him or her polish manuscripts prior to submission.

Some writers are scared to death of reading work out loud and letting other writers criticize their writing. As a beginning writer, I had a great fear of criticism. It took me a couple of years to come out of my writer's isolation and join a critique group. It didn't take long for me to realize, however, that it was the best thing I had ever done for my writing career.

If you as a writer work in isolation, you have no one to point out problem areas or those silly little mistakes we all let creep into our writing. But getting involved in a writing group can help your work mature and improve considerably. Many published writers give a great deal of credit to their writers' groups—and some even owe lifelong friendships to those groups.

Some groups are more successful than others; the important thing is to find a group that works for you. Writers' groups can meet weekly, biweekly, or monthly. Some groups are area-wide, others are statewide. Some focus on instruction, others on critique, when discussing each other's written work.

The format for these meetings varies, but most run something like this: Each person brings a piece of writing—an article, short story, or book chapter—to read aloud to the group. After each person reads, the group comments on the piece, going around the circle one by one. Since everyone knows they are expected to comment, they become more actively involved in the process, and participation improves. It is an unwritten rule that group members start with a positive comment, followed by any suggestions for improvement. The writer is not allowed to refute any of the comments. In any writers' group there will be differences of opinion on what changes should be made, so the writer must process the suggestions and decide which to incorporate. Because the members of the group may be from diverse religious backgrounds, they comment only on the writing, not on the theology. In some groups, members are not allowed to attend meetings if they do not bring something to read, or if they miss bringing something one or two times in a row.

Obviously, with a group of four to eight members, each person taking a turn to read and receive critique, meetings can run long. Because of that, some groups limit the number of readers or the length of time allotted to each reader for the reading/critique combination. That time allocation allows the group to stay on schedule. The easy way to fit everyone in is to ask how many are reading and divide your time by that number. A timer/alarm clock can be used to keep things moving, if necessary.

Some group meetings begin with members reporting their successes and rejections from the previous month. Since members usually take turns being up or down, this provides a good opportunity to encourage all participants at their various stages of writing and publishing. Some groups also have members take turns bringing refreshments to share at the end of the meeting during an informal social time. Other groups skip that part.

When you set up a group, plan the components to meet your group's particular needs. Some groups meet in the evening, some during the day, and some provide both a daytime and an evening meeting. Some of the smaller, more intense groups may meet weekly or biweekly. Some groups don't read aloud, but ask members to bring enough copies of their manuscripts for the other members to read and critique individually.

Another possibility, good especially for those unable to attend writers' groups (for whatever reason, perhaps because they live in a remote area or have a long-standing illness), is the round robin. Here's how it works: Either by email or "snail" mail you send each other manuscripts to critique. Once manuscripts are critiqued, they are sent back to their authors. This doesn't provide that in-person social interaction many enjoy, but it does allow you to keep in touch with other writers and get personal feedback on your work.

Writers' Conferences

I am often asked how important it is to attend a writers' conference. My answer? Very important—on more than one level. First, it is the best place for the beginning writer to get basic knowledge and background information in a short period of time. A person would have to dedicate large amounts of time to reading numerous books and articles on writing—and even then, they couldn't attain even a *portion* of the helpful information available at *one* conference. Even if you've read a lot before attending, conference workshops and seminars will help you put your writing knowledge into perspective as well as answer those nagging questions you had about publishing.

If you are a beginning writer, I suggest you attend a conference every year or two to learn about writing and to grow as a writer. Because so much is offered at these conferences, it is normal to feel frustrated because you can't take every workshop or remember everything you hear. That is all right. At each conference, focus on what you need to learn right then or in the near future. Then, the next time you attend, you will be at a different place and will pick up on other things, things you need then. That is the value in attending often. And as you move into new areas of writing, you will be able to take in relevant and helpful workshops in those areas. But don't go without a little research: At this early stage, look for conferences that offer the best teachers and a well-rounded teaching program.

For the more advanced writer, the conference serves a different purpose. Although advanced writers will still look for interesting classes and experienced teachers, they will be most interested in the number and quality of editors present. As the number of Christian agents grows, we will also see more of them attending conferences—another important consideration. In Christian publishing, as in any other field, it is not what you know (or what you can write), it's who you know (or who might contract for your manuscript). Since it is getting more difficult to find editors who will read unsolicited submissions sent to their offices, advanced writers should consider attending one or two conferences a year where they can interact with and get acquainted with the largest number of editors. You may not have something to sell to a particular editor right now, but realize that the editors will be looking more long-range—seeking out authors with potential who might fill a need in the future.

Another tip for the seasoned and/or professional writer: Look for conferences that offer an advanced track, something that goes beyond the basics to deal with your special needs. Such tracks often deal with the business end of being a writer, rather than with writing techniques. In the advanced track you will cover topics such as book-contract details, income tax, marketing, and current trends. That track often provides question-and-answer panels with editors and allows you close interaction with editors and conference speakers.

Meeting with editors

After registering for a conference that boasts a good number of editors (some have as many as fifteen to thirty), check the brochure for a list and prepare to meet with those editors. Determine the editors you are interested in and either match them with appropriate manuscripts or write a new query, book proposal, or manuscript to meet their specific needs. Even if you don't have time to prepare something special for every editor, at least come up with a possible idea you can pitch, or take along one of your published manuscripts in their topic area and use it as a springboard to launch other ideas that might interest them.

In one of the first conferences I attended, I took an idea for a children's picture book. I showed the manuscript to seven different publishers during the week. Of those, five showed an interest. Only one, though, was interested in the book as I presented it. The other four suggested variations, different approaches, or other products that I could develop from that same basic idea. An idea—any appropriate one—nearly always leads to a productive conversation with an editor. But if that first idea falls flat, be prepared with several others to keep the interaction going. Sometimes simply discussing the smallest kernel of an idea will develop it into a "mighty oak."

Are you reserved? Too uncomfortable to make an appointment to talk with an editor on a formal basis? Then at least try to sit next to a different one at each meal and learn all you can about the editor and the periodical/house that editor represents. Even if you don't ask questions, listening to how others interact or present their ideas will help you understand how the process works.

A great by-product of the writers' conference is the people you meet and the contacts you make. Among my best friends are those I've met at writers' conferences. Many other conference attendees have proved exceptional contacts, providing needed information in their areas of expertise or referring me to important resources. Writers help writers and the writers' conference becomes central to making that happen.

For a complete list of conferences nationwide, see the *Christian Writers' Market Guide.* Request information from any that interest you. Read the materials and brochures carefully. And make use of any special services the conference offers even before the conference begins. These can include a pre-conference sign-up with editors. Or they may include the opportunity (sometimes for a fee) to have your manuscripts or proposals reviewed and critiqued by professionals a few weeks before the conference begins. These extra services are often worth the cost of the conference.

Start with Articles

I meet a lot of people who have never written anything before but are working on, or want to write, a book. Although many writers start this way, most of them would benefit greatly by writing for periodicals first. Working your way through shorter stories or articles can teach you many skills and prepare you for writing that book in a number of different ways.

It polishes your writing skills. You learn how to get words on paper; you learn how to cut unnecessary words; you begin to refresh your technical skills in grammar, punctuation, and spelling; and you develop your own voice and writing style. Many first books show obvious lack in those areas. I know of numerous writers who skipped the preliminaries and started right off with book writing. They look at those first books with regret, though, wishing they could have written with more honed writing skills.

It helps you establish credibility in a certain field or with a particular topic. Most people aren't aware of the benefit of beginning with article-writing. If you are published regularly in connection with a particular topic or are known for a type of writing, you will start to develop a solid reputation among readers and editors. Not only can you get visibility for writing on certain topics, you can get visibility for the *types* of writing you do (some of these types include feature articles, historical material, humor, short stories, essays, material for children or teens, and Bible studies). Once a writer becomes well-known as an "expert" because of writing credits in a certain area or because of success with a type of writing, editors start coming to that writer and asking for articles or books on that topic. If you never establish that reputation, you will never get into any editor's prospective authors' pool.

Publishing frequently on "your" topic or type of writing establishes you as an expert and gives you a better chance of then selling a book. Even if you don't have formal credentials or a college diploma in your area of expertise, the publishing credits alone become your degree and badge of authenticity.

My own experience proved this to be true. After twenty years' experience in Christian education, I started writing regularly for every Christian education periodical on the market. Later I wrote seven books in the field of Christian education. Did I have a degree in Christian education? No. Did anyone ever ask me if I did? No. Why? Because I had established myself as an expert by being published regularly in the field. In *your* area of expertise or interest you can do the same.

Finding Your Voice

As we start writing for publication, we suddenly become very aware of how our words "sound" on paper. At first, many of us strive for a what we think is a "literary" tone, and we try using big words or high-sounding phrases or flowery language.

But that doesn't work. It isn't until we get a few more words—and a few rejection slips—under our belts that we begin to realize that something is wrong. We discover that it's not those big words and high-sounding phrases that make a good writer. It's finding and developing our own writer's voice (or style).

And we do that how? By writing, like the most successful writers, with straight-forward simplicity. Be yourself. Avoid the big words and flowery language that aren't *you*. And unless you are writing for an academic audience or in a highly technical or specialized field, the rule of thumb in writing is this: Never use a big word when a small one will do.

Some people can hear a passage from a certain work, recognize the style, and know immediately who the author is. So what, exactly, defines a writer's voice (or writing style)? And how can a new writer develop his or her own unique style?

Your voice emerges when you reach the point where you can write honestly, when the things you say ring true, and the real you begins to filter through in your writing. Often those around you, like those in your critique group, will begin to recognize that voice before you do. That voice usually surfaces more readily when you are enthusiastic or care deeply about what you are writing. That doesn't mean you should resort to shouting on paper, it means letting your passion bring power to your words so that your voice can be heard. Voice is simply your personality on paper. Write until the words reveal the real you.

Some have found that writing regularly—and honestly—in their journals helps to bring their true voice to the surface. Once you have mastered it in your journal, start transferring it to other kinds of writing. Constantly strive for authenticity in your life, and your words will bring power and clarity, force and flavor, to your voice.

Trying to imitate various writers' styles can be a useful exercise for beginning writers—especially as you are learning to recognize style or voice. Never, though, take on someone's style as your own. Trying to adopt another's style, or writing things you don't believe passionately, will leave your voice flat and without that ring of truth.

No one can teach you how to have that authentic voice; it comes from a personal writing journey in which you open up your life to your readers.

Professionalism

It's important to be professional in your writing, even though you may be a beginner. As you enter the marketplace, apply the etiquette you find in such writing and publishing books as this. Different books will give varied advice and direction, but most books agree on the general guidelines. If they don't, don't panic: When presented with two different approaches, do something that honors the spirit of the rule and best suits your publishing needs. (Rest assured, guidelines provided in this book fall within the acceptable range for the publishing industry.) Chapter 2, "On the Basics," shows you how to adapt guidelines as you prepare and submit your manuscript.

The rules for writing are like any other rules—you need to learn them well, following them faithfully until you are comfortable enough with the whole process to break the rules when it makes sense to do so. Ignoring protocol *before* you have paid your dues, though, can cost you your good reputation as a professional with the editors and publishers you are working with.

Professionalism is a state of mind—an attitude toward your work. It is *how* you view (and present yourself in) the business of writing, more than how you actually function as a writer. I developed that professionalism only later. When I started writing, I had no background or education in writing and no real personal desire to write. It was only because I sold what I wrote at the beginning that I stuck with it. Not until I realized God had called me into this role did I begin to take writing seriously. God expected a professional response to a spiritual call—and I had a responsibility to become the best writer I could be.

The writer who feels called to write should proceed with the attitude of a professional. This includes being dedicated to that calling and not letting anyone talk you out of it. There are a lot of would-be writers who either never believed in themselves enough to actually write, or have let friends and family convince them they could never be a writer. But a professional writer—a successful writer—writes.

Am I Really a Writer?

The concern I hear most often from writers or would-be writers is "How do I know if I have any talent—if I have what it takes to be a writer?" Usually writers are afraid of one of two things: that they have no talent or that they won't be successful.

Some writers have obvious talent, and I have seen them either succeed or squander that talent. Many others I have seen have developed their lesser talent, with hard work and determination, into a successful writing career. Some of you may have to work a little harder. *The important thing is to be a caretaker of the talent you have been given and determine to become the best writer you can be.* Although I recognize that I do have some talent for writing, I also know that my skill has developed through the hard work of learning the craft over the years. I have no delusions of becoming a literary giant—there are few of those in this world—but I have worked to be the best writer I can be, no matter what the final results of that effort might be.

Remember that doing a job well means avoiding putting up roadblocks for yourself. Follow the writer's path laid out before you—step by step. If you are given the opportunity to write, and the desire, follow that opportunity until some roadblock closes that path. A blocked path may mean (among other things) that you are unable to sell your work. But it *doesn't* mean that because you lacked writing discipline or allowed less important things to fill your time, your road is blocked. That is *your* roadblock, not God's.

Real success is not in the accolades or royalties you receive, but in a job well done. Joe Bayly, one of my first writing mentors, once said, "God is not served by technical incompetence." Years ago I learned that hard work and a professional attitude are my responsibility. God is in charge of the results.

Writer's Block

Writer's block is one of those things people either believe in or they don't. Generally I don't. Sure, there are times when all of us get "stuck" in our writing, but usually there are good reasons for it.

For those of you experiencing this mysterious writer's block, I can offer no magical cure for this creative paralysis. I can, however, offer some practical suggestions for getting the words flowing again.

The first thing to consider is the obvious one: You may simply be burned out on writing—a result of pushing your mind and spirit too hard. Writing is like any other endeavor: You don't work at your peak if you are too tired or your creative juices haven't had opportunity to rest and revitalize. A writer friend of mine suggests that just as the land needs a fallow season after it has been overworked producing crops, so writers need a "fallow" season too. Give yourself a well-earned break so that you can return to that blank sheet fresh and excited about writing again.

A block can also be caused by the following: your regular editors have stopped asking you for new books or proposals for no apparent reason; your latest book has been a big success and you're sure it's a fluke and you'll never be able to do it again; you are overwhelmed with too many deadlines and don't have enough time to meet them.

These can be cases of losing your nerve or belief in your writing. At times like these, you may need the objective opinion of a qualified outside person to evaluate your work. If you don't have a writing friend or a writers' group that can be objective about your work, hire a professional to critique your recent work (see the Editorial Services listing in the *Christian Writers' Market Guide)*. Your writing may need a simple adjustment by a professional, similar to the tune-up golfers get to improve their swing.

Other times, when a block comes, you simply need to write in a whole new genre. If you have been writing a serious feature, take a break to write a children's story or a humor piece. Give your mind and emotions a change of scenery. Also, if you tend to write only from what you know, pick a subject that takes research, and research until you *have* to start writing.

If you experience a "block" as you try to get back to a writing project from the previous day or week (or even longer), here are a few simple tricks that can get you going again:

1. Reread what you wrote last to get yourself back into the mood of the piece. Editing or polishing the previous writing can also get ideas flowing.

2. Instead of stopping for the day at the end of a paragraph, idea, or chapter, stop where you know what comes next so you can easily pick up where you left off.

3. Do some physical exercises. It will get your body moving and perhaps get your mind unstuck.

4. Generate some new ideas by reading the work of one of your favorite authors—or by starting to type a page from someone else's book.

5. Sit down and start typing anything that comes into your head. Don't stop until you start focusing on the project at hand or until you come up with an idea for a new project.

6. Give yourself permission to write badly. Perfectionism often keeps us from getting started with new ideas or projects. (Don't worry, you can rewrite it later.)

7. Write up one of your own experiences as an anecdote.

8. Skip over the beginning of a book or article if you're

stumped. Start in the middle or start at the point you *know* what you want to say. Writing the lead to a piece will be easier once you get into it.

9. Switch from typing on the typewriter or computer to writing longhand (or vice versa) until you get ideas going.

10. Read an article in the magazine you're trying to write this piece for. Convince yourself you can write your article better. Figure out *how* you will write yours better and then proceed.

11. Write at the same time everyday and for the same length of time. If you can't think of anything to write, sit and look at the screen until your time is up. Something will come to you.

12. When writing, don't think about the magazine, the book publisher, the money, or the fame. Think about and write directly to your reader. Put the reader in a chair opposite you and begin to tell your story.

13. Don't fall into the trap of thinking you can only write when you feel like it. A real writer writes when the writing needs to get done, not just when the muse is present.

14. Put yourself in the position that if you don't write, you don't eat. (Of course, don't take it to extremes.) It does wonders for writer's block!

Specialize or Diversify?

Many writers ask this question at some point in their career. Should they develop one area of expertise and stick to it, or should their writing be more diverse?

That is a question each one must answer for his or herself. Some writers are writing because of a life-changing experience that becomes the topic for every article or book or that colors all of their writing. For some that will be enough.

Other writers will gravitate naturally to one area or another based on their interests or experiences. Try a number of different fields. Look for your strong areas. Even while I was writing Christian education materials, I wrote material for children, as well as inspirational articles. Because I was successful at all three, I stuck with all three. Sometimes it is a matter of testing the market to see which markets are the most open or which ones you are most successful in. Don't devote a lot of your time to writing material for which there is little or no market.

Each of us has certain innate strengths we need to recognize and use. For me, it is how-to material. Even though I have written in a number of different areas, my basic strengths as a writer center on the ability to organize material, teach others, and provide practical help. Once I recognized those strengths, I was able to better direct my efforts into the areas that would take the best advantage of those skills.

Recognizing Salable Themes

Once you get tuned into looking for ideas for stories and articles, you will find them everywhere. The trick is learning to identify which ones are most likely to sell. Here are some of the underlying principles that work for me.

The key, obviously, is selecting a subject of high personal interest to your readers. We as writers tend to want to write about what interests *us,* but every piece you write needs a definable potential audience of readers. Perhaps it is an audience of homemakers, hockey players, businessmen, retirees, children, or home-schoolers. Perhaps your audience contains two thousand or two million. But you need to know your audience: its size and its tastes.

You can write an effective article on almost any topic as long as you determine how that topic will interest and affect people and then write it with that slant. Even if you are reporting on a new street being built, the focus of the article should not be what kind of blacktop they are using, but how that new street will have an impact on the people in the area. That basic principle (writing about what *affects* and *interests* your audience) should apply to every article you write.

"What do readers want?" is the underlying question.

- *To learn.* Readers want to learn about all kinds of things. Writing how-to and service pieces will help meet your readers' need for learning how things work, how to do something, or where to go for help.

- *To have new experiences.* Readers want new experiences, even if they get those new experiences vicariously as they read about others. Inspirational or human interest stories often fulfill such a need.

- *To read about themselves.* Not only do readers want to read about themselves, they want to read about others like themselves: suburbanites, people in business, mall-shoppers, those involved in the PTA. Personality profiles, interviews, and personal experience pieces will catch readers' interest.

- *To keep up with trends.* Readers want to keep up with the latest developments, gossip, and trends in their areas of interest, in their neighborhoods, in their businesses. They want to be prepared for the future—physically, socially, economically, and spiritually. Articles on such things as new exercise programs, diets, investment opportunities, or Bible study methods will fill their needs in this area.

❖

Obviously you cannot meet all of these needs, but with every idea that interests you, ask how a book or article with this idea as a focus can meet the needs or interests of your readers. Look for solid life applications. And remember, if you are not highly interested and enthusiastic about the topic, you are not likely to interest an editor or, ultimately, your readers.

Writers need to keep up with what is happening in the world around them and to be constantly on the look-out for current universal themes that, given the right twist, will meet the needs of their readers.

Criticism

I have been asked why anyone would want to get into the business of writing—a business based on criticism and rejection. I suppose that is true. This can be seen as a real negative by beginning writers. Yet, though criticism has a negative side, it can also be the key to success in this business.

Later in the book, we will talk about rejection slips—which can be a big discouragement in the writing life—but here I want to focus on criticism. The first important lesson to learn about writing is that criticism (as well as praise) is essential to growth. When we have written about our most intimate thoughts or experiences, we are often tied too closely to our words to remain objective. Even if we are writing about how to wash the family dog, we have still created something that is open to criticism, whether it is criticism of our words or of our method. Accepting criticism in either case is not easy. Laying a manuscript open to criticism is like asking for an honest opinion of your newborn baby. All you want to hear is how wonderful it is—not that it has big ears, a red face, and its father's unruly hair. This can be painful!

The key to surviving that painful criticism is to detach yourself emotionally from your writing. When you seek criticism of your work (yes, I encourage you to *seek* it), remember that it is the *manuscript* being critiqued, not you. I did not grow as a writer until I started seeking constructive criticism. (And it is important to ask for *constructive* criticism, as it focuses on the positive: pointing out the weaknesses of a piece in order to improve it.)

My first experience with critique was after the close of a writers' conference. For a fee, interested writers could stay and work with an accomplished and respected author on an individual basis. In my first session, I took a copy of a recently published article. The author and I went over the article line by line, and she showed me where I could cut or tighten it. Although the article was only 1,100 words, we were able to cut that published article by fifty words. Inspired, I went back to my room and cut 100 words from an article I was working on. That meeting was a turning point in my writing career. For the first time I was able to view my writing through someone else's eyes.

Although inviting criticism is important to your success, be careful whom you ask for such help. I tell most people: Cross your mother off the top of the list, along with your spouse, children, sister, brother, best friend, and favorite aunt. This is especially true if they do not have experience critiquing writing—pointing out weaknesses while developing strengths. Often the only thing they tell you is how wonderful your piece is. So, if possible, go to a *professional* who knows how to write and understands writing for publication. A trusted writers' group that is set up solely for critique would be the next-best option. The last choice is avid readers, who can often be helpful critics. Still you are usually better off getting professional and detailed advice. (A word of caution: Do not expect to get such a critique from a busy editor. Although it would be wonderful if we could get a letter outlining exactly why we got each rejection, it *will never happen*. It is up to us to find people who can provide helpful critiques of our manuscripts.)

Whomever you get feedback from, watch for recurring criticisms. If you hear more than once that your dialogue is stilted, your plots are weak, your leads are boring, or your endings lack punch, take note. Instead of defending yourself, get a helpful book on the topic or take a class in order to improve in those areas. You can even learn on your own by analyzing good writing and taking particular note of how successful authors deal with the things that are trouble spots to you. Read their work, underlining the leads, endings, transitions, or whatever sections that pertain to your writing needs. Study to discover why they are successful in those areas. You might even want to start a notebook of ideas and good examples that help you work through those trouble zones. Criticism from others serves no purpose unless you are willing to act on the evaluations and improve your writing.

When you pay for a critique, go over all the comments and corrections. Study them carefully. Learn from your mistakes. Even when you have a manuscript accepted for publication, learn from the final version: Compare your original manuscript to the finished product. Note the changes or corrections that were made. Some changes any editor might have made, while others are changes unique to your book's publishing house or the magazine publisher. Learn from both kinds of editing—the first to improve your writing in general—the second to better understand how to write for that particular publisher.

Chapter 2

On the Basics

In any business, you need foundational know-how. It's no different with writing. This chapter gives you the basic steps you need for writing and marketing. Guidelines presented in this section may vary somewhat from guidelines elsewhere, but slight variations are to be expected. The following guidelines will put you well within acceptable limits with any publisher. Use your common sense to adapt these guidelines to your specific needs.

The following topics will be presented alphabetically. For a list of topics, see the table of contents.

Counting Words

On the first page of your manuscript, you will need an approximate *word count*. This count is used by the publisher to determine three things: whether the piece is within the established word-length limit for the publisher, how much book or magazine space it will require, and (for a periodical) how much you will be paid for the piece.

For a book manuscript, round off your number to the nearest 100. For an article, round off to the nearest 50. The exception is with *fillers* (usually anything less than 800–1,000 words), where the publisher will want the exact number of words. Since these are used to "fill" extra space at the end of a full-length article, an exact word count will help determine which piece will fit the available space.

For computer users, word count is not a problem. The computer does it automatically. Gone are the days when we struggled over *how* to count, or *which words* to count. A useful thing about the computer's automatic word count is that you can periodically check word count as you go along, avoiding those surprises at the end of your piece when you come out 500 words over your limit.

If you do not have a computer or word processor to count for you, there are ways to figure out word count without counting every word (unless, as mentioned above, you are writing for fillers).

Base your count on averaging—the kind you did in grade-school math. If it's been too long since your last grade-school math class, follow these easy steps.

For short manuscripts:

1. Count the number of words in three lines of type. Divide that total by three to get the average number of words per line. (Example: 30 words total divided by 3 = 10 words per line.)

2. Count the number of lines per page. Multiply that number by the number of words per line in order to get the number of words per page. (Example: 25 lines x 10 words per line = 250 words per page.)

3. Multiply the number of words per page times the total number of pages. (Example: 250 total words x 10 = 2,500 words.)

For longer pieces or books:

1. If your manuscript has 25 pages or more, count the number of words in 3 full pages. Divide that total by 3. This is your average word count per page. Now multiply that by the total number of pages you have.

2. If the manuscript is 50 pages or more, count the number of words in 5 full pages. Divide that total by 5. Now multiply that by the total number of pages you have.

❖

Obviously the number of words per page will vary depending on whether you are writing for children or for academia. But if your writing doesn't swing too wide into those variables and you use the same font size throughout, you can come up with a page average that will work most of the time. Just so you have something to compare your count to, the average page count for Pica type is 250 words per page; for Elite it is 300 words per page.

Cover Letter

When submitting a book proposal or book manuscript you will always include a cover letter, but with periodicals, whether to send a cover letter or *not* send a cover letter is often the question. My answer: When in doubt, use a cover letter. But this comes with a warning: Be brief, as editors are looking for a *quick* introduction to your submission.

Be sure you've checked a market guide for publishers' information regarding cover letters: Some publishers prefer no letter. Sending a letter when a letter is not necessary is as bad as not sending one when it is expected. It's a point to be careful about.

When sending a letter, include the following information.

Use the *cover letter* to answer questions that might arise in the mind of the editor concerning your authority as a writer, your sources, and the potential readership. Always keep these comments as short as possible. If it is important that an editor know, *briefly* explain your reason for writing that article or book; how you came to know this information; why you are using a pen name; and how your credentials, experience, and source of research relate to your work.

Refrain from giving your life story or from getting off on a tangent unrelated to the book or article. When submitting to a Christian publisher, you also might include a sentence or two concerning your Christian commitment. If it is a denominational publisher and you belong to that denomination, mention that. If your article or book is about a person or group that is part of that denomination, mention that as well.

Your letter should introduce your piece and whet an editor's appetite to read your submission. Never use it to explain the purpose or intent of the piece—it needs to stand on its own. It is an important letter as it provides a first impression of you as a new author and reveals something of your personality or background. If the piece is how-to, your letter should reflect careful organization; if it is a humor piece, the letter should provide a touch of humor (just a *touch,* don't overdo it!); if the piece is serious or reflective, the letter should convey the same tone.

Remember that your submission should stand on its own; your cover letter should only provide information that cannot be found elsewhere.

Always personalize the cover letter to the specific publication (for instance, by mentioning the name of the publisher or periodical) to give them the impression that you have selected them specifically. Always check your current market guide to see if it lists a specific contact person who can receive your submission. If no name is available or your market guide is out of date (anything over a year), call the publisher for the appropriate contact person (make sure you get the correct spelling!).

Here are a couple of things to avoid: Don't direct your letter to "Dear Sir" or "To Whom It May Concern." Use Ms. or Mr. only if you are certain of the person's gender. When gender is not obvious, address your letter to the editor's full name (ie. "Dear Leslie Jones").

Editor-Author Relationships

If you don't yet have a working relationship with an editor, begin by getting your foot in the door. Since some editors rely heavily on freelance submissions—this is especially true in the world of periodicals, where editors are often limited to publishing the best of the submissions—many editors are on the lookout for good writers to assign specific assignments. Show them, through your submissions, that you understand their publishing house's needs and can supply appropriate topics. In that way you put yourself in a position to be on the receiving end of some of those assignments.

This means that instead of writing only what you want to write, you work to understand the needs of their book company or periodical. To some, writing for the market may sound like a sellout, but it is the reality of the publishing business; it's the reality of the first step of working with editors.

Once you've started working with an editor, it is important to develop a good relationship. Although the editor isn't your "boss," editors, for a short time, have that "boss" role—at least during the time you are freelancing, writing an assignment for them, or selling them a manuscript. Because of that, it's good to work as a team.

The first thing to remember is that editors have no special powers or mandate from God to rule over the publishing industry. What editors *do have* is a knowledge of what kind of writing meets the particular needs of their market. Editors' primary concern is getting the kind of material they need for their book or periodical company. We need editors as much as they need us. We write for their reading audience and editors, in turn, help us hone our craft and understand how to *better* write for that audience. This is what a good working relationship is all about.

How do you nurture the editor-writer relationship? Simply work with and for them as you would any employer. Don't put an editor on a pedestal and don't be afraid to develop a personal friendship. Follow their lead. If and when they move to a first-name basis, do the same. If you have a good relationship with a certain editor or publisher and will be in their area, call and ask if you can drop by. Usually they are happy to meet with you and give you a tour of their offices. Invite them to lunch, if they have time.

With access to editors becoming more limited, you need to go out of your way to make personal contact with them at conferences and trade conventions (the big one for the Christian marketplace is Christian Booksellers Association or CBA), or by making office visits. Some publishers are already accepting submissions only from writers they know or those they have met at conferences.

Follow up any meetings, lunches, extended phone calls, or conference contacts with editors with a letter reiterating what you talked about. Send them Christmas cards. Send a thank-you note or email after they publish your book or after they take you to lunch. Share with them copies of encouraging letters from readers. But always remember to keep correspondence or phone calls *short*. Don't call unless you know they welcome calls (or it is an emergency). Don't send anything unless it is your best work. Be open to editing suggestions and learn from them. Know the publishing company's guidelines and work accordingly. And don't forget that although there are certain general editing standards, every editor edits slightly differently—some better than others.

Though you may do everything to develop a good relationship with your editors, be prepared for times when things won't run smoothly. Editors may ignore your submissions, fail to return calls, or not edit your work thoroughly. Your best way to deal with these problems is by keeping a strong sense of self-respect. Remember: What you do is every bit as important as what the editor does. The editor may sometimes forget that, but if you respect yourself as well as your editor as you try to resolve the situation, you will probably meet with success.

Following are some typical problems and possible solutions/responses regarding editors:

➤ *Editors send you a form rejection slip.* Although frustrating for the writer, form rejects are standard. Most editors are overworked and do not have time for personal responses to each submission. Don't expect or ask for a personal critique; it will label you as both a beginner and unprofessional. Do, however, take seriously any comments of encouragement they may scribble at the bottom, and as soon as possible send them something more targeted to their publishing needs.

➤ *They request a rewrite.* Editors don't ask for rewrites to aggravate you; they ask for rewrites because they want to use your piece even though as is your piece doesn't suit their audience or their needs, or it doesn't happen to be the right size. Writers typically hate rewrites, but it is one of the best ways for you to learn how to rework a book with a specific audience in mind or rewrite a piece for a particular magazine. Being willing to rewrite lets editors know you are willing to work with them. Pay close attention to the types of changes they request: Keep those suggestions in mind when you are writing new pieces for them. If an editor requests a rewrite and you—without good reason—refuse, it shows a lack of professionalism and will probably hurt your reputation with that editor.

➤ *They change your intent or meaning.* On rare occasions an editor—either purposely or inadvertently—will edit your article or book and change your meaning. This can sometimes happen when an editor shapes your piece toward a specific reading audience. Editors correct grammar, spelling, consistency, style, and length problems, among other things. They should not, without your permission, change the overall meaning, intent, or theology of your piece. If this happens, call or write the editor and explain calmly and clearly what change was made and why that significantly changed your work.

On books, you as a writer should be able to okay all major editorial changes. But for articles, correction may be impossible before it goes to press. If a serious problem occurs, ask your editors how their publishing house usually corrects such errors. If *they* don't suggest a retraction (or other appropriate action), *you* should make the suggestion. Their attitude and reaction to your call or letter will be a strong indicator for you as you decide whether or not you want to submit to this publisher in the future.

One note of warning: Your editor may be more aware of your market than you are and may have merely edited with the best interest of your work in mind. It's difficult to have your work edited because you are so close to what you've written. You want to ensure the integrity of your piece, but not at the cost of your professional reputation with editors. If you ask for a retraction and your publisher does not see a valid reason for it (or you are unbending when it comes to editorial changes), be aware that they might not want to work with you on a future project.

➤ *They give you the silent treatment.* One of the biggest complaints I hear about editors is that they do not respond to submissions (queries or manuscripts). The market guide you are using or the publisher's guidelines will tell you how long you can expect to wait for a response. It can vary from one week to a year or more—so check. It is safe to add a week for mailing time, plus another four weeks for good measure, and then follow up on the submission with a letter.

When you send a letter, explain what you sent (title/description), when it was sent, and to whom. Say you are checking to be sure they received it and would like to know its current status. Be business-like and professional—not accusatory. If your letter brings no response, wait another four weeks and call, asking for the editor you sent it to.

To the letter or to the call, you are likely to receive one of the following responses: they returned it, they can't find it, they never received it, they are holding it for a final decision, they are publishing it, or they will pull it from the bottom of the pile and make a decision on it. If they didn't receive it, ask if you can resend it. If they tell you that they can't give you an answer now, ask when you might expect a response from them and wait that length of time (or wait another month if they don't give you a time). If there's still no response, you can either leave it there indefinitely or send a registered letter withdrawing the manuscript for publication and telling them you will be submitting it elsewhere. You may not get the actual manuscript back, but you are then free to send it out again.

The following paragraphs refer to writing for periodicals, because book publishers are obligated to keep to the terms and dates agreed upon in your contract.

➤ *The periodical pays for but doesn't print your piece.* Occasionally a publisher pays for a story or article but doesn't print it even after many months or years. If you were given a publication date but your article didn't appear, you can inquire about why it wasn't in that issue and ask if it has been rescheduled. The publisher may then give you a new date if they have one. If you are not given a publication date, wait about a year and inquire again.

At this point you have a few options: You can let the publisher print it if and when they please; you can ask if you may offer one-time or reprint rights to other publishers while waiting for publication; you can ask for the rights to be returned to you if the publisher has no plans to use your piece.

If the publisher does return the rights to the story or article, you are not obligated to return the payment.

➤ *They accept but don't print your piece.* This is similar to the previous issue except in this case they pay on *publication,* rather than on acceptance, and you have not been paid. Follow the same steps given above, omitting any references to payment.

➤ *They are slow or provide no payment.* When publishers accept pieces they usually tell you when and how much you will be paid. If that payment does not come as promised, do not be afraid to follow up. Give a month's grace period and then send a polite letter, reminding them of the promised payment. If you previously received a letter from them giving the projected time and amount of payment, make a copy and send it along, pointing out that the designated time of payment has passed and requesting payment. If within thirty days you still have no response, invoice them for the amount due.

Fog Index (Reading Level)

Writers for a popular reading audience need to write for the reading level of their readers. Writers can determine this by use of the *fog index.* Some computer programs will calculate this for you automatically, but if you don't have that capability, you can follow these instructions:

1. Calculate the average length of your sentences. Here's how: Take a section of your manuscript, count 100 words or to the end of the sentence closest to 100. Now count the number of sentences in that 100-word section. (For a more accurate test, do this at the beginning, middle, and end of your manuscript. Add the total results and divide by three to find the average.) Divide the total number of words in each 100-word section by the number of sentences in that section. The result is the average sentence length.

2. Next, calculate the percentage of "hard" or longer words in the passages. In each section of 100 words, count the number of words having three or more syllables.

   Do not count capitalized words, words that are combinations of two short words (such as *housekeeper* or *butterfly*), or verb forms that have three or more syllables as the result of adding *-ed* or *-es* (such as *created* or *trespasses*).

   Now divide that number of long words by 100 (or the number of total words in that section). That will give you the percentage of long words.

3. Finally, to determine the fog index, add the average sen-

tence length to the percentage of long words and multiply by .4.

Here's an example: I counted the first five sentences in the section below under "Typeface" and came up with 113 words. So 113 divided by 5 = an average of 22.6 words per sentence. Then I counted the three-syllable words in the same section and found 7. And 7 divided by 113 = .06. I added 22.6 to .06 and got 22.66. Then I multiplied 22.66 by .4 and got 9.1 (or slightly above ninth-grade reading level).

Check your result against the list below. Keep in mind that anything between 17 and 13 will be at too high a reading level for a popular magazine.

17 = college graduate
16 = college senior
15 = college junior
14 = college sophomore
13 = college freshman
12 = high-school senior (level of *Atlantic Monthly*)
11 = high-school junior (level of *Harper's*)
10 = high-school sophomore (level of *Time*)
9 = high-school freshman (level of *Reader's Digest*)
8 = eighth grader (level of *Ladies' Home Journal*)
7 = seventh grader (level of *True Confessions*)
6 = sixth grader (level of most comic books)

An index of 6–10 indicates an easy reading level. If you are trying to write for a popular-level reading audience, but your manuscripts show a higher fog index, that higher level of reading difficulty will prove a problem for your audience. However, if you are writing for an academic or college-level audience, it is appropriate to have a higher index.

Typeface

Today, with so many different *typefaces* (sometimes referred to as *fonts* or *typestyles* in this computer age) available at the click of a button or touch of a mouse, writers are even more confused than ever about which one to choose for their manuscripts. The thing to keep in mind is that editors read a lot and appreciate not having to strain their eyes to read your manuscript, so choose a typestyle and size that is easy on the eyes.

Writers should choose a clear typeface and a point-size that makes reading easy. With most typefaces, a 12-point type size works well. (What works best for me is the Times Roman typeface with 12-point type.) Do not use a *sans serif* type: That is a blocky typestyle without the serifs—those small additional lines or squiggles at the tops and bottoms of each letter. For some reason, typefaces without serifs are much harder to read.

Typeface should be your main consideration when thinking about presentation of a manuscript to an editor. Don't get carried away with all the bells-and-whistles design options that your computer offers. Although you have the capability of making fancy headings, using various typestyles, or adding graphics—*don't*. Not only do those "extras" come across as unprofessional in the industry, they do not allow an editor to easily calculate the length of the finished piece. For that reason, you will want to use the same typestyle and size throughout.

A word about underlining, italics, and boldface: Most publishers avoid using underlining and boldface, preferring instead to use italics for such things as emphasizing a word or phrase, giving the title of a book, or introducing a foreign word. But avoid overuse of italics, especially when using them as emphasis for emotional effect. Of course, with a typewriter authors would underline what they wanted to italicize. But with today's word processors you just italicize it yourself.

Mailing Guidelines

The following guidelines should be followed when sending out manuscript submissions.

The addressee

When preparing your mailing, address the envelope to a specific editor. Do all you can to ensure that your submission gets into the hands of the correct person. Editors' names can be found under publishing houses listed in most market guides.

If you can't find the correct information in your market guide, or if you are mailing to a new publisher, or that press has a new editor, call the publisher's office and ask for the editor's name to whom you should send your submission. And even if it's not an unusual name, ask them to spell it (an incorrect spelling may come across as carelessness on your part).

Check your market guide's listing to see if your submission is going to a publisher who prefers you submit your proposal simply to "Editor." Those cases are few, however. When possible, avoid addressing a package to "Acquisitions Editor" or "Editor"—it may convey laziness in research or a lack of professionalism, or it may reduce the chances of your submission being seen by the right person.)

The S.A.S.E.

In publishing there is a certain protocol for mailing a manuscript submission. The general rule is to include an *S.A.S.E.* (a self-addressed stamped envelope) with your submission. Make sure that your S.A.S.E. is a large enough envelope and has the *correct* return postage on it. Most publishers will toss your manuscript unless you include that extra stamped envelope, so in order to get the manuscript back if it's rejected by the publisher, you must include an S.A.S.E.

With the use of computers, however, it's so easy to print out a fresh copy for each submission that some people don't want their manuscript back. If that is the case, include a #10 business-sized envelope for an acceptance or rejection slip, and then in your cover letter request that the #10 envelope be used for a response and that the manuscript be discarded.

Be aware that some publishers no longer return manuscripts,

even if you do provide an S.A.S.E., so take note of those publications and save yourself the postage.

When a manuscript requires more than one first-class stamp, as most will, realize that the second and subsequent stamps are less than the first. If you are not sure of the current rates, check with your post office. (Buying an inexpensive postage scale will save a lot of trips to the post office.) Make sure the stamps are attached, not paper-clipped or left loose in the envelope. Never send a check for return postage; editors don't appreciate having to cash the check and prepare your S.A.S.E.

When you start sending out manuscripts, check with your local post office for current mailing regulations. These regulations change constantly, so keep yourself informed. You may want to take advantage of the cheaper rate for manuscripts and printed matter. Ask your postal worker how you should mark the outside of the envelope for that manuscript rate (currently "Media Mail") and also what you should write below your return address in order to have your manuscript returned to you if it is undeliverable. Though it's more expensive, it may be worth the cost to send packages via Priority Mail: It ensures a speedy delivery and return if the package is undeliverable.

Never bind or staple a manuscript. Send out a clean copy of your manuscript with the pages left loose. If your manuscript is returned from the publisher with a rubber band around it or a paper clip on it, and the clip or band leaves a mark, *don't* send that used-looking copy out again. Make a new copy that doesn't look like it's made the rounds. If the article with a paper clip still looks fresh, just send it out with the paper clip left in place.

Although shorter manuscripts (up to three pages) may be folded in thirds and sent in a #10 envelope, many publishers prefer to receive submissions unfolded and in the larger size manila envelope. This saves the editor the extra step of unfolding and makes your submission easier to process. It also saves wear and tear and offers your manuscript a longer life if you plan to send out the same copy again. (For those of you who send many submissions out, here's a little hint that might be helpful: If your manuscript is returned a little dog-eared, you can sometimes just retype or reprint the first page in order to give your submission a fresher appearance.)

You can do one of two things regarding your S.A.S.E. You can include an S.A.S.E. that is slightly smaller than the outside envelope in order to keep all your materials flat (an outside envelope of 9½ x 12½ -inches or 10 x 13-inches allows for the smaller 9 x 12-inch S.A.S.E. to fit neatly inside. The other option is a #9 envelope enclosed within a #10). Or you can fold your S.A.S.E. in half, including it in your submission package. Don't worry—a folded S.A.S.E. is the exception to the publishers' no-fold rule.

If you're submitting an entire book manuscript, send unbound/loose pages in an appropriate-sized box, such as a manuscript box sold for this purpose or a typing-paper box. This box can be enclosed in a large padded mailer. If you prefer not to use a box, you can put a protective sheet of cardboard on the top and bottom of the manuscript and hold it together with rubber bands, placing the manuscript in a padded mailer envelope. Instead of an S.A.S.E., enclose a mailing label addressed to yourself, plus enough postage for the return of the manuscript and instructions as to whether to return by Priority Mail or Special Standard Mail. I usually enclose these in a small envelope marked, "Label and postage for return of [manuscript title here] by [your name]." Paper clip this to the title page or to the cardboard on the top of the manuscript. In this package you may also wish to enclose a self-addressed postcard that the publisher can return acknowledging that your manuscript was received.

Keeping a record of costs for tax purposes

You will want to keep track of all postage costs, both for the mailing and the return. Even if you are not claiming your writing as a small business, keep track of the postage, as you may be able to claim it as a deduction. (See "Income Tax" in chapter 3 for details.)

Mailing Guidelines: Foreign Countries

When mailing to Canada or other countries, it is important to keep in mind that you cannot send U.S. stamps on an S.A.S.E. When submitting a manuscript to a foreign publisher, go to the post office and request International Reply Coupons (IRCs). Foreign publishers can redeem these coupons for local stamps at their post offices. The coupons are not inexpensive, and each coupon is worth about a half-ounce, so you will probably need several coupons for a larger manuscript. If you write regularly for a foreign publisher, you may wish to request another arrangement, one that allows you to send checks periodically to cover postage. Ask the editor how best to handle it.

Manuscript Format for Periodicals

When I sent out my very first manuscript to a periodical, I didn't have a clue as to how I was to lay it out on the page. I broke every rule. Back then I didn't even know there were rules regarding the layout of the manuscript. To avoid making the same mistakes I made, follow these guidelines regarding format for articles, fillers, and stories. (Format guidelines for *book* manuscripts can be found in chapter 9, "On the Writing of Books.")

First page format (For a sample first page, see figure 2-1.)
Margins. First set your margin at 1¼ to 1½ inches on the left side of the page. Put a 1-inch margin on the right side as well as the top and bottom. Use 20-pound white bond paper (never use onion skin or erasable bond).

Upper left-hand corner. In the upper left-hand corner (below that 1-inch margin), put your name, address, phone number, fax, and email address (this is optional)—put all these on separate and successive lines. On the next line, put in your Social

Security number (a publisher must have that to send out a check). Make sure that the name you've put in this upper left-hand corner is the name you want your check made out to, if the publisher should buy it.

Upper right-hand corner. In the upper right-hand corner, you will put what kind of rights you are offering, usually "First Rights Offered." (See chapter 3 under "Rights and Reprints" for details about rights.) Under that line, put a line identifying what kind of piece you are including, such as "A How-To Article" or "A Teen Short Story." Under that, put the approximate number of words. If you are sending a filler piece, put down the exact number of words (for example, "About 1,500 Words" or "Exactly 546 Words").

On the next line, you can put "Pix on Request" informing them if you have pictures available. Knowing this, they can request them if they are interested.

On the last line, put your copyright notice: © 2003 [Your Name]. (For more information about this, see chapter 3's sections on "Copyright Law.")

Middle of page. Next, drop down to just above the middle of the page (to leave editor room for making notes) and, in all capital letters and centered, type in your title. Drop down 4 lines and type in your byline, centered again, "By [your name]." If you are planning to use a pen name with the piece, put that pen name here (leaving your real name in the upper, left-hand corner). The name on this byline will be the name that appears on the piece when it is published. (For more information about this, see chapter 3's section "Pen Names/Pseudonyms.")

Text. After the byline, drop down 6 lines to start the text. Indent the first line of each paragraph consistently (5 to 10 spaces). As you type, do not put an extra linespace between paragraphs. Double-space your text on only one side of the paper. Your first page does not get a page number; only the second page and subsequent pages should be numbered.

Second and subsequent pages

On the second and all subsequent pages of your submission in the upper left-hand corner just below that 1-inch margin, you should put in a header: Use a key word from your title along with your last name (for example, Key/Stuart). In the right-hand corner, put the page number in, such as "Page 2." If you are using a typewriter, you will have to type this at the top of each page. With a word processor or computer, headers are easy to put in automatically.

The end

When you reach the end of a manuscript, it is not necessary to type in "The End." Just stop. If there might be some doubt as to whether it is the end (if your piece ends at the bottom of a page, for example), you can indicate the end with a "- 30 -" or a "###" typed in below the last line.

Text tips

If you are including a song, poem, or long quotation in the middle of your text (called an *extract),* indent the whole poem or quotation five to seven spaces more than the regular text indentation. You don't have to leave extra lines before or after the quote, but you do need to double-space the text of the extract.

Occasionally a publisher will ask that you submit your manuscript on a thirty-five character line (or a length of the publisher's choice). This doesn't mean you have to have exactly thirty-five characters on every line, but you should set your margins so there are thirty-five characters between the two margins. Once you have your margins set at thirty-five characters, you can begin typing your manuscript, simply breaking at the end of the line as you normally do. Some magazines are set up with columns of a certain width and when you adapt your margins to their specifications, they can easily determine the length of your piece as it will appear in their magazine.

If you are using a typewriter, type the same number of lines on each page. This helps the publisher calculate the length of your piece. Computer users don't have to worry about this, as the computer does it automatically.

Figure 2-1

Ready Writer
1500 Your Street
Anywhere, USA 12345
Tel.: 000-000-0000
Fax: 000-000-0000
E-mail: xxxxxxx@aol.com
SS# 000-00-0000

First Rights Offered
A How-To Article
About 1,200 Words
Pix on Request
© 2003 Ready Writer

HOW TO TYPE A MANUSCRIPT

By Ready Writer

Manuscript appearance

The appearance of your manuscript is one of the most important indications of your professionalism. You won't have a second chance to make a good first impression. There should be no errors on the first page, and the rest of the manuscript should be as near to perfect as possible. With a computer spell-check, that is an easier task, but always proofread a hard copy before you send it off—it's amazing how seeing your manuscript on paper can reveal errors you never saw on your computer screen. If you are using a typewriter, correct all errors with a correction ribbon or white-out (avoid correction tape or strips from which the white rubs off). Don't type over a mistake hoping that no one will notice the double marks. Also, if possible, avoid hand-correcting mistakes. If you must, cross out the error and rewrite the correction legibly above the crossed-out word. And don't allow more than three such corrections per page. If that happens, retype it.

It's important to have a professional-looking manuscript. Be sure your typewriter or printer has a new or nearly new ribbon or printer cartridge in it before typing or printing out your final copy. And avoid sending a messy or dog-eared manuscript; it may get your piece placed at the bottom of the pile. Some editors never give a piece the chance it deserves, based on looks alone.

When sending a manuscript, *don't* send your only copy even if it is in your computer. Always make an extra copy or two for your files. This is especially important for those who are sending *typed* manuscripts—you don't want to lose your only copy in the mail.

Poetry format for periodicals

For poetry, put the same information at the top of the first page as described above, identify it as "A Poem" (in the upper, right-hand corner), and indicate the number of lines instead of the number of words under that. Always prepare each poem as a separate manuscript; never put two or more poems together, even if they are short. Although you may send more than one at a time to the same place, editors will want to select the ones they want and return the others, so each must be clearly identified.

When preparing your manuscript, if a poem is short enough

to fit on one page, simply center it on the page under the title and byline. If it is too long for one page, start your title just above the middle of the page, as you would with other manuscripts, and continue over onto the next page or more as needed. (See the section below on "Submission Guidelines" for more information on submitting poetry.)

Games, puzzles, fillers, and miscellaneous items

As described above for poetry, each of these specialized submissions must be sent as a separate manuscript, even if you are sending more than one to the same publisher at the same time. Use your common sense when it comes to arranging them on the page, since these submissions rarely fit the rules. If it is a filler, handle it like you would any other article manuscript, starting just above the middle of the first page. For games or puzzles, center the game/puzzle on the first page, with the solution at the bottom (if it is short) or on the next page, if longer. The game or puzzle should have a name and the solution should be clearly identified if it is on a separate page.

Some publishers expect camera-ready artwork for some puzzles, such as crossword or word-search puzzles, so check their guidelines before submitting such material.

Manuscript format for books

Book manuscript formatting guidelines will be covered extensively in chapter 9, "On the Writing of Books," but I'd like to include a brief word here about the basic difference between the book and periodical formats: Instead of providing your essential information in the upper corners of the first page (as with a periodical manuscript), you provide that information on the title page of your book manuscript.

Rejection Slips

In the "Criticism" section of chapter 1, I mentioned that rejection slips are part of that critical cloud that follows writers around. But one of the first things you as a writer need to do when beginning to submit manuscripts is desensitize yourself to the inevitable tide of rejection slips. Don't worry, it's not as hard as it sounds.

When I tell people that I sold the very first articles I ever wrote and nearly everything I have written since, those people assume that I have never received a rejection slip. They are wrong. I literally have *hundreds* of them. Rejection slips have never deterred me. I am persistent and keep submitting to different publishers until someone buys the manuscript.

What's the secret to my persistence? Early on I learned that rejection happens. You just can't please everyone all the time. No matter how good you are at writing, there will be someone who won't like you or won't like your work. Rejection is as much a part of the business as mud and dirt are to the construction worker. But mud doesn't stop the builder from building. And rejections shouldn't stop you from submitting manuscripts. Rejection slips can in some ways be a good sign—because if you aren't getting rejection slips, you aren't working very hard to get your work out.

Another thing I learned is that there are a lot of reasons for rejection—and it's often not based on the value and quality of a manuscript. An acceptance (or rejection) by an editor is based on a multitude of factors, many of which the editor has little control over. Perhaps there is no room for a piece in an upcoming issue of their periodical, or a book manuscript doesn't meet the demands and interests of the market, or there isn't enough money left in their budget to pay for another book or article to be added to the publishing schedule, or they can't accept a piece because it is too much like something they have already done or have scheduled, or you've written for them before and they won't publish a string of articles by the same author too close together, or the publisher won't publish something controversial because it will upset their readers—and those are only a few of the possibilities.

It is true that editors make whopping mistakes and don't see the value in a certain book or article. I know a few editors who confess to having made poor judgment calls, telling me their horror stories about the one that got away—the article they rejected that won a prestigious award, or the book that became a bestseller.

The worst thing to do is take a rejection slip personally and assume it means your manuscript isn't any good. *Rejection slip:* I know of writers who don't like that term, so they, instead, call them *pre-acceptances.* Maybe that will make it easier for you to tolerate them. A pre-acceptance is not a rejection—it doesn't mean your manuscript is bad—it just hasn't found a home yet.

Before you ever send out that first manuscript, expect pre-acceptances back and get proactive: Devise a plan. Prepare a list of other places you can send your work. When it comes back, don't you dare put it in a drawer and forget it. Determine that you are going to get it off to another publisher on your list within that same week.

If I've had a secret to my success, that's been it: To keep those submissions going. If I believe in a manuscript—and I never wrote one I didn't believe in—I keep sending it out as long as there is anyone left to send it to. One general-interest article that I wrote has sold eighteen times—which is quite a record. But the truth is, I've sent it out at least *150* times.

A rejection slip may be written on a very small slip of paper, but for some writers, that piece of paper seems big and has the power to destroy what might have been a promising writing career. But if a writer can simply view it as a step toward the goal of being published (or of getting this piece published), it can take you step-by-step to success.

One last word about rejection slips. If you get a slip with an encouraging word from the editor, such as "This almost made it," or "Try us again," or "I like your writing," *don't* ignore it. Editors don't take the time to encourage bad writers or writers they don't want to hear from again. Take those comments as an invitation to submit again, and do it soon. Study the periodical, book guidelines, or catalog, and send something else that you think would have an even better chance than the previous submission. Don't give up until you make that sale.

Submission Guidelines

Along with learning how to prepare and mail a manuscript, there are a few other publishing-etiquette issues that you should know regarding submissions. Understanding and implementing these will add to your professional presentation.

Periodical submissions

Avoid simultaneous submission unless. . . When submitting an article or story to a periodical, it is the usual practice to send your manuscript out to one publisher at a time, wait for a response from that periodical, and then resubmit it elsewhere. There are, however, some exceptions. If the piece is timely (tied to a current event, season, or holiday), then you may send it concurrently to several editors (this is called a *simultaneous submission;* there's a detailed explanation of this later in this same section). If you are sending a simultaneous submission, write something in your cover letter to that effect. Something like this would work: "Due to the timeliness of this piece, I am making a simultaneous submission to several different editors. I will, however, sell first rights to only one. Other interested editors may purchase reprint rights following first publication." This way you will likely find an interested editor before it is too late.

Reprint rights. Another exception to the no-simultaneous-submissions rule is if you are offering reprint rights (see "Rights and Reprints" in chapter 3 for details). In that case, you may send the article to as many publishers as might be interested. The way I determine how many to send out at one time is based on the market for a particular piece. When I used to sent out Christian education articles as reprints, I'd send them out one at a time because of the limited market. Now, if I have a general-interest piece that has a good number of potential markets, I send it to, say, three to five periodicals at a time. As it is hard to keep track of multiple submissions, sending out any more than five at a time can be an overwhelming task.

Multiple articles and pen names. There's another problem with sending out too many at a time. If you are sending to a limited market (say, Christian education), you can easily flood your own market. Many editors do not like to publish too many articles by the same author in a short span of time, so they may reject good articles because they have recently published something by that author. If you find yourself being told that your work is good, but there's too much of it out right now, you can offer to have your articles published under one or more pen names (find out more about this under "Pen Names, or Pseudonyms" in chapter 3).

Book submissions

Did you know that most books are sold before they are even written? It's true: most publishers prefer to be approached with a good book idea—especially if it's nonfiction—instead of a completed manuscript. (See chapter 9 for more details about writing book proposals.) That gives you a lot of freedom, because at any stage of the book-writing process you can approach a publisher with your idea. In fact, it's almost better to be at the idea stage than the have-already-written-it stage because it's easier to adapt an idea to a publishing house's needs than revise a completed manuscript to fit.

If your idea is a bit unusual or of limited interest, you may want to start with a query letter sent simultaneously to any number of appropriate publishers. In the letter, present your idea as clearly and succinctly as possible and ask if anyone is interested. That can save you a lot of time. The publishers will not make a commitment of any kind based on a query letter only, but you will find out who is interested. There are also a few publishers who will only accept a query letter initially (check your market guide), so this will have to be your first step in those cases as well.

Most publishers prefer a full book proposal (see chapter 9 for preparation details), and many authors will send that proposal to one publisher at a time. However, to save time, you can check your market guide for those who accept simultaneous submissions, and send the proposal to all those potential publishers at once. Indicate in your cover letter that you are making a simultaneous submission (this can be done as a P.S.), but let the publisher know you will send the full manuscript to only one at a time after getting their go-ahead. (This gives a sense of urgency to the publishers receiving your letter, letting them know if they fail to respond promptly, they may miss the opportunity to read your full manuscript until another publisher has looked at it.)

If you are a new writer, an interested publisher will usually ask to see the full manuscript before they will make a firm commitment or offer a contract. At that point they may also make some suggestions or ask for some changes from what you outlined in your proposal. That is the value of working from a proposal: the editor can have input before the manuscript is actually written. If you have a good track record, or have written other books for the same publisher, they may offer you a contract based on your proposal alone.

Just as there are publishers who will accept only *proposals,* there are also publishers who will accept only *complete* book manuscripts. And some will accept either. This information can be found in your market guide. Send each publisher what they want or, when given a choice, do what seems the most logical. The general rule of thumb is that it is better to send a proposal initially to test publishers' interest, so as not to waste time writing a book that no publisher wants.

Poetry submissions

For periodicals. Even though each of your poems is prepared as a separate manuscript (as described above) most publications accept more than one poem at a time. In the periodical listings of your market guide, the poetry section in each listing will indicate the maximum number of poems an editor will accept in one submission. That may vary from one to twenty.

For book manuscripts. Poetry manuscript submissions should not be sent as a proposal, the way fiction or nonfiction is sent. Instead, send poetry as a complete manuscript or a short sampler of your poetry, unless you are a well-established poet. Most publishers will want to see the complete manuscript before contracting. As to format: Keep in mind that unless they are short poems or the poetry format dictates something different, each poem should begin on a new page. Poetry books are among the most difficult to sell, and nearly impossible for the unknown poet to sell, so establish yourself by writing poetry for periodicals first.

Simultaneous submissions

For books and periodicals. When you send a *simultaneous submission,* you are sending the same manuscript, query, or proposal to a number of periodicals or publishers at the same time. Don't do this unless the publications you are sending to are listed in your market guide as being willing to receive simultaneous submissions.

When sending a simultaneous submission, make it clear in the cover letter to all the receiving editors that you are doing so. Never make a simultaneous submission without informing everyone involved. (If you make such a submission, however, it is not necessary to tell the editors whom else you are sending it to.)

Make it clear in your letter that although you are making a simultaneous submission, you will sell first rights* to only one publication. Or, if it is a simultaneous query (rather than a manuscript), that you will send the completed manuscript to one at a time for consideration. Of course, any interested editors could buy reprint rights if they are still interested after the piece appears the first time.

Another option when making a simultaneous submission to a periodical is to offer "one-time rights" to each interested editor. Make that offer only to those publishers whose listings indicate that they accept both simultaneous submissions and one-time rights. Generally speaking, that will be publishers from non-competing markets, such as denominational markets or newspapers where they know their constituency will not be

*For more information about rights (first, one-time, and simultaneous rights), see "Rights and Reprints" in chapter 3.

reading periodicals from other denominations or reading areas.

The last possibility is to make a simultaneous submission offering simultaneous rights. You normally limit this option to those times when you have a timely piece or something you think would be of interest across denominational lines. When making such a submission, you would tell the editors in your cover letter why you are offering simultaneous rights and to whom they are being offered. List the others you are sending it to so they can verify that they are non-overlapping markets. In this case, you will sell the piece simultaneously (offering simultaneous rights) to everyone who wants to buy it, and they all buy the same rights at the same time.

Greeting card submissions

At the back of the *Christian Writers' Market Guide* you will find a listing of greeting card publishers that accept ideas for greeting card verse or text. These have their own particular submission guidelines: Most publishers prefer that you submit each idea either on a 3 x 5-inch index card or on a manuscript page—remember one idea per card or page. The greeting card ideas you submit should be complete: including caption, inside/outside message, closing tag line, and, for Christian publishers, an appropriate Scripture verse.

Since these card ideas will generally not have a title to identify them, as an article would, you will need to include a separate copy reference number with each idea. You can use any method for numbering or labeling that you devise, as long as it makes it easy for you and the publisher to identify each idea. One method that works well is to use a combination of letters and numbers. Say you have three ideas for Christmas cards, you could use this coding: Ch-1, Ch-2, Ch-3. If they are valentines, use V-1, V-2, V-3. Birthday cards could be BD-1, BD-2, BD-3. Come up with an identity system based on letters, and number all the ideas under that code. That way, an editor can simply notify you that they want to buy Ch-4, V-8, and BD-5 and 6. The appropriate code should be used at the top of every manuscript page or index card.

Unless you are an artist (many card manufacturers are open to freelance artists), you don't need to supply the artwork for your idea. Card companies use their own artists to prepare the art. If, however, you have an idea for the art or how the card might be laid out, you may include that as a rough sketch. Most of the greeting card companies have submission guidelines, so send for those before submitting anything. Unfortunately, most companies will not send you a copy of their catalog, so you may want to check with your local Christian bookstore to see if they have any catalogs you can look at. Also, in your local store's card section, look at actual cards from the various card publishers and see the types of card each company produces.

Submission tips

In chapter 7, "On Marketing," we will learn how to determine *where* to submit material, but here I just want to add a short note to encourage you to do your market study and research first. Before you even send out a query or manuscript for the first time, create a thorough list of potential publishers to send to. Then, if it comes back rejected from one place, you will have other places on your list to send it. When a rejection comes, give yourself a deadline for getting it back into the mail to another place. Two to three days is best—don't let it go longer than a week before resubmitting, otherwise procrastination takes over. Rush to get a piece out, but don't be careless—consider each publisher you wish to send to. Before sending out your query letter or complete manuscript again, you may need to revise it to reflect the needs of the new publisher's market.

Tear Sheets

Occasionally you will hear from a publisher or find a publisher listed in your market guide requesting *tear sheets*. What they are asking to see is copies of articles or pieces you have previously published in other periodicals. The term *tear sheet* is a reference to pages torn from a magazine, but you probably won't want to tear out the pages—use a razor blade or knife to get a clean cut. In many cases you won't have an unlimited number of copies available, so it is acceptable to send out photocopies of your published articles. And if you don't have any tear sheets, say so.

If you have a lot of published articles, send those that are similar (in subject and tone) to what you are offering this editor. So, for example, if your submission is to a family magazine, send tear sheets of your best family-related articles. If you don't have anything that particularly fits, then send them the best you have.

Tracking Submissions

Before you send manuscripts to editors, it is important to have a good tracking system in place. Your system should keep track of the following:

- where each manuscript has been sent (along with a record of both the sending date and the receiving-word-back date)
- which manuscripts are still out to publishers and periodicals
- who has already rejected or accepted each manuscript
- who owes you payment or royalties (for a book contract)
- for a periodical: what rights you have sold on each piece of writing

If you don't start with a good tracking system, it's easy to lose both money and manuscripts in the confusion. At one point in my career when I was writing a lot of articles, I often had as many as 150 manuscripts in the mail at one time, both new pieces and reprints. Without a system to keep track of that volume, I would have quickly reached the point of self-destruction. Fortunately I had a good system.

Make sure your system works whether you have 5 or 150 manuscripts making the rounds. There are any number of new tracking-system programs available for the computer—a good basic personal office manager program would work, as well as programs designed specifically for this purpose. There are also books and booklets on personal management or manuscript tracking that can be helpful. The key is finding something that is easy to use and works well for you. Some people like an organizational system (even systems within systems) that covers everything, down to the smallest detail. Others like a general organizing structure and little more. Explore the resources available to you and also ask your friends who are writers for ideas on a tracking system that has worked for them.

If you prefer keeping your records by hand—although this is easily modified for the computer—feel free to adapt my favorite method:

1. Keep your records in a full-sized loose-leaf notebook that has alphabetical dividers.

2. Either hand-write records on notebook paper or prepare typewritten or computer printed records on regular paper, then use a three-hole punch on the paper so you can file them in your notebook.

3. Make up a separate sheet for each article or piece of writing you are submitting. In the upper right-hand corner put the title of the piece, a short descriptor (article, short story, poem, etc.), and the word count.

4. Then record the following information: The publisher's name (where you sent it), the date sent, the date accepted or rejected. If accepted, also indicate when paid, when it appeared.

Figure 2-2 provides an example of how this could be set up.

Figure 2-2

Beating the Winter Blahs
Family article
1,200 words

MOODY MAGAZINE
Sent query: March 18, 2002. Received go-ahead letter March 30, 2002.
Sent manuscript: May 21, 2002
Result: Rejected June 15, 2002. Note on rejection slip: "We have an article on this topic scheduled for next month."

CHRISTIAN PARENTING TODAY
Sent manuscript: June 25, 2002
Result: Sold! July 21, 2002. Scheduled for 2/03 issue.
Paid $150 August 2, 2002. Appeared in 2/03 issue.
(Include any other information on this sale that is pertinent.)

5. After the piece has appeared in print, you can indicate you are now offering reprint rights and continue with the same kind of listing. Here's an example:

Figure 2-3

REPRINT RIGHTS OFFERED:

PENTECOSTAL EVANGEL
Sent manuscript: March 10, 2003
Result: SOLD! Reprint rights June 2, 2003. Paid $75 on June 20, 2003. Being held for future use.

6. Once the sheets are made up, they can be filed alphabetically (by title) in the notebook. More sheets can be added as needed for additional records on each title.

7. In the front of the notebook put a routing schedule. This

schedule tells you at a glance what pieces are out and how long they've been out. As you make each new submission, write the current date, the title of the piece just sent, and the name of the receiving publisher on one line across the page. When the next submission is sent, list it under the previous one. If a manuscript is rejected, cross it out. If it is sold, circle it in red and write "Sold!" next to it. With that kind of system, you will be able to tell at a glance what has sold, what has been returned, and what is still out to publishers.

8. When a manuscript sells, but you have not yet been paid, put that information on a sticky note. On the slip, give the date, the name of the piece, when payment is due (if known), and the amount promised or expected. Put that sticky note on the back of the tracking sheet. As these are paid, record it on the appropriate sheet and discard the note. If the due date passes with no payment, follow up with another polite note.

9. Periodically you will need to follow up on the oldest of your submissions that haven't been returned or received a response.* Send a polite note giving the name of the piece, when it was submitted, whom it was addressed to, and ask about its current status. In your records, write a note stating that you requested information on this title, and then put a date beside the request so that you can keep track.

10. In the back of the notebook, you might want to keep various lists. For instance, you might keep a list of the different pieces you have sold and tally how many times each piece has sold. Another adaptation of that is to list the specifics: Write down each manuscript title along with the publica-

*For information about waiting on submission response, see *They give you the silent treatment* in this chapter's "Author-Editor Relationships" section.

tions that have bought that particular piece. Listing by publisher is another possibility: Write down each publisher who has printed your work. Under each publisher, list which of your pieces they have accepted.

11. Book manuscripts can be tracked in the same way. You may want to keep them in a separate section at the back of the same notebook, or they can be mixed in alphabetically with the periodical titles.

Chapter 3

On the Business of Writing

- Jane sold all rights to her article on gardening to *Garden Gate,* and then turned around and offered the same piece to *Country Gardens.*

- Lee was in a hurry to get his article on a current event out as quickly as possible, so he made a simultaneous submission. When five publications showed an interest, he sent it to all of them, offering first rights.

- John was so afraid someone would steal his material that he registered his copyright on every article he wrote before sending it out.

- Shirley liked another author's material on parenting so well that she adopted it as her own and included it in her new book.

- Alan just got a big advance on his first book and wants to start claiming his writing as a small business, but he has no record of his income or expenses for the year.

- Susan doesn't want anyone to know she is the one writing her article on child abuse, so she is submitting it anonymously to publishers, including only a pseudonym.

All of these writers are heading for trouble because they don't know enough about the business side of writing.

Most writers would rather write than administrate. But, like any other business, writing has certain business-related or legal ramifications the writer needs to watch. Many writers are uncomfortable dealing in these areas because they are not well enough informed to make appropriate decisions. In most of the following areas it is a matter of knowing enough to make informed decisions and to protect your rights. One of the real problems for writers is that they are often dealing with editors or publishers who do not know very much about these areas either.

Fortunately, we do not have to know a lot to protect our rights. My intention here is to give you the basic knowledge that will stand you in good stead. I challenge you to take a few minutes to read and review this information until you understand it. Then review it from time to time until you can remember the basics, especially in the areas of rights, copyrights, plagiarism, and libel—the areas where you are most likely to lose rights or trample on someone else's. Other sections in this chapter will deal with income tax and record keeping for tax purposes.

Rights and Reprints

Before we get into the ins and outs of the copyright law, I want to lay a foundation by explaining something about what rights you are selling when you sell a manuscript to a publisher. We have touched on some of these in earlier chapters but will cover all the various options here.

When you sell a book, the rights and copyright concerns are spelled out in the contract. The book is copyrighted either in the name of the author (preferred) or the name of the publisher, and all subsidiary rights are negotiable. But this is not the case with articles and other small creative products. When you offer these, such as a magazine article, a photo, or a cartoon, for publication, you will put the rights offered in the upper, right-hand corner on the first page. You have several choices of rights to offer:

First rights

This is usually your first choice, unless this manuscript falls into a category described below. It offers the publisher exactly what it says—the right to publish your piece for the first time. When you sell first rights, such as first rights to an article on family Bible study, as soon as the piece is actually published, the rights automatically revert back to you. At that point you can offer reprint rights (see below), put the material in a book, or do whatever you like.

Serial rights

Sometimes you will see the term *serial rights*, which refers to use in a periodical (as opposed to serialization) and is always used in connection with some other rights. For example, "first serial rights" means first use in a periodical, and "first North American serial rights" means first use in a periodical in North America.

One-time rights

This also means what it says: the right to publish a piece one time. The difference between first rights and one-time rights is that with first rights you are selling the right to publish it the first time. With one-time rights, they may publish it one time but not necessarily the first time. You may sell one-time rights to as many publishers as are willing to buy them. Generally, you sell one-time rights to publications with non-overlapping readerships, such as newspapers in different areas of the country or different denominational publishers. The sale of one-time rights is common with photos or graphic material.

All rights

Most writers avoid selling all rights except in special cases. If you sell all rights, it means the material then belongs to the publisher, and you have no more control over how or when it is used. When you sell all rights, those rights will nevertheless revert back to you after thirty-five years. Some types of material, such as curriculum, are almost always sold this way since they are used over a longer period of time, reissued in various forms, and so on. I don't mind selling all rights in such a case since there would not likely be an additional market for it anyway. Aside from material like curriculum, I usually will only sell all rights if the payment is high, the market is very limited (I'm not likely to sell it elsewhere), or if I want to add a particular periodical to my list of credits. For example, I would sell all rights to a high-profile general market or a top Christian market so I could say I had sold to that publication.

The phrases *all rights* and *exclusive rights* mean the same thing and are used interchangeably. All or exclusive rights to your work cannot be sold unless the transfer is specifically stated in writing. An acceptance letter may say something such as, "We will pay you $X for all rights to your article entitled . . . " Also watch for wording on the back of your payment check that may say, "Endorsement of this check indicates the transfer of all rights." If you receive such a check, and you have not agreed to sell all rights, return the check and ask them to send a new check without that imprint.

The choice is always yours. If a publication offers to buy a manuscript, but will only accept all rights, then you will have to decide if you want to make the sale. If not, you politely let them know that you are not willing to sell all rights. In some cases, especially if it is something they really want, they will be willing to accept only first rights—even if it is against their usual policy. Fortunately there are few Christian periodicals that require all rights.

Simultaneous rights

This means you are selling the right to publish a piece to more than one publisher. Such sales are usually to non-overlapping markets, such as denominational publishers, or are of a timely nature. For example, you could sell an article on your trip to a war-torn country to several different newspapers at the same time in different areas. However, never sell simultaneous rights unless all parties know about it and have agreed to it. (See "Submission Guidelines" in chapter 2 for more information on offering simultaneous rights.)

There is not a lot of difference between simultaneous rights and one-time rights. Simultaneous rights are offered and sold to several publishers at the same time, whereas one-time rights may be offered and sold at different times.

Reprint rights

After you have sold first rights to a publication, you wait until your piece is actually published and distributed in the periodical, at which point the rights revert to you. You may then offer that piece to other interested periodicals who accept reprint rights. Their listings in *The Christian Writers' Market Guide* will indicate which ones do, and in the topical listings the *R* following a periodical's name indicates that they accept reprints. That will make it easy to quickly select possible publishers for your reprints.

Since some Christian periodicals don't pay a lot, this is a way to make additional money for the same piece, as well as get your material out to new readers. I have sold many pieces five to eight times, and a couple as many as fifteen to eighteen times. For example, you might sell that family Bible study article to a general publication such as *Discipleship Journal,* and then resell it to your church's denominational magazine and to your college's alumni magazine.

Formerly when submitting reprints it was not necessary to include a cover letter. However, the reprint market is changing. There are still a lot of publications that use reprints, but many are becoming more particular about where and when a piece previously appeared. They now want a cover letter that gives that information. In your market guide, you will find a reference as to whether or not they want such information. If they do not ask for it, go ahead and send your reprints without a cover letter. Simply put "Reprint Rights Offered" in the upper right-hand corner of the first page.

As a general rule, reprints work best for denominational publishers or publishers in specialized areas. Although some major publishers will accept reprints, they are less likely to buy those that have appeared in another general-interest publication to which their readers might also subscribe.

Nonexclusive rights

As stated earlier, when you offer a manuscript for publication, you need to specify what rights you are offering in the upper right-hand corner of the first page. If you do not specify the rights you are offering, and they do not specify what rights they are buying, you have sold nonexclusive rights. That means that after they publish it the first time, they can reuse it in a succeeding issue of the same periodical (but not in any other periodicals they may publish) without further payment. However, you may also sell reprint rights to the piece, since their rights are nonexclusive.

Keep copies of all correspondence concerning publication and accurate records of what rights you have sold. If you sold manuscripts in the past before you understood about rights, and you do not know what rights those publishers have purchased, you can write to them and ask.

Works for hire

Occasionally you may have a publisher send you a work-for-hire contract for an article or story they plan to buy from you. I do not recommend that you sign such a contract. The work-for-hire provision of the current copyright law (see details below) was intended to cover writing done by an employee while being paid a salary. The provision says that such work belongs to the employer. It was not intended to cover work done by freelance writers and offered for sale to a periodical. As with all rights, this is an outright sale—the publisher has full control—but the rights will not revert to you after thirty-five years as they do when you sell all rights.

However, there are exceptions to this recommendation. For example, many writers sign work-for-hire contracts when producing Sunday school curricula, Bible study guides, or compilations of quotes and writing under very specific guidelines. Such work is often considered a legitimate use of the work-for-hire contract. The product of such a contract is not so much a creative product as it is a piece of work done to the publisher's specifications.

Copyright Law: The Basics

The copyright law can be intimidating in its entirety, but fortunately the part you need to know and understand as a writer is fairly small. It is, however, extremely important that you take the time to learn and remember the following material in order to be in a position to protect your rights when necessary.

I have talked to enough writers who had concerns about the copyright law to know that most tend to be overly concerned about protecting their rights. Fortunately, there are not writers or editors on every corner waiting to steal your material. It does happen rarely—even in the Christian market—but generally the copyright law gives you reasonable protection. To be constantly worried about that possibility would be like worrying about being hit by a truck every time you stepped out of the house—counterproductive.

The current copyright law went into effect on January 1, 1978, and generally affects only material that was printed on or after that date. I will mention the differences, as we go along, for material published before that date.

The first thing you need to know is that everything you write has copyright protection from the time it reaches a tangible form (such as being typed or entered in your computer). This protection is automatic—you do not have to register the copyright. Note that registering a copyright is what most people consider the appropriate protection, but the automatic protection is just as viable. This copyright protection gives you control over how and when your material can be used.

This law originally said that a manuscript had to have a copyright notice on it to get the protection, but a later court ruling changed that, so now you are still protected without the notice. However, I recommend that writers always put their copyright notice on a piece before sending it out. It is your responsibility to do that before distribution. I have heard some writers comment that they don't put the notice on because the editors tend to misunderstand or label you an amateur. That may have been true initially, but now it has become standard practice for most professional writers.

There are three necessary elements in a copyright notice. It should include:

➤ a C with a circle around it (or in parentheses) or the word *Copyright*

➤ the date of creation or first publication

➤ the copyright holder's name (yours).

My copyright notice looks like this: ©2003 Sally E. Stuart. I use the date of creation until it is published, then switch to the date of first publication. Do not change that date each time it is published.

Anything that is published or distributed to the public without a copyright notice goes into public domain. If a publisher merely forgets to run your piece with a copyright notice, however, the copyright law provides for correcting this (request Form CA). It will restore the copyright and also protect any infringers who used the copyrighted material thinking it was in the *public domain*. Public domain refers to material that is not protected by a copyright either because it was originally distributed without copyright protection or because the copyright has expired. Anything that is in public domain can be used by anyone without permission, but he or she still needs to give credit to the author. The law cannot restore the copyright to any work already in the public domain.

Publication is defined as distribution of copies by sale (or other transfer) to the public. Even just offering to distribute something constitutes publishing it, so if you run an ad in a magazine offering to sell a book called *100 Favorite Hamburger Recipes*, even if no one buys a copy it is considered published because you offered it to the public. However, a public performance does not constitute publication, so you can participate in a poetry reading without losing the copyright protection on your poem.

Most government publications are not copyrighted, so you may use the information in them freely without having to get permission. See the next section on "Fair Use and Permissions" for more information on when and how to get permissions when needed.

The next question, then, is how and when do you register a copyright? In most cases you won't. I have never registered a copyright myself. My books are copyrighted by the publisher in my name (usually). Generally speaking, I don't recommend that writers copyright their material unless they have produced something unusual based on a good deal of research or have come up with some original statistics someone else might want to steal. The only reason you need a registered copyright is so you can sue someone for infringing on it. For personal or financial reasons or because there is not enough money at stake, most of us wouldn't consider suing. Usually the only time that kind of money is involved is if your story was stolen and made into a movie or put into a form that would generate a lot of revenue. For most of us, that simply isn't the reality.

If you do not register your copyright when you write the manuscript (or when it is published), you can still do so within five years of first publication. You can even register a copyright after an infringement if you decide to bring suit. If you don't register until after the infringement, you can sue for damages but not for attorney's fees. The suit must take place within three years of the infringement.

If you want to register your copyright, you will need to send for forms to Copyright Law, Library of Congress Copyright Office, 101 Independence Ave. SE, Washington, DC 20559-6000; or call 202-707-3000. Forms can also be copied off their website at *www.copyright.gov.* There are a lot of different forms, depending on what you are copyrighting, so you will need to request or select forms by name. For most articles and stories that is Form TX, for published and unpublished, nondramatic literary works. There are also categories for performing arts (Form PA), visual arts (Form VA), and sound recordings (Form SR). See their website for additional information.

When you get the form, follow all instructions and submit it (you will need one for each piece being copyrighted) with a fee of twenty dollars for each copyright requested. You also have the option of copyrighting groups of material under one copyright, using Form GR/CP. For this option you must sort your manuscripts into two categories. The first is all unpublished manuscripts for the year. Put them in a loose-leaf notebook and give it a title, such as "The Unpublished Writings of John Doe 2003," and register them under one thirty dollar fee. If you want to register all your published manuscripts for the year in a similar way, each must carry a copyright notice on the piece itself when it is published. It is not enough that they were protected under the blanket copyright of the publication. If you plan to do this, you must ask each publisher to print your piece with a copyright notice at the bottom, otherwise you cannot include them in this blanket copyright of published pieces for that year. Put the qualifying published pieces in a notebook under one title also.

When you register a copyright it is for the author's lifetime plus seventy years. A copyright is also a tangible asset and can be left to someone in your will, which can be especially important for books. After you are gone, your family will then have control over when and how your material is used.

If you have a piece printed in a copyrighted publication, your piece has copyright protection under that publication's copyright. If the publication is not copyrighted, you will want to ask that they carry your copyright notice at the end of your piece. To find out if a periodical is copyrighted or not, you can check their listing in the *Market Guide* (it will tell only those that are not—the rest should be), or check their masthead.

Copyright Law: Fair Use and Permissions

Authors often struggle with issues related to copyright as they do their writing. For example, do you need permission to quote an author in your article? The law says that you don't if your quote falls within "fair use." What's that, and how do you proceed? Unfortunately the law does not give us specific numbers, only some general guidelines to consider when making that decision for ourselves. Here is the definition of *fair use* and the four factors we must consider.

Fair use

Fair use states that "the right to use a copyrighted work for purposes such as criticism, comment, news reporting, teaching, scholarship, or research is not an infringement of copyright. In determining whether the use made of a work in any particular case is a fair use the factors to be considered include:

1. The purpose and character of the use, including whether such use is of a commercial nature or is for nonprofit, educational purposes.

2. The amount and substantiality of the portion used in relation to the copyrighted work as a whole.

3. The nature of the copyrighted work.

4. The effect of the use upon the potential market for or value of the copyrighted work."

The guidelines are vague and leave a lot of room for interpretation. I will try to clarify each point here:

1. *Use.* It is more likely to be fair use if you want it for nonprofit or educational purposes, rather than to put it in an article or book you are going to sell. You may still be able to use it for commercial purposes if it qualifies under the other three guidelines.

2. *Amount/proportion.* Look at how large a quote you are using in relation to the entire piece you are quoting from. It is more likely to be fair use if you quote three pages from a four-volume set, than if you quote a paragraph or less from a short article. Also, look at how much of *your* piece the quote constitutes. If you use someone's short story as a ma-

jor part of one of eight chapters of your book, then that story constitutes a large proportion of your work.

3. *Nature.* It is almost impossible to quote (without permission) from things such as poetry or song lyrics. Anything other than the title of a song requires permission, and even one line of a poem may also. It is usually easier to quote from an article or book without getting permission. However, if you are using tables, graphs, or results of original research you should also get permission. Think of it this way: the more creative the item you are quoting, the more likely it is to require permission.

4. *Effect.* How will your use of this material affect the copyright owner? Here you simply need to use your common sense. Ask yourself: If the material was yours would you expect the author to ask for your permission? And, more importantly, is the quote you are using going to have a negative effect upon the author's ability to sell his or her work in the future? For example, quoting an anecdote or idea from a book called *Ten Keys to a Happy Marriage* is likely to be fair use, but if you pull out the ten principles on which the book is based and write your own book using those as a basis, it would not be fair use.

Anytime you are unsure as to whether or not to ask permission—ask. Don't go overboard and ask permission for every line you quote, but err on the conservative side. Also keep in mind that it is not always best to use a direct quote. You will want a direct quote if the person is an authority and you need his or her specific words, or if the way the person said it is as important as what was said. However, sometimes you can simply paraphrase the information and make a stronger point to fit your particular need. You will still give them credit, but you won't need permission.

Ask permission to quote anything in its entirety or to translate someone else's work. Keep track of all your sources as you write in case you have to go back and get some permissions later.

Also be aware that almost all the Bible versions or paraphrases are copyrighted, so you must follow the guidelines for their use. The King James Version is the only one in the public domain. Each version has its own guidelines for when it is necessary to ask permission, but most of them allow up to five hundred verses without asking permission as long it does not include an entire book of the Bible and does not constitute a major portion of your work. (For example, you can't reproduce a chapter of Romans from the New Living Translation, typeset it nicely, and call it your own.)

You need not obtain a copy of the complete copyright law from the Copyright Office, but you may want some of their pamphlets. The Copyright Office provides a number of circulars dealing with various aspects of the law that are helpful. They can supply you with a free ten-page booklet called "Publications of the Copyright Office," but some of the most helpful are R1: Copyright Basics; R22: How to Investigate the Copyright Status of a Work; R31: Ideas; and R34: Names & Titles.

How do you obtain permission?

When asking permission, you usually start with the original publisher. Write them a letter explaining what you want, and if they do not hold the copyright, ask them to forward it to the author or copyright owner. With an older or more obscure quote, it may be harder to track down the copyright owner, especially if the publisher has gone out of business or the author is deceased. Do not assume that either of those situations frees you to use the quote without permission. Someone still owns or controls those copyrights and you'll have to do your best to find them, or delete the quote from your work. Anything that is more than seventy-five years old is automatically in public domain, so subtract seventy-five from the current year and anything published prior to that date you can use.

When asking permission you must be very specific about exactly what the quote includes and how you are going to use it. See figure 3-1 for an example of a permissions letter.

If you cannot find the copyright owner through the usual channels, you can contact the copyright office and they will help you track down the copyright owner. They won't clear the copyright for you, but will they forward your request to the appropriate publisher or copyright owner.

Sometimes you will have to pay for the permission to use a quote, especially for things such as poetry, music, graphs, cartoons, or illustrations. Occasionally the cost will be too high to justify its use, and you will have to drop the quote or substitute another one.

Figure 3-1

Dear Copyright Holder (use actual name if available):

I am writing a book called ___________________, to be published by ________________, and am contacting you for permission to quote the following material from *(title of book)* , by *(author's name)*. I will be quoting page ___, line ___, through page ___, line ___, for a total of _________words. Said quote begins "______________" and ends "_______________."

Permission should cover my aforementioned book and any future revisions or editions, including nonexclusive rights in all languages. Such permission will in no way restrict your use of this material or affect permissions already given or to be given to others. If these rights are controlled by another party, please let me know whom I should contact.

I will use the following credit line and copyright notice, if that is acceptable to you: *(indicate)*

I need this permission soon and will appreciate your timely response. Please sign and date this request below, returning one copy to me and keeping one copy for your records.

Cordially,

(Your name, address, phone, fax, email)

I (we) hereby grant the permission as outlined above

Date _____________

Signature ____

____

Income Tax: The Basics

As soon as you start selling your writing, you will need to deal with the question of income tax. You will not necessarily have to start claiming your writing as a small business at that point, but you will need to determine whether your writing is a business or a hobby. Those are the two options given you by the IRS, and they will not be interested in whether you consider it a ministry.

Writing as a hobby

If you write for fun and have no real profit motive or expectations, then you are likely doing it as a hobby, and you can deduct your writing expenses up to the amount of your income. So if you make $200 (or whatever) on your writing during the year, you may deduct up to $200 (actual amount) worth of writing expenses. Always claim the income (if for a hobby) on your regular Form 1040 under "Other Income." The expenses (up to that amount of income) can be deducted on Schedule A under "Miscellaneous Deductions," but this amount is subject to the 2 percent limitation. Consult your accountant for details.

A profit motive

If, on the other hand, you are trying your best to make money at your writing, then you may consider it a small business and fill out Schedule C to go along with your personal tax forms. As a small business, you can deduct most or all of your expenses, even in excess of your income.

The guideline the IRS uses is that you make a profit three out of five years. That means they give you two years to run in the red, but then they expect you to start turning a profit. They will not automatically reject the claim that you are a business if you don't make a profit, but you may be called upon to prove your profit motive. As a writer, you can do that by keeping good business records, sending out manuscripts on a regular basis (keep the rejection slips and copies of letters from editors to prove it), and showing evidence of contests won, writers' conferences or classes attended, etc. Some writers keep a log of how much time they actually spend on writing and related activities. If you are audited before your five years is up, you may be asked to sign a Presumption of Profit form that says you will make a profit three out of five years. You do not *have* to sign it, so don't unless you are sure you can do it. Instead, rely on the other evidence to prove your profit motive.

Keeping tax records

Your case in favor of a profit motive is helped if you keep complete and accurate records of your submissions, sales, and expenses. Be as diligent as you would be with any other kind of business. Keep your financial records in a separate ledger or in a financial computer program, such as Quicken. I suggest you start keeping official records as soon as you start making money so you'll get into the habit and have the necessary records in case your business suddenly takes off. Here are a few suggestions:

1. *Keep all your receipts.* Without receipts, you can only claim small deductions if they are reasonable expenses for a writer, such as for paper or computer disks. If one of your regular suppliers doesn't provide sales slips, take along your own receipt book for them to use. Next to my desk I put out three manila envelopes each month—one for household records, one for business expenses, and one for business income. All my receipts go into one of these envelopes.

2. *Track expenses and income.* A simple system for tracking expenses and income is to use a 3x5-inch scratch pad and make up a slip to attach to every receipt. On the slip put the date in the upper, left-hand corner, the category (office supplies, postage, repairs, etc.) in the upper right-hand corner, and a description in the middle (computer paper, printer ribbon, etc.). Staple the slip to the receipt and put it in the appropriate envelope for future entry. Attach the slip to check stubs or to a photocopy of the check.

3. *Keep a ledger.* If you are doing the bookkeeping by hand, keep a running ledger of all income and expense items as they come up. If you do this once a month (or even wait until the end of the year), it is a simple process to put the slips in order by date to enter them, then to reorder them by category in sequential order and make a list for each category. Then you simply add up each category and enter the totals in the appropriate place on your income tax form or in an organizer for your accountant.

   Likewise, every time you get a check or payment, enter the date, the amount, the name of the periodical or source, and the name of the manuscript sold. If using a computer program, enter the income amounts and it will automatically calculate the total income by month or year, as well as put everything in order and sort by categories.

4. *Keep separate accounts.* As your writing business grows, you may want to open a separate savings or checking account for your business funds, and write all your business-related checks on that account. Some writers also have a credit card to use only for business expenses. Both of these options make the finances easier to track.

What's deductible?

What kinds of things are deductible? Generally, all writing-related expenses, but the following is a list that will cover most of them:

- All office supplies, such as paper, computer disks, ribbons, toner, envelopes, file folders, etc.

- All related postage. Either buy stamps to use only for writing and deduct that amount when you buy them, or keep a record of the stamps used as you use them, add it up, and record in your ledger at the end of each month.

- All photocopying or printing costs.

- Rental, repairs, or maintenance costs on writing equipment, such as computer, typewriter, printer, tape recorder, or camera.

- Writing courses or conferences (registration, travel, lodging, and meals) are deductible only if taken to improve your writing skills, not to learn how to write, and only deductible above the 2 percent of Adjusted Gross Income. If you don't have receipts for meals and lodging, the IRS provides Per Diem allowances based on the location of the conference.

- Dues in writers' organizations as long as the purpose of the group is not entertainment.

- Mileage for travel on related trips (post office, bank, library, editorial offices, critique meetings, office supply stores, etc.). Actual cost or the current amount per mile allowed by the IRS (no limit on miles). Also parking or toll fees or actual cost for public transportation. Keep a mileage log in your car to track all business-related trips as well as the total mileage for the year. Add the total number of business miles and calculate what percentage of all miles traveled was for business purposes. You may then deduct that percentage of all your car-related expenses or the allowable rate per business mile, whichever gives you the highest deduction.

- Business-related long-distance phone calls, but not any part of your monthly base fees, unless you have a separate business line or fax line (in which case all fees are deductible).

- Research fees.

- Books, tapes, videos, or software on how to write, or those used as research for a writing project.

- Depreciation of equipment having a useful life of more than one year and a value over $150 (may vary). You may take the full depreciation in one year for equipment costing up to

$19,000 (if it doesn't exceed your income). These numbers may change, so check with an accountant for current limits.

- Fifty percent of the cost of meals for a person being interviewed, or for meals when traveling on business. Receipts are required if over $75. The IRS requires that you keep a log or journal when traveling or claiming deductions for meals. Keep accurate records of who, where, when, why, amount, and business discussed.

- Typing fees, secretarial costs, or critique/editorial services.

- Photo developing or printing when writing-related.

- Office space rental fees, fully deductible if office is used exclusively for writing.

- You may deduct 60 percent (at least until 2001) of health insurance premiums for yourself (and family members) if you are self-employed and have no benefits available through a working spouse. (Check with your accountant after 2001.)

- Interest on business assets.

- Legal and accounting fees.

- One hundred percent of most decorating or improvement costs for a home office. Check with an accountant for limitations.

- Home office expenses (can't go over your net income after all other business expenses are deducted). For details, see IRS Publication 587.

- Business gifts; limited to $25 per person per year. Would include gifts or cards sent to editors or suppliers.

- Subcontract labor or employees, such as a secretary.

- Bank charges or fees, or percentage of fees used for business. If separate accounts, all fees are deductible. If you don't have a separate account, figure the percentage of checks used for business and take a deduction for that percentage of all bank fees paid during the year.

- Publications purchased, or subscriptions if related to writing. Would include writing publications and any publications you subscribe to in order to analyze them for future submissions.

Note: Always check with an accountant for the most current rules.

Estimated tax payments

Publishers don't withhold taxes when they pay you, so if at the end of the year you owe $500 or more in unpaid taxes, you will need to start making estimated tax payments. If your income is increasing regularly, and you think you might owe that much, call your local IRS office and ask them to send you Form 1040-ES. It will help you figure out if you need to make the payments and show how much you will need to pay quarterly to cover your estimated tax liability for the current year. If the calculations show that your tax debt will be less than $500, you can forget the quarterly payments for now. But if the calculations show you will owe at least $500, you cannot wait until the end of the year to pay, so you will have to make quarterly payments.

The exception will be if you or your spouse have paid in enough excess taxes on another job to cover this tax liability. For example, when I first started making enough that I owed the $500 at the end of the year, my husband always had enough of a tax credit to cover it (it just meant we got a smaller refund on our joint return).

If your calculations show that you should be making quarterly payments and you don't, you will be charged a penalty. However, there is no penalty if you pay at least 90 percent of your actual final tax bill for that year or 100 percent of what your tax bill was the previous year. But if this will be your first year (and you don't have a previous year to go by) it is especially important that you track your income and be sure you pay at least 90 percent of the taxes you're going to owe for the year. After you make estimated payments for that first year, the following year all you have to do is take that first-year total, divide it by four, and pay that amount as four equal payments. So, if you pay $800 in taxes for the year 2003, during 2004 you simply pay $200 each quarter, equaling $800 or 100 percent of the year 2003 total. That probably won't be the correct amount, but you can pay more (or get a refund) when you file your taxes, and there will be no penalty.

Self-employment tax (Social Security)

When you start making $433 per year or more in net profits, you may need to pay self-employment taxes (unless you've already paid the year's limit for Social Security through another job). When figuring your taxes, fill out Schedule SE. Unfortunately, the self-employed rate is double that which you pay as an employee. (As an employee you pay half the Social Security taxes, 7.65 percent, and your employer pays the other half. When self-employed, you pay both halves, 15.3 percent.) The good news is that 50 percent of those Social Security taxes for the self-employed are tax deductible.

If you consider your writing a hobby—but you have book royalties to report—they can be reported on Schedule E, rather than Schedule C. In that case you will not have to pay self-employment taxes on those royalties since you do not consider yourself self-employed. However, if you are planning to claim deductions for expenses against those royalties (in excess of the royalty income), the IRS will consider you self-employed and expect you to report royalties on Schedule C.

Business use of your home

If you set up an office in your home, you may be eligible to deduct it as a business expense. However, they will not let you use that deduction until or unless you deduct all other expenses and still have enough income left to cover that amount. For example, if you deduct all other expenses and still have $500 in income, but your home office deduction would be $1,000, you could deduct only the $500. But you can then carry the excess $500 over to the next year in case your excess income is large enough to cover it at that time.

You may have heard that business use of your home is the one deduction most likely to trigger an audit, so don't claim it unless you are sure you qualify and have nothing questionable elsewhere in your return. Actually, I have claimed it for years and have never been audited, so if you do qualify, don't fail to claim it just because you fear an audit. Note: There are special ramifications concerning business use of your home when you sell that home, so always check with your accountant for information on appropriate tax planning.

The current IRS guidelines for claiming business use of your home are as follows:

1. It does not have to be a separate room; part of a room may qualify.

2. The room or partial room must be used exclusively for business. If your kids use your computer to play games or you have your ironing board set up in your office, it won't qualify.

3. It must be your principle place of business—the place where you do the majority of your writing.

4. The space can be used for more than one business, so if you have more than one business or your spouse runs a different business using the same space, it will qualify as long as the other criteria are met.

Miscellaneous tax tips

Of course, only an accountant can give you all the advice you need for your taxes, but here are a few more tips:

➤ Prizes and awards you win for your writing are taxable—

even if goods or services—unless the award was unsolicited (some exceptions).

- If you have had a book published, keep accurate records of books purchased for resale and books sold. Your tax form will ask for beginning and ending inventory each year.

- Interest on business equipment is deductible, so it may pay to finance the purchase of major expenses like a new computer.

- You may combine business and pleasure when traveling in the U.S. If a trip is primarily for business, the cost of travel is fully deductible even if you tack on a few days of recreation. Expenses at the destination that are for business are fully deductible, but don't deduct the pleasure expenses. If a trip is primarily for pleasure, you can still deduct any business-related expenses. Keep a daily log of activities to back up your deductions. Regulations for foreign travel are more stringent, so check on those before you plan or take a trip.

- If your spouse helps in your business (doing filing, typing, mailing, or whatever), pay him/her a wage, but put all the earnings in an IRA so you won't have to pay taxes on them.

- If you reach the point where you need secretarial help, be aware that if you bring someone in to do typing for you on *your* computer or typewriter, he or she is considered an employee, not contract labor. So, if that is what you need, you will be better off paying someone, perhaps at a secretarial service, to do the typing in their home or office using *their own* equipment. The expense is tax deductible, but you won't owe the payroll taxes and benefits that go with having an employee.

Libel

Most writers are not concerned about libel. We are not writing things that are potentially libelous. However, every writer should at least be aware of what libel is and the consequences involved, even if you never have or never intend to write anything nasty about anyone. You can be guilty of *libel* if you defame someone by an opinion or a misquote and put their reputation in jeopardy. The libel laws do vary from state-to-state, so if this is a concern, find out what your state laws are.

Be sure the facts in your article are accurate, especially if you are writing news, features, and particularly exposés. If you don't get your facts straight, you could be in trouble, so always double check. Be careful of your quotes. If you quote someone else's libelous statement you can be held responsible. Write only what you know to be true or what you can prove.

Don't assume that if you get sued your publisher will back you up. With book publishers, that possibility is covered in the contract. With magazines you never know, but assume they aren't going to help you out. Also, don't assume that if you change someone's name and location (or a couple of key facts) you can't be sued. If there are enough facts left to identify the person, you are still liable. To be on the safe side, change key facts or come up with a composite of two or three different people. In most states you can't libel a dead person, but check to be sure. Also be aware that fiction writers as well as nonfiction writers can be sued for libel if you base your characters too closely on someone who is recognizable from your description.

Some authors fear that if they don't quote an interview subject word-for-word they will get in trouble. Basically, you can edit quotes for length, grammar, or other legitimate reasons as long as you don't change the meaning of what was said.

If you do get into legal difficulties, look for a local chapter of Volunteer Lawyers for the Arts, which has chapters around the country. If you can't afford a lawyer, they can provide much-needed legal advice or representation where you pay only for out-of-pocket costs and legal fees. Check your local yellow pages or visit their website at *www.stus.com/ncs/vla.htm* (lists lawyers by state).

Pen Names, or Pseudonymns

Most writers are curious about pen names—when you should use them and why. Usually you won't use a pen name unless you have a good reason. If you are trying to build a reputation as a writer, you will want to see your name in print as often as possible. There are, however, some good reasons for using pseudonyms:

- If you are writing something of a sensitive nature and you want to protect your own identity or that of your family or friends.
- If you do a lot of writing for the same publication, or the same few publications. You or the publisher may decide to use more than one name so it doesn't look like everything is written by the same author.
- If you have a name that is impossible to spell, pronounce, or remember. Also, if your name is the same as another writer.
- If you choose to use different names when writing in different areas or genres. For example, a book author might use one pen name for romances and another for westerns, children's books, or nonfiction titles. Magazine writers might use one name for children's stories, one for Christian education material, and another for family-oriented material.
- Sometimes a female author will use a man's name when she's writing in a genre that is more readily open to male writers, or vice versa.

If you decide to use a pen name, there are a few things you need to know. First, in preparing a manuscript, put your real name in the upper left-hand corner and your pen name in the byline. If you do receive a check made out to the pen name, you can either return it to the publisher with a request to reissue it in your name, or let your bank know that you might receive checks made out to the list of pen names you provide.

Further, if you are using a pen name on a particular article, include a cover letter to the editor explaining your reasons for doing so. Never withhold your real identity from an editor. Other than that, no legal steps need to be taken before using a pen name. In most cases you will want your copyrights to be in your name, not the pen name.

There are no rules to govern your choice of pen name. Sometimes writers use a maiden name or family name, a name they have always liked, or a name that fits the genre. Select a name you can live with because you may be stuck with it for life. I have even heard of instances where the editor has selected the pen name for a prolific author.

Plagiarism, Piracy, or Infringement?

A lot of writers seem to be confused about what plagiarism is, so I want to begin by comparing *plagiarism, piracy,* and *infringement.* We talked about infringement earlier under Copyright Law, but basically it means that you use someone else's copyrighted material without their permission (i.e., outside the bounds of fair use). Piracy is when you take someone else's work (copyrighted or not), exactly as they wrote it, and put your name on it—offering it as your own.

Plagiarism, then, is different from piracy in that the writer tries to rewrite it enough to make it sound like he or she is the author. Most of us were probably guilty of plagiarism as children when we used to write those school reports by putting into our own words what the encyclopedia or other reference books said.

Because plagiarism is so hard to prove, few cases actually go to court. It is simply too expensive and uncertain. There are some steps you can take, though, if you find strong evidence that someone has plagiarized your work. (Don't take the following actions if you just find a similar article—there must be several documentable similarities.) Start with a cordial letter to the editor of the publication where the offending material appeared. Give them all the facts with the assumption that they will want to make it right (chances are the editor doesn't know about the plagiarism); indicate that you can prove your claim with original manuscripts and notes; send all letters registered so you'll have receipts; and request the specific action you want taken—a retraction or apology, proper credit, and/or payment. If results are not forthcoming, be persistent in your demands. Leave a lawyer (or even threat of a lawyer) as a last resort.

A word of caution. Writers are often quick to assume that someone with a similar article has stolen or plagiarized their idea. Keep in mind that ideas cannot be copyrighted, so if you see your idea for making a birdhouse out of a tuna fish can in someone else's article, you don't have grounds to sue them. Anyone can pick up and repeat your *idea;* the only thing protected is your description of how to actually make the birdhouse.

I often hear horror stories from writers who are sure some publication stole their idea for an interview or article. Generally speaking, editors do not steal ideas—especially in the religious market. Usually when I check out such allegations I find that a writer had sent a query for an article that was rejected, only to have the same publication come out with a similar piece the very next month. Was it stolen? Unlikely. First, publications typically work from three to twelve months (or more) ahead, so by the time the editor saw the query, their piece was already into production. Second, the old adage "There's nothing new under the sun" isn't an old adage for nothing. It doesn't surprise me anymore when I talk with two different authors at the same conference who have articles or books in the works that are almost identical. Remind yourself that if you got the idea, someone else is just as likely to have come up with it too.

Do writers get ripped off? Sure they do, but not often—and certainly not often enough to make it a primary concern. The truth is, unless someone steals your novel and makes it into a multi-billion dollar movie, it is probably not worth the time, headache, and money to pursue the case. You will not find an evil editor behind every desk, and it is counterproductive to go looking for them.

Chapter 4

On Setting Up Your Office: Paper and Electronic

Now that you've decided to write, it's time to find a place to work. Your office need not be spacious, just a defined area that you can call your own. If you have a spare bedroom to turn into an office, that's ideal. But even a desk somewhere will do. Put it in the corner of a bedroom, family room, living room, dining room, or even in a large closet. If you have a separate dining room you never use, consider making it your office.

Of course, you could work on the kitchen table, but there is something about having a place to *go* to write that helps get the creative juices flowing. You are more likely to write in small snatches of time if you don't have to get everything out each time you want to work. If you are using a typewriter, it is possible to drag it out when you need it, but a computer will require a permanent spot. I encourage you to find the best place to work that your circumstances can provide. After all, you may be launching a new career.

Office Setup

My office will never appear in a magazine for its beauty, but it is functional. Because I work full-time at this business and have nearly full-time help, I have a separate office where much of the work goes on with the *Christian Writers' Market Guide*. That office holds the copy machine, work table, books, the assistant's computer, office supplies, and various files. I also have my own writing space in about half of a bedroom.

Because so many people ask me, I will tell you how my space is set up, but I encourage writers to arrange their office in a way that works best for them, depending on the kind of writing they are doing. I have found it to be a process—one you perfect as you go along.

I have an inexpensive *computer table* that quickly got too small to hold a new computer (with internal fax), two printers, a scanner, and papers. When that happened, my husband painted a sheet of 5/8 inch plywood that is somewhat larger than the desk. I laid it on top of the table, and it's perfect. To my left and at right angles to the computer table, I have a large desk where I can do noncomputer work, edit, open mail, etc. I try to leave as much clear space as possible, but the desk also has three stacking letter bins. The top bin is for incoming mail or material that needs to be dealt with soon, the middle bin is for material that is pending—I'm waiting for a response from someone or more information before I can act on it. The bottom bin holds things that aren't urgent but that I need to or may want to deal with later.

Next to the bins is a *tickler file* (see "Organizing Papers and Files" below). The desk is deep enough that I can put my most frequently used books along the back edge against the wall. On the other side of the desk is an upright file that holds frequently used files, and a telephone. I also have a Rolodex file for addresses (I keep a separate one for email addresses), pencil holder, tape dispenser, stapler, calculator, stamp pad, and various rubber stamps.

On the wall over the desk is a bookshelf (four shelves) for writing books. Over the computer table are two deep shelves (12 x 13-inches) that hold computer manuals and well-marked cardboard project bins—one for each project I'm working on. On the wall opposite the computer (behind me) is a large, four-drawer filing cabinet I got inexpensively from a doctor's office that was liquidating. I have often said I wish I had bought two of them, but by having only one I am forced to clean it out regularly and discard or store files I don't need nearby.

I have a secretary's chair and a vinyl mat to roll easily from my desk to computer and back. The chair should be comfortable and give your back the support it needs. If your desk has drawers, don't put anything in them except those supplies or materials you use most often. A wall calendar is also essential (see chapter 6, "On Time Management," for tips on using it).

The rest of your bookcases can be elsewhere in the house, depending on space. I have my writing books in my office, and some reference books that I use the most, but most of my other books are in other rooms. However, when I have had room to keep most of my books nearby, I have tried to organize them on the shelves for the greatest efficiency. At one point I had them divided like this (reflecting my particular interests at the time): writing books, speaking books, time-management books, general reference books, Christian education books, Bibles/Bible reference books, autographed books, and books waiting to be read.

The last, but one of the most important features of your office, is the lighting. Since I am using the desk and the computer in the same area, I have a two-tube fluorescent fixture suspended from the ceiling that covers both work areas. It was inexpensive and simply plugs into a socket—not fancy, but very functional. If that won't work in your situation, find desk lamps (or even floor lamps) that provide sufficient light in the right places.

Most people prefer an office in a quiet place with few distractions, but that isn't necessary or possible for everyone. When I first started writing, I had three small children, and a quiet place did not exist at our house. At that time I learned to write in the midst of chaos when I had to, and so can you. If you are serious about writing, you will not wait for the ideal time or place. One of the most productive times of my writing career was when I had moved into a new home and worked off a card table in the middle of an empty room. I had just enough room on the table to put my typewriter on one side and still have a little writing space on the other. All my papers and files were in piles on the floor around me.

I have a friend who writes in a noisy fast-food restaurant because that noise is less distracting than her own phone, doorbell, or housework crying to be done. Never wait for the ideal setting—it is rarely available.

The bottom line here is that a writing space is as individual as the writer. You need to find a setting and arrangement that makes you comfortable and helps the writing flow. My space rarely stays the same two months in a row. I am constantly changing it as I strive to make it more workable, and you should too.

Organizing Papers and Files

Because ours is a paper-oriented business, finding a place to put or file all that paper is an ongoing problem. In my experience, organizing paper is like setting up your office space—it takes time and refinement to make it work for you. Although I have a natural bent toward organization, I have also learned to keep it as simple as possible. Even if you are naturally disorganized, some of these ideas will work for you. Simply pick what sounds reasonable and find your own ways to deal with the rest. Below are some ideas for filing or organizing different types of materials that are common to the writer.

Writers' guidelines

You will quickly amass a collection of writers' guidelines from various publishers. You need to keep them handy so you can refer to them quickly and easily. I suggest putting them in loose-leaf notebooks, using one for periodicals and another for book publishers if you have collected a lot of them (or in the same notebook if the number is limited). Add alphabetical dividers, and file the guidelines alphabetically by title of periodical or company name. Put this on or near your desk for easy reference.

Sample copies and book catalogs

Samples take up more room but still need to be in a convenient place, at least until you become more familiar with them. I find that the cardboard or plastic magazine file boxes work well for organizing samples and catalogs. Sort the periodicals by the categories you write for. For example, put all the children's publications in one box, teens' in another, Christian education or pastors' in another, etc. These can correlate with the categories in the *Christian Writers' Market Guide* or the specific kinds of things you write, such as poetry, devotionals, teen short stories, Bible studies, etc. Send for new guidelines and sample copies if yours are more than two or three years old, and ask for new catalogs every other year if you are likely to write for that publisher. Keep up to three of the most current sample copies for each magazine. Throw out samples of periodicals you are sure you will never write for, and save your limited space. Book catalogs and larger categories of magazines can be kept in storage boxes with lids.

Published/Unpublished manuscripts

Make up a file folder for each manuscript as soon as you have a rough draft. Put the title on the tab and file it alphabetically in a manuscript file. When you complete the piece, put the final draft in the folder, and eventually all your rejection slips or correspondence concerning that manuscript, a copy of the periodical when it is published, and anything else related to that sale. If you sell a lot of reprint rights to a particular piece and the folder gets too full for all the magazines, keep a list and the first published copy in the folder and store the others elsewhere. When a piece sells for the first time, put a red line across the top of the folder tab. That way you can tell which manuscripts have sold and which have not.

Topical files

Most writers have rather extensive topical files that they use for research. One of the biggest problems is figuring out what kind of topical material to keep and how to file it. We all see articles or bits of information in our areas of interest that we want to keep for future reference, but how do we avoid being buried under tons of paper in the process? Even after setting up some topical files, I struggled for a long time with what to include in those files. Eventually I decided that I couldn't have a file for everything. I needed to be selective.

My first lesson was setting up fat files, not skinny ones. If your topics are too narrow, you will have too many folders and it will be hard to find what you need. I started with a file for each of the broad topics I was writing about or hoped to write about at some point. If I expanded into a new area, I added a new folder. I also found that there were certain topics that always attracted my attention, even though I didn't know enough about them to write on them. I began to recognize that those might be areas I'd move into in the future, so I added folders for those. As you sort accumulated resources they will likely suggest their own topical files. As files get too full, you will want to divide them into smaller categories, but not too many. Divide one fat folder into two to four new files, not ten to twelve.

I have learned a couple of other lessons about filing. One is that if you want to keep related files together, you need to use file titles with subheads. For example, if the topic is family, you would label your files like this: Family: Activities, Family: Finance, Family: Discipline, etc. Otherwise all that related material will get scattered throughout your filing system.

I've also discovered that if I use one of my files to write on a certain topic, it doesn't mean I should discard that file when the article is published. Instead, I keep an eye out for additional resources to add to the folder, and when I have enough new material, I consider doing another article on that topic incorporating the new information.

Writing how-to

I love writers' magazines but don't have room to keep them indefinitely, so I have found a way to keep the information I want at my fingertips. First I set up file folders for the topics I teach or am most interested in, such as marketing, children's writing, copyright law, and income tax (I actually have three boxes full of different topics). I also have one magazine file box labeled for each different writing magazine. As those magazines arrive, I read them and file them in their box. When each box gets too full, I remove the oldest copies, tear out the articles I want to keep, file them in the topical files, and discard what's left. If you have room and can't bear to discard the magazines, simply tear out (or copy) the table of contents from each magazine and keep those contents pages chronologically in a looseleaf notebook. Stack the magazines in order somewhere, and when you want information on a certain topic, the contents pages will send you to the right issue and page number.

Files are time and space consuming, so never file something if there is somewhere else you can go to find the same information—such as in a book on your shelf or on the Internet. Never file anything you aren't likely to need again, and finally: purge your files of outdated material every two to five years.

Office Supplies

The particular office supplies you might need will vary depending on the kind of writing you are doing or how much you are doing. So set up your office space as professionally as possible by getting the supplies you need to do the job right. You could write on the child's tablet with a crayon if you had to, but there is something positive that happens psychologically when you have the supplies that help you think of yourself as a professional.

Whether you are using a typewriter or a computer with a printer, keep extra ribbons, toner cartridges, disks, etc., so you will not lose valuable time waiting to get to the store to replace them. You will eventually want letterhead stationery, envelopes, and business cards, but if you have a newer computer and a high quality printer, you can print them up quickly and inexpensively for yourself. Check at your office supply store for a wide variety of paper choices and business cards ready to print out by the sheet. Even if you don't have your own computer, you may have a friend who can do the printing for you.

If you have room, set up a mailing center or find a plastic bin to hold your mailing supplies in one place. Get a postal scale (inexpensive) so you can mail your manuscripts from home and save a lot of trips to the post office. You will need stamps in a variety of denominations, various-sized manila envelopes, a self-inking stamp or labels for return addresses, self-addressed #9 and/or #10 business envelopes, a "First-Class" stamp and a "Media Mail" stamp that allows you to send your manuscript at a cheaper rate. Sending out manuscripts can be a tedious job, but it goes a lot more smoothly if you have all the supplies you need in one place.

Do I Need a Computer?

My purpose in this section is to help you determine whether or not you should make the leap to a computer if you haven't already done so. I know a good number of writers who are not yet using a computer (but that list gets shorter every day). A typewriter or word processor has served them well up to now. One writer friend commented ten years ago that he wished he had been born fifty years earlier so he wouldn't have to contend with the computer. Well, he wasn't and he has had to—and now he wouldn't trade his computer for anything. The pain comes not in using a computer, but in having to make the transition to one.

My first computer sat in a box in the corner for six months before I even unpacked it. I turned it on for the first time the day I started work on the second edition of the *Christian Writers' Market Guide*. By the time the guide was finished, I was at least comfortable with the computer. It's been a step-by-step learning process since then.

At this point, it is not a question of whether a typewriter or a computer is better. The reality is that within a relatively short time, the computer will no longer be optional for writers. At the rate technology is advancing today, if you are not able to use a computer, you may be left behind. As more and more publishers get their equipment up to speed, they will expect writers to be able to submit their material not just on disk, as we had imagined the next step would be, but downloaded directly into the publisher's computer.

I am reluctant to tackle this topic simply because I know almost anything I say will be obsolete before it gets to the publisher—much less to you. One of my biggest frustrations is knowing that no matter how much I try to keep up with what is happening in the world of technology, I'll never catch up. If you are a writer working at home alone, and not out in the business world where your coworkers and regular networking keep you up on the latest developments, you can be at a real disadvantage.

I suppose my first word of advice is not to lose any sleep over it. Fortunately, although you need a computer, you have little need for all those bells and whistles. Word processing is pretty straightforward and can even be done on—heaven forbid—a "dinosaur" computer. Although the outrageous promises offered by some of the new computers are enticing, few of those features will help you be a better writer. When it becomes necessary to find a new computer, my bottom line consideration is what do I need to do and how can I do it as efficiently and inexpensively as possible. If you are happy with what you are using, and it is compatible with your publishers, then stick with it until you have a good reason to upgrade.

When it is time to upgrade, don't let a salesman talk you into more than you need. Take a friend or acquaintance with you who knows something about computers and knows specifically what you need. It also helps to find someone who knows enough about computers to help you when you run into problems or when you need to learn the next step. Many computer "geeks" are willing to help individuals at an hourly rate lower than most professionals you could hire. For example, the young man who handles all the computer problems in the company my daughter works for helps me after work at a reasonable rate and is worth every penny.

Email

I realize that getting a new computer so you have access to email and the Internet is a big temptation. I did it because it makes sense for the kind of business I do related to the *Christian Writers' Market Guide* and because I needed a way to keep in touch with editors and writers more easily. Email is a quick way to get messages and information to people painlessly, but you also may get barraged with advertisements and jokes you don't necessarily want.

For the isolated writer, email can provide a vital connection to other writers. One of the most frequent complaints I have heard from writers is that they feel alone. They don't know any other writers in their area, and they have no writers' groups nearby. Email has addressed and often alleviated that problem by keeping those writers connected to writers all over the country and even around the world. There are Christian writers' email groups where members can ask questions, share frustrations (or even prayer requests), get feedback on their manuscripts or article ideas, discuss current trends or controversial issues—all the things we have longed to do with writing friends.

Others have started round-robin writers' groups by email where they send their manuscripts around to other members to be critiqued and then returned. When one writer finds out about a new market, contest, or writing opportunity, he or she can share it with other writers by email. Personally, I find that writers are much more likely to send me market update information by email than they were when they had to mail it. It speeds up and facilitates communication among writers and editors.

These days most editors have email and many prefer it as a way to communicate. However, there are just as many who don't like that form of communication, so check with your market guide to see the particular preference of each publisher—and honor that. The *Christian Writers' Market Guide* now tells you which editors prefer or accept email queries and which do not.

Never submit complete manuscripts to a publisher by email unless you have gotten a go-ahead from them to do so. Some publishers have email systems where every message that comes in is automatically printed out. In those cases, editors are not happy to have complete, unsolicited manuscripts printed out without prior knowledge. Your market guide should also tell you whether the editor wants the material sent as an attachment or pasted into the email message. Because this use for email is relatively new, move slowly and cautiously until you can determine how a particular editor is going to respond.

Internet

Even if you don't own a computer, or you have a computer without access to the Internet, most of you will be aware of the potential the Internet offers. Every day I find a new site that is potentially helpful to me as a writer or to the writers I am trying to help. As I started preparing the last *Christian Writers' Market Guide,* I spent a good deal of time searching the Net for new markets and for the websites of established markets. I found plenty of both.

In checking out the websites of both periodicals and book publishers, I found that I learned a lot I didn't know about them. Of course, some sites are more helpful than others, but I soon found that I could learn about the denomination or sponsoring organization by visiting the various sections of their website. Some even had guidelines I could print right off the site. (The *Christian Writers' Market Guide* indicates which ones have guidelines by email or on their websites.) On others I printed out the portions that helped me better understand who they were and what they wanted. I could often find a list of recently published articles and even print out one or two to analyze more closely before I submitted anything to them. I am now recommending a complete study of each publisher's website as a necessary part of the marketing process. To help in this process, visit my website where you can link directly to the websites (or email) for all the Christian book or periodical publishers that have them: *www.stuartmarket.com.*

Internet Research

Some writers do not do a lot of research, so fast and easy Internet access is not an issue for them. If you already do a lot of research, then it will be worth the money to ensure that you have the fastest and easiest access possible. However, if you don't need much Internet access now, then don't spend money on it yet. The technology and resources are growing and changing so quickly that what you buy now may be outdated by the time you actually need it. The bottom line is that the Internet can be a tremendous time drain, so unless it will save you as much time as it is going to cost you, then avoid getting entangled with it.

If research capabilities are important to you, however, then you will need a computer and modem of the size and speed to support such activity. If owning your own system has to wait, check out the resources available at your local library. Many libraries will let you rent time on their computers and give you access to specialized resources.

Once you have access to the Internet, the possibilities are endless. Virtually every research source has their own website and access to almost any kind of information you might want or need. See appendix B for information on how to get the booklet called *Electronic Research Sites and How to Use Them,* compiled by Deborah Page. It lists all the best sites, describes what you can find there, and actually includes a copy of the home page for thirty of the best sites so you can see exactly what information it will link you to. It's an essential resource for anyone wanting to do research on the Internet.

Actually, a lot of the information I find most helpful comes via email by networking with other writers on writers' email groups. It is also a lot easier to keep up with what is happening with publishers when I have access to them via email. (I hesitate to call them but feel comfortable emailing them with quick questions or to verify manuscript changes or information.)

Often you will be able to find websites or groups that deal with your primary areas of interest and also provide regular newsletters that keep you up-to-date on developments in the field. For example, since I regularly evaluate contracts for writers, I'm especially interested in a newsletter that tells me what's happening with book contracts.

I am always on the lookout for sites of interest to Christian writers, and you'll find a list of the best ones in the current edition of the *Christian Writers' Market Guide* under Resources for Writers.

Software programs

Once you have a computer, you can get a software program to do almost any job that needs doing. You will find programs to track your manuscripts, help with research, plot your stories, name your characters, organize your markets, or aid you in hundreds of other writing-related chores. You will want to be on the lookout for those that will be particularly valuable to you, but keep in mind that you are looking for programs that will save you time—not ones that will eat up your available writing time. As my husband says about saving money, "You can't save money (no matter how good the sale) if you are spending money." You have the same problem on the computer—a program will never save you time if you spend more time figuring it out or playing with it than you save using it.

Talk to your writing friends and ask them to recommend those programs that they can't get along without. The current edition of the *Christian Writers' Market Guide* will list some of the best resources I have found. Now, forget about the mechanics of your office set-up and get to work!

Chapter 5

On Part-time/Full-time Freelancing

As I wrote in the "Income Tax: The Basics" section of chapter 3, writing can be either a hobby or a business. But there is a problem differentiating between *hobby* and *business*. The truth is that most people who write are so passionate about it that they would hardly call it a hobby—yet they don't make enough money at it to call it a business. For most of us herein lies our dilemma: Can we make enough money at writing to call it a business?

Though most of us try our hand at writing to see what will come of it, in the back of our minds is the hope that writing will pay so well that we can quit our regular jobs. Is it possible? Perhaps. The key is to make sure your *enthusiasm* for turning your writing into a business *matches up* with the *practical issues* at hand. Here's a story that illustrates this: At a conference I taught a class of beginning writers. In that class a woman explained that she was a single mother with three kids, and that she worked as a nurse. She asked me, "If I quit my job tomorrow, can I make at least as much at writing as I'm making as a nurse?" When I asked her how regularly her writing sold now, she admitted that she hadn't actually sold anything yet. I suggested she keep her day job.

But that wasn't the end of the story. About three years later I taught a class at another conference. I shared this woman's question to me with the class. As I finished the story, the class laughed. Then a woman raised her hand. She admitted to being the one in the story, but she wanted to report that she had given up her dream to write full-time in order to support herself—she'd married a doctor instead. Probably a wiser choice.

Can I Make a Living at Writing?

That previous illustration aside, some of you have serious questions about how much money you might expect to make as a freelance writer (part-time or full-time) and whether it is realistic to attempt a full-time writing career. These are not easy questions to answer. There are many factors involved: Your potential for income has a lot to do with how good a writer you are, what kind of writing you do, your flexibility as a writer, the diversity of topics you can write about, your degree of self-discipline, and how aggressively you market and promote your work. There are no across-the-board answers here, but there are some general guidelines and information that can help you make that decision for yourself.

The latest statistics I read regarding the average income for freelance writers had the average at $4,600—well below the poverty level. There are, of course, those who make a comfortable living at writing and even some who make a fortune. Unfortunately they are few and far between. Although there are writers who earn regularly from their writing, most of them have a spouse who supports them, or they work another job to supplement their income, doing things such as taking and selling photos, providing critique or editorial services, and teaching or speaking. One writer I know used to make about $1,000 a month by selling stories and articles. But to do that, he had to average one sale a day, 365 days per year—a daunting task. He could make more at the same level of production today, but it would still mean keeping about 300 articles (new and reprints) out in the mail at any given time.

If you have been making regular sales by working at writing part-time (and that is where I suggest you start), you already have some idea how long you had to work to do the writing and make the sale, and how hard it would be to do that on a regular basis. Obviously, there is going to be a big difference in the amount you make, based on whether you are selling short stories to take-home papers for $35–85 apiece, or selling features to top magazines for $500–1,000, or more. If you are writing books, the difference is in whether you are selling them to smaller publishers (with an advance of $0 to $3,000) or to larger houses (giving advances of $4,000 to $40,000 or more).

Until someone has worked at writing as a part-time business long enough to have a realistic view of his/her own income potential, that writer should not consider writing as a full-time business. If you are having extraordinary success with your sales—selling nearly everything you send out on the first few tries and to the top markets—you can be at least reasonably certain that working at it full-time could increase your sales significantly. On the other hand, if you are selling infrequently to only the smaller publishers and periodicals markets, there is no reason to expect that working at it full-ime would produce enough income to live on.

If you are serious about someday quitting that day job—or at least supplementing the family income—there are ways you can prepare for that:

1. Write and submit as much as time allows right *now.* Don't just talk about what you could do if you had more time.

2. Clear your time schedule to make as much time as possible to write (chapter 6: "On Time Management/Self-Discipline" provides helpful tips on this).

3. Assess where you currently are in your writing career. Create short-term and long-term goals for yourself and determine to follow up on them.

4. Develop a professional mentality. Think of yourself as a writer: Learn to say, "I am a writer" without flinching. Treat writing as a profession that demands respect. Begin to inform and educate the people in your life about the writing

life and the seriousness with which you are taking your writing goals.

5. Start building your reputation as a writer who has expertise in specific areas. Establish your name in one or more genres, such as how-to and self-help books or feature writing and family/marriage articles for periodicals. Have it be your goal to be established and recognized in those areas so that editors will think of you for assignments.

6. Nurture relationships with editors. Make yourself known to the periodicals and publishing houses that you want to sell to on a regular basis.

7. Start sending out queries on a regular basis and determine what percentage of them actually produce a sale. It takes a while to get into the rhythm of how many queries to send to produce the number of go-aheads to fit into the time you have available to actually write the articles. If you can do it successfully on a part-time basis, it will be easier to do when you go full-time.

8. Determine how much you are making an hour by what you sell. Start tracking the amount of time it takes to write different kinds of stories, articles, and books. Compare that time amount with the cash amount you are paid for those projects.

9. Be willing to invest in yourself and your future. You are a potential income-producing property. Part of that may include convincing your spouse and family that the time and effort is going to pay off in the end. You will likely lose money the first few years—consider it an investment. Being willing to invest in yourself involves some sacrifice: pay off bills, simplify your lifestyle, and learn to live on less—now.

10. Work hard, but be patient. The average business takes from

five to eight years to get off the ground and only achieves real financial success at about ten years. There's no reason to expect a writing career to blossom much faster.

11. Work toward writing books. As a full-time writer, you will need book royalties to boost your income. If you plan to write books exclusively, you will need to produce two or three books a year (unless they reach bestseller status) to maintain a steady cash-flow.

12. Look for opportunities to write regular columns or features. Those regular paychecks are invaluable for full-time writers.

13. Think *marketing*. Work to discover the best potential markets for your work. (See chapter 7: "On Marketing" for help in perfecting your marketing skills.)

When/How to Take the Leap to Full-time

If you are able to follow the above advice, you begin to produce some positive results, and you feel strongly about expanding your writing into a full-time career, there is much more you need to consider. And the more you have worked at the above steps, the less overwhelming the following steps will be. Going full-time as a writer is like starting any other kind of business. It would be foolish to jump into it without taking all the necessary preliminary steps to determine your potential for success.

Following are some wise steps to consider as you move slowly toward your goal.

1. *Save your money.* Start putting aside as much money as you can. You will need a nest egg large enough to support you for at least six months—preferably a year. Also investigate retirement or investment options with a financial planner, and arrange to set up a Keogh or other retirement vehicle.

2. *Plan your future.* Spend at least a year ahead planning and preparing to make the move to full time. This will include following through on the suggestions below.

3. *Bolster income.* Start pursuing sources of regular income, such as writing columns, positioning yourself to get assignments, teaching classes, editing, speaking, etc. When you are freelancing, any income you don't have to work for right now, such as book royalties, becomes crucial to your survival.

4. *Read.* Read everything you can on how to write, how to be a successful freelancer, how to run a small or home-based business, etc. Find the books, magazines, and newsletters that provide the best marketing tips, information on trends, and hints on potential new markets.

5. *Take classes/attend conferences/listen to tapes.* Identify your areas of weakness and attend classes to strengthen your skills in those areas. Also attend conferences that offer helpful sessions as well as a large number of editors in attendance. (See chapter 1's "Writers' Conferences" for tips on how to make the best use of that opportunity.) Many conferences tape all sessions, so order tapes from sessions or conferences you are unable to attend. Work at increasing your knowledge in all areas of the writing business.

6. *Develop a network.* Writing can be an isolated business, so begin developing a network of other writers—especially those who are at your writing level or above. Seek out mentors with success in the writing field who are willing to encourage you and give advice. Join a critique group of successful writers in your area, online, or via mail.

7. *Develop a personal budget.* Come up with a realistic personal budget that will take into consideration all your current expenses that will be ongoing, plus any new ones that will

result from your move to full-time (such as insurance, self-employment taxes, etc.), minus expenses you will no longer have (such as transportation or other job-related costs). Continue to pay down all consumer debt.

8. *Find affordable health insurance.* If you currently have medical insurance through a regular job (that you will lose when you quit), and it is not available through a spouse, you will need to find new insurance. Individual health insurance is very expensive, so get some figures you can use in calculating your personal budget plan.

9. *Work out a business plan and budget.* Based on your part-time experience, come up with a probable budget for your business. Writing doesn't have high overhead, but you do need to plan for postage, new equipment, and office supplies. Based on the combined needs of both your business and personal budgets, develop a business plan that will determine how many sales and what kinds of sales you will need to produce the income necessary to satisfy those budget needs. You will quickly learn that your income per hour is more important than your income per sale.

10. *Set up bank accounts and credit cards.* If you are going to run this as a business, you will want to set up a separate checking account (and perhaps a savings account) for your business. Check out the options offered by different banks and select the one that best serves your needs. You may also want a separate business credit card to use for charging any business expenses so you have a record of those transactions. If you don't have an accountant to prepare your income taxes, now would be a good time to find one.

11. *Review equipment needs.* Determine what additional equipment you will need for the business, or what equipment you will need to upgrade, such as a computer, copy machine, tape recorder, camera, fax, scanner, answering

machine, etc. Buy or replace as much of that as possible before you launch your business.

12. *Survey educational needs.* Being a full-time freelancer does not have any educational requirements in itself, but the areas you plan to write in might. Determine if you need to bolster your credentials by pursuing additional classes or even degrees.

13. *Seek speaking opportunities.* One of the best ways to supplement your writing income is through speaking, whether on the topic of writing, on your field of expertise, or on the subjects that you are currently writing about. Offer your services to writing conferences you have attended. Find out about teaching adult education classes through your local community colleges. Many do not require a college degree–just experience in the field.

14. *Research support services.* Find out which companies in your area offer the best prices on photocopying, printing, phone service (you also might want to research the cost of separate fax or phone lines), mailing services, typing, transcription, or any other services you are likely to need. If you will need them, research editorial services and literary agents.

❖

The above list may not cover all your needs, depending on your business plan, but following it *will* move you a long way toward your goals. It may also move you in the other direction—toward the realization that you don't want to freelance full time.

Although it does have rewards, full-time freelancing is not an easy way to make a living. It requires that you be self-motivated and self-disciplined. Full-time freelance work requires that you schedule and divide your time well, spending about half your time writing, a fourth marketing, and the last fourth reading, researching, and running your business.

Many who are just getting started work night and day, taking every assignment that comes along just to make ends meet. But I determined that if I ever got to the point where my life was no longer my own, I'd get out of full-time freelance writing. So far I'm still here.

Chapter 6

On Time Management/Self-Discipline

Because so much of what goes into being a freelance writer—part-time or full-time—is dependent on self-discipline and time management, we will want to look more closely at what part those disciplines play in the writing business. As I talk with writers, I find that one of their main concerns is finding time to write. It is a universal problem. I may not have any magic answers to make the problem disappear, but I have learned a few things over the years that may help.

One of the first things I have learned about time management or self-discipline is that some people are naturally organized or disciplined and some are not. Those who *are* naturally organized tend to readily accept any suggestions in this area, while those who are not don't understand what all the fuss is about. The organization tips seem much too rigid and confining to them, and they tend to ignore them all. You probably know immediately which camp you fall into—and it is important to recognize your style—but even if you dislike the more rigid approaches to self-discipline, I encourage you to determine where you need the most help. Read the suggestions I make and pick three that you believe will best lead you to greater productivity. Concentrate on troubleshooting in a few areas at first so you are not overwhelmed or discouraged. Look back on the rest of the suggestions later and consider incorporating a few more into your work style.

The amount of discipline you are able to muster often has to do with the kind of writer you are and your motivation to write. Types of writers include those who:

- are totally committed to writing and would have to write no matter what (even if never published)
- work at a full-time job while writing (always their first love) is on the side
- write because they believe it will provide wealth or fame
- write a lot and get excited about several projects at once, but seldom finish anything
- spend their life (or at least their writing life) writing one story or experience
- are obsessed with a single idea that is written and rewritten
- write, submit, and sell, year in and year out.

Recognizing what kind of writer you are is often helpful in determining what changes you need to make to gain the level of success you are seeking. Make sure you have chosen the role you are in and have not simply fallen into it for lack of direction. Each of us can either accept where we are or determine to change by learning some self-discipline. At some point we need to make that choice and set a goal.

Making Time to Write

Start by looking at your time and setting priorities. Where is writing going to fall in your life? *If you are serious about writing you will have to give up other things you are doing.* Early in my career, I was almost running a church single-handedly—and was quite good at it—but when I realized I was being called to be a writer, I had to give up most of those reponsibilities so I would have time to write. Now I select my outside activities very carefully, choosing either those that feed into my writing or those that do not interfere with my writing.

For example, when I had children at home and was also writing for children, I volunteered to correct sixth-grade spelling papers at my son's school. Correcting those original sentences gave me helpful insight into how kids think. I worked in the school library, so I got to eavesdrop on the kids' conversations with the librarian about what they liked and didn't like in the books they read. That was a job that fed into my writing.

By contrast, I now volunteer to keep the church kitchen stocked with supplies because I can do it on my own schedule at times that don't interfere with my writing time. I avoid committing myself to any activities that will eat up time I should spend writing, or that sap the energy and creativity I need to write effectively.

If you are already over-committed it is often hard to get out of activities, but it can be done. The first step is to accept the fact that the activities can get along without you. It was helpful for me when I realized that just as I had been called to write, others have been called to their particular tasks. So if I am not writing as I should be—doing something else instead—I may be interfering with someone else doing the job they were called to. Once you recognize what your job is and begin to arrange your time to do that job, you will be managing your time, rather than it managing you.

There may be times during your writing career when you will have to be very creative in finding the time you need to write or to complete particular assignments. For some people that may mean getting up earlier, going to bed later, or being released from family duties for the time necessary to complete the assignment. One writing friend shared that he was offered a lucrative assignment with a short lead time that would mean he would have little time to spend with his family for the next month. He took the assignment, but only after going to his wife and children and asking their permission and dispensation for that time commitment.

Another writer who had both a full-time job and a family to care for also had to find time to complete a book on schedule. She determined that she would have to "create" a time to write. To do so, she went to bed right after dinner in the evening (her husband agreed to get the kids to bed), slept for four hours, got up and wrote for four hours, went back to bed for three or four hours, and got up in the morning to get the kids off to school and go to work. She was able to maintain this schedule until the book was completed. This example may be an unrealistic answer for your situation or personality, but the point is: If you are serious about writing, you will find or create a time to do it.

Friends and Family and the Writer

It is essential to establish and maintain a good balance between your writing and your family, friends, and/or spouse. Writing can easily become all consuming, but recognizing that and working to prevent problems on the home front will make for better writing and a happier home.

Start by asking for family support. The amount of support you need will depend on the age of your family and what place writing is taking in your life. If you are just getting started, share with them your goals for writing and where you want it to take you and them. If you need to make more time to write, take that time from expendable outside activities before taking time away from your family.

When I had children at home and was writing on the side, I usually put whatever money I made into a savings account and used it to send them to camp or to pay for vacations or special activities. Since they knew that, they were usually quite willing to cooperate with my writing schedule.

A transition to full-time freelancing may require a greater sacrifice on the part of your family. Be sure they are with you before deciding to take that plunge.

Involve your family in what you are doing as much as possible. Ask your spouse to proofread for you; have the kids stamp envelopes, sort, and file; share all your rejections and acceptances with them. Include the whole family in celebrations of the successes. Be available to your family except at specified times set aside for your writing.

Once you have the support of your immediate family, you may find there are still problems with friends and extended family who expect you to do things with or for them because you "don't work." This problem calls for some re-education.

- Set specific office hours or hours you will be working each day and let others know (firmly) that you are not available during that time, except for emergencies.

- Use an answering machine or voice mail to screen calls. If you do answer, let the caller know you can't talk now, but will call them back at a specified time (after office hours).

- If your mother, sister, friend, or neighbor gets upset for being put off, make it up to them by inviting them to dinner or lunch (or some other activity) at a time convenient to you. Start setting up some new relationship patterns that won't interfere with your writing time.

- Maintain a balance. Although I have set office hours, I can be talked into a day at the beach or a shopping trip, especially if I recognize my need to get away and be refreshed—or that my husband or family are needing some time with me.

Setting Goals

If it is any consolation, probably 95 percent of the writers I know struggle with self-discipline. A lot of that has to do with the fact that writers have to be self-starters—we don't have a boss looking over our shoulders to see that we get our work done. As someone has said, you have to tempt yourself with a carrot, swat yourself with a switch, and then pull the cart as well.

One of the pitfalls we face is the illusion of busyness. There is a big difference between being busy and being productive.

The successful writer must be a productive writer. If I don't plan my work and set goals for myself, I focus on the motion—but it is motion without meaning.

Every January, a writing critique group I was in exchanged lists of our writing goals for the year. At the end of the year we reported on how well we reached those goals. That was very helpful for me because it gave me a specific yardstick to use in measuring my progress for the year. I met more of my goals when I knew I was being held accountable for reaching them. If you aren't in such a group, share your goals with a supportive spouse or friend who will encourage you during the year. Three-to-five-year goals are also helpful in giving your career a specific direction.

Your goals might include any or all of the following:

- the number of books or articles you plan to write each year (or each month)
- the number of queries you'll have out
- the number of conferences where you'll speak/teach
- the number of manuscripts you'll keep in the mail
- the number and types of books you'll read
- the number of days per month you'll spend in the library, on the Internet, or researching at book stores.

Customize these goals to fit your particular needs and realize that they tend to change from year to year.

For some it will be helpful to set goals for your actual writing schedule. Estimate a minimum number of words for a set period of time—so many per day or week. Be realistic; start low. Even twenty words per day is a marked improvement if you are doing little or nothing right now. Work up to the point where you are comfortable but challenged—and don't go beyond that. We usually fail in meeting our goals when we push them beyond our reach.

Write every day if possible, but if not, determine what schedule will work best for you. Using a chart or graph will help establish a workable pattern. Record the amount of time spent and the number of words written each day. Using that information, set a length of time you can comfortably write without it being a chore—say ten minutes. Set a timer for that length of time and when it goes off, quit (whether you want to or not). This kind of regimen will help develop your self-discipline. As you get better at filling the time, set the timer for longer periods.

Another friend has come up with the following system. Each morning she sets a goal for the number of words or pages she wants to write that day. She then divides that among the number of hours she has available—say, one page per hour. At the beginning of the hour she sets out to write that page, and if she finishes before the hour is up, she spends the rest of the hour doing other office chores. At the beginning of the next hour she starts the next page. That way she meets her writing goal without being diverted by the other chores.

I often find myself torn between too many different projects calling for my attention. Rather than picking one and letting the others fall behind, I try to divide my day accordingly. For example, if I have three or four different projects in the works, I simply divide the day into one- to three-hour segments of time to spend on each different project.

Meeting Goals

Setting these goals is often the easy part. But it is important to realize that setting them is not enough. They will serve no purpose unless we start moving toward them. But how? Like the time-management gurus have told us—the same way we eat an elephant: one bite at a time. The next step, then, is to take each goal and break it into the bite-sized steps it will take to achieve it.

For example, if one of your goals is to write a book in the next year, based on the length of the book figure out how many pages you will have to write every month, every week, and every day. Or if research, travel, or other activities are involved, work those into the equation as well. Have specific goals for each step of the process. If you meet those goals, the book will be finished on time. The small-bite-plan also makes the task seem less intimidating.

Managing Time

The real key to achieving any goal is the proper use of your calendar. Time is managed with calendars, not with clocks. Even if you set priorities, if you don't plan for them on your calendar, they will give way to the priorities of your spouse, family, friends, boss, or church. In that case, you will be living your life by others' priorities, but you will still be personally responsible for how you use your time.

So use your calendar, not only for appointments, meetings, and special occasions, but also for the small bites of your elephant. Write in the days and hours you need for writing, time at the library, reading, and other writing-related activities, and honor those commitments as faithfully as you would any other meeting or appointment. Then when you are asked to do something else, you can honestly respond as to whether or not you have the time. I use a monthly calendar to set the daily priorities, and a yearly wall calendar to plot the big picture.

On the one-year wall calendar (where you can see all twelve months at one time, with room to write), I use different-colored, self-adhesive dots to help me track my writing schedule and speaking trips. First I put a red dot on each day I'll be out of town speaking at writers' conferences. I then use a different color for things such as personal travel days, regular column deadlines, and local meetings. That way I have a visual picture of what my schedule looks like for the year. This system will work just as well to schedule writing days, trips to the library, writing field trips, interviews, or whatever your writing life entails.

By using a calendar to work your priorities into your daily routine, you will not only be more likely to achieve your goals, but you will have ordered your life around your writing goals and not around the plans of others. However, you need to set and incorporate similar goals in each area of your life—time with spouse, family, friends, church, and community—so your writing doesn't eclipse the rest of your life.

To-Do List

Basic to any time-management program is the *to-do list*. This is a tool that needs to be personalized to your specific needs. I have used different types of to-do lists or systems over the years, depending on my current needs. I change from time to time because if I use the same type of list for too long I start ignoring it. Changing to a new system tends to get my attention—at least for a while. Some people instinctively know what needs to be done next and don't need a list for the day-to-day activities. They might, however, have a list of jobs that are on the back burner or that have no particular deadline. On the other hand, for many, it is the day-to-day list that is most needed. Probably the simplest way to make a day-to-day list is to divide a yellow pad into three sections: Must Do Today, Should Do Today, and Do Later. This could also be typed up as a form and duplicated for daily use.

Wall to-do list

You might also try a wall variation of that idea. This works well on a blank wall or bulletin board. Using 3x5 sticky notes, label columns across the top: Do, Doing, Deadlines, Calls. Spaced down the left-hand side of the open space put smaller sticky notes indicating: #1–Priority, #2–ASAP, #3–Later. Then put each chore, deadline, or call to make on a separate sticky note and stick it to the wall in the appropriate section and in the order of priority. This system makes it easy to remove, add, or reorder the slips as necessary.

Master file system

Another option is to use a *master file system.* This works especially well when you are juggling a number of different things in your life. Start with a loose-leaf notebook—a small one will do. In the notebook, keep one master list of everything you have to do. In its simplest form, that means that every time you think of something that needs to be done, whether personal, business, or writing-related, add it to the bottom of the list. The list could include everything from "finish the Johnson report," to "interview with Mr. Harris on Friday," to "buy Jane a birthday present," to "make a hair appointment."

If you prefer, the list can be broken into different sections with a master list for each different category, such as personal, work, writing, church, community, etc. That way you put the items on the appropriate list. Don't make too many lists.

Use this master list to make up a daily to-do list. Read through everything on the list (or lists) each morning and add the most pressing tasks to your daily list. When a task is completed, cross it off the list.

Tickler file

When you get very busy or start juggling a lot of different activities, a *tickler file* is invaluable. I wouldn't be able to function without one. (A tickler file will not be as helpful if you have little to do or if you do not use it regularly.)

First, prepare a set of files that includes one file folder for each month (labeled with the name) and thirty-one additional files for each day, labeled 1–31. Put the day files in front and the month files in the back. The daily files should be in order with the current date in the front. The monthly files should have the next month's file in the front.

Start putting in the file: reminders of things to do, appointments, meetings, deadlines, letters to answer, calls to make, and anything else you need to keep your writing business or your personal life running smoothly. Also put in bills or greeting cards on the days they need to be mailed, reminders of errands to be run, or other things you need to be reminded of at a particular time. If the reminder is for something happening in a future month, put it in the appropriate monthly folder. On the first of each month, distribute anything in that month's folder into the appropriate daily folder. Use your tickler file to remind you of everything in your life, including the small bites of your elephant noted on your priority calendar.

❖

Your prioritizing system will probably change over time. If you find yourself in a rut with a familiar system, try using another for a time. Whatever system you use, the key to a successful to-do list is to do things in the order of their importance. Most of us make the mistake of doing the easiest things first "just to get them out of the way." The problem is that you then rarely get to the most important things and even if you do you don't have enough time or energy left to tackle them well. Start with the most important; it is easier to find the time and energy to do the little jobs if the big ones are already out of the way.

Time Wasters

Writers used to contend with two major time wasters: mail and the phone. Now most must deal with two more as well: email and the Internet. While these things are valuable parts of a writer's life, they need to be kept under control or they will control you.

Mail

Every writer I know loves mail and often considers the arrival of the mailperson as a highlight of the day. Just don't let that mail bog you down. Make use of an executive tip: Handle each piece of paper only once. As you open the mail, immediately discard outer envelopes, fillers, junk mail, and anything else you don't need. If you are using a tickler file, file the bills on their mailing date, activity announcements on the appropriate date or day before (as a reminder), and find a place for anything else that can best go into that file, rather than leaving items in a pile on your desk.

If you aren't using the tickler file, a simple system is to have three folders on your desk labeled: To Answer, Bills, Future. Into those put any mail that needs an answer, bills, and anything else that must be held for future action. Add to those three a folder for each group or organization you belong to, including your church. File all mail that you need to keep from that group in the appropriate folder. When possible, write dates and details on the calendar and discard original mail.

As you read each letter, highlight any parts that call for action or a response from you. Have a supply of generic or nice postcards on hand to answer letters right on the spot if possible.

Phone

For many, the phone can be a bigger time waster than the mail. It may be more efficient to send ten postcards with a response than to make ten phone calls. Don't let phone calls steal prime time for writing. That may mean letting an answering machine pick up your calls, or asking people if you can call them back later (at your convenience) if it is not an emergency. Often it is a matter of educating your friends and family about what time of day is appropriate to call you. In some cases it will mean being diligent to break the bad habits of others that infringe on your writing time, such as a mother, sister, neighbor, or friend who calls every day "just to talk." Setting aside specific time for writing and specific time for talking on the phone allows you to give more of yourself to each activity at its respective time.

Email

Email is becoming more and more of a problem for some writers. If you get a lot of junk email, when possible, ask to be dropped from mailing lists, or get information from your Internet provider on how to stop all junk mail. Be selective about what you read. If the message isn't personal, chances are you don't need to read it. Realize that you will get as much or more junk mail on email as you do in your mailbox and treat it accordingly. If something comes through that seems to be of interest, print it out to read later.

Unless you are expecting an important message, pick one to three times a day when you will read and answer your email. For me that is first thing in the morning, before I quit working for the day, and at bedtime. Having such a schedule also helps you tell others when you will likely read a message they might send during the day.

Internet

By now, we are all aware of the bountiful resources we have on the World Wide Web, but if you've ventured into cyberspace you also know that it can consume copious amounts of time. If you have specific research needs, enter at your own risk, but limit the amount of time you will spend on the Internet. Set specific time slots—write it on your planning calendar—for such research. Avoid the peak hours when everyone else is online. That way you won't have delays on connecting and receiving information. If you feel like you need more time to get acquainted with this new resource, or to research in more general areas, try to plan those forays during non-productive time slots—perhaps when the kids are around disturbing your concentration anyway—and set yourself a time limit.

Qualities of Time

The underlying basis of good time management is recognizing and honoring the differing *qualities of time*. Discovering this concept has been more helpful than any other time-management concept I have run across. Look at the different segments of time you have available during an average day and recognize the quality of time each offers.

For example, when I had school-aged children and was working at home as a writer, my day fell into identifiable segments with very specific qualities. From the time I got up until the last child left for school (they were all on different schedules), life was hectic, so I used what extra time I had to straighten up the house or do mundane chores. From the time the last child left in the morning until the first one returned in the afternoon was my prime time of the day—the time I set aside for creative writing. I guarded that time carefully against outside interruptions.

However, when the first child returned from school, I knew that segment of time was over and I switched gears. I had a chair across from my desk where they could sit and share their day while I started addressing envelopes, filing, sorting material, or doing whatever required minimal attention. After dinner I wanted to be with the family watching TV or doing homework; I joined them but used that time to peruse newsletters or magazines, cut out articles for my topical files, or do other busy work that allowed me to interact with them at the same time. If I was on a tight deadline, I could work after the last child went to bed until my bedtime. By recognizing that my day was divided into distinct segments with very different qualities, I soon learned to assign each project to the appropriate time of the day, thus making the very best use of the time I had available. Although your daily schedule may differ widely, I encourage you to start recognizing your own qualities of time.

Chapter 7

On Marketing

One day at the end of a class I taught on marketing, a young woman made her way to the front of the room so excited she could hardly contain herself. She explained that she had been trying unsuccessfully to sell her writing for some time, but all of a sudden it was as if a light had been turned on. "I work in marketing for a big corporation—that's my job—but it wasn't until today's class that I finally realized that everything I know about marketing on my job can apply to marketing my writing. Why hasn't anyone ever told me that before?"

I've been teaching workshops on marketing for a good number of years now. In all that I teach in this area, there are two underlying principles. The first is that as a freelancer, the stories, articles and books you write are a product that you are selling, and the second is that they are sold as you sell any other product.

Before we go any further, however, I want to say something to those who view Christian writing as being too commercial—those who see the emphasis at conferences or in books like this as being too obsessed with selling. If you as an author are able to give your book or article away, then you need not read this chapter. But most authors want to see their writing sold so their words will influence the lives of others. Although for many of them, ministry is more of an issue than money, the ministry does not happen until the message reaches the marketplace. For that reason, it is important for us to recognize the need for marketing skills.

While saying that, I must admit that I rarely run into writers who bubble and gush about marketing being so much fun they can hardly wait to get started. Most of us are creative people, and we'd rather spend our time creating—not selling. I can't promise I will change that for many of you, but I hope I can make it a little easier, more understandable, and less intimidating. When we get to the bottom line, we all want to know which publishers are going to buy what we write. That is not only a beginner's question. I hear it from more experienced writers as well—those who have not figured out how the marketing process works. By the time you finish this chapter, you should have a clear picture of that process.

Marketing: A Business

Before we get into the actual details of how to sell your writing, lets go back for a minute and look more closely at how selling your writing compares to selling anything else. For example, let's assume that rather than selling manuscripts, you were going to sell cookies. Before you opened up your cookie shop at the local mall, you would not only need to develop some great cookies, you would also need to know who your customers are and what they want. You are not going to open a recipe book and start making any old cookie. You're going to find the best recipes—the ones people love and are most likely to buy.

It must be the same with your manuscripts. It doesn't make sense to start cranking out manuscripts if you don't know who your customers are and what they are in the market for. That is a very basic marketing concept, but the one most writers miss or tend to ignore. You must have a clear concept of who your customers or potential customers are. Think of going home and making a dress and then going door-to-door looking for someone to buy it. You would have to find a woman who was the right size, who liked the style and the color, who needed or wanted a dress, and who had the money to buy it. The odds of finding such a person would be pretty slim; no one would be so foolish as to approach marketing in such a haphazard way, yet we do exactly the same thing every time we write a manuscript with no particular market in mind. There is a better way. Learning this process will make the difference between selling your manuscripts and dooming them to the rejection pile.

Market Guide

If being successful in a business means knowing our customers and what they want to buy, then that is our goal in this study. If we want to know more about our potential customers, it's time to turn to the *Christian Writers' Market Guide*. It will be your primary resource for the Christian market. If you are writing for other markets, you will need appropriate market guides for those particular markets. The process is pretty much the same no matter what the target market.

If you already have a market guide and are familiar with how it works, that will speed up this process considerably. If you are new to the market guide, you will want to spend some time getting better acquainted with it so you can move about within its pages with ease. (See the section on "How to Use This Book" at the front of the *Market Guide*).

If you are serious about selling, you will always have the most current guide. Trying to sell your writing without the most current edition is like trying to build a house with bent nails—slow, if not impossible. I do not update the *Market Guide* every year because I need something to do, but because the information changes so quickly that that is the only way to keep all of you as up to date as possible. You will waste more in bad postage sending manuscripts to the wrong address or to defunct publishers than you would spend on a current guide.

Understanding the Market

Before we get into the actual plan, I want to give you a little background information that will help you better understand how this market is structured, so even the new or would-be writers will understand more about the world of marketing, especially as it has to do with the Christian market. I realize for many, this is like entering a foreign country where the customs and language are strange and unfamiliar.

Market divisions

In writing for the Christian market, you have many different options. You can write for magazines, Christian newspapers, or newsletters. You can write tracts, pamphlets, booklets, or books. The books will include most genres of fiction, as well as all types of nonfiction books, including gift books. These are listed by their various categories in the *Christian Writers' Market Guide.* The guide also includes a section on greeting card and specialty markets—markets for all those gift items you find in a Christian book store that include some kind of text. Each of these different areas offers opportunities for the freelance writer. That, by the way, is what you are if you want to write for publication—a freelance writer. It simply means you are not salaried as a writer, but work when and where you can find a publisher to pay you.

Although the *Market Guide* includes almost 1,000 markets, it helps to be able to categorize those a little more closely so instead of looking at those hundreds of markets as one pile, you can at least begin to break them down into separate and definable categories.

Denominational markets

Some of the markets (both books and periodicals) are denominational, which means they are sponsored by the various denominations—Baptist, Catholic, Assemblies of God, United Methodist, etc. That information is given in the individual listings, as well as in the Denominational Index at the back of the *Market Guide.*

Denominational publishers like you to understand their denominational slant, or at least those things that distinguish them from other denominations. Some use only writers who are a part of their denomination, or prefer to, while others are open to any writers who can write to their needs. By reading their publications and guidelines, you can begin to identify any specific taboos they might have.

Denominational publishers are always interested in articles or stories on their own members or churches. That means if you are doing a personality profile, consider selling it to or doing another piece for that person's denominational magazine. Also watch for churches in your area or places you visit that have significant programs in the community that could be written up for the denomination. In recent years, many denominational publications have expanded their scope to be of interest to readers outside the denomination, so they are also more open to outside writers.

One big advantage of denominational publishers is that they tend to be non-overlapping or non-competing markets (they each have their own readership), so you can offer the same article to any or all of them (if appropriate), either as a simultaneous submission or by offering one-time or reprint rights.

Organizational/educational publishers

Some of the publishers are tied to religious or para-church organizations or colleges (such as Focus on the Family, the Billy Graham Association, or Moody Bible Institute). When you see such a periodical or book publisher, you will find that the focus of the publisher will reflect the focus of the ministry, so if you are familiar with the organization you will already know a lot about the publication.

Keep in mind that both organizational and educational publishers tend to be extremely conservative in their approach to publishing and controversial issues. Most of these organizations are dependent on the financial support of their readers, so they are not likely to print anything that will alienate any of their donors.

Independent publishers

Some publishers are independently owned—which means they have no particular sponsoring denomination or organization. For that reason they are not as limited theologically, and see the entire Christian community as their potential audience. Some independent book publishers have a specific publishing image or niche, while others tend to be more general. More and more of these independents, magazines and book publishers, are ending up as part of one of the larger conglomerates, such as Christianity Today, Inc., or Cook Communications.

We often find that some of the newer, independent publishers are more likely to tackle the controversial issues because they are not governed by a long-standing, conservative constituency.

General publishers who do religious books or have a religious division

Another category of book publishers you need to be aware of is the general publishers who publish a few religious books. Keep in mind that these are religious books, not necessarily Christian. These publishers are very broad in their definition of "religious." They will not do books that are strongly denominational, theological, or evangelical. They will be books of a religious nature, more likely about God than about Jesus (except from an historical perspective). These books are more likely to sell in the mainline church market, rather than in the evangelical. Books for this market must be geared to a broad cross section of the religious community. Study their catalog and decide if you would be comfortable having your book included in their catalog.

❖

Now, with that information as a background to help us put these publishers more in perspective, we can move on to the how-tos of marketing.

Market Plan for Periodicals

With the current market guide in hand, it is time to look at a specific plan for selling. Unfortunately this is not a magic formula, but a plan that works only if you are willing to work the plan. The key to the success of this plan is time. As with any other business, if you are going to be successful you must invest a substantial portion of your time developing a marketing plan. If there is one sure way to fail in selling your manuscripts, it is by not investing enough time in this area.

The underlying purpose in the following plan is to start determining which specific periodicals are the best potential markets for the things you are going to write. With almost seven hundred periodical markets included in the *Market Guide*, obviously you cannot (nor would you want to) submit to all of them. This plan will help you refine and narrow that list to those you can best identify with and that are most likely to buy from you. *Marketing is not finding editors who will publish what you write, it is finding publishers you can write for.*

As you begin writing, you will likely try your hand at a number of different types of writing. That is fine; it is one way to help determine what topics or kinds of writing you are most qualified to tackle, what kinds you most enjoy, and what types sell best for you. It is a natural part of the process. However, once you have begun to recognize your strengths, it is time to determine what topics or types of writing you want to target during the next three to five years. This is an important, but often overlooked part of the process. One of our goals as writers is to have editors start recognizing our strengths and then give us assignments in those areas. If you write too wide a diversity of material, your name will never be associated with any particular areas of expertise.

Establishing those areas of expertise also prepares the way to write books in the future. One of the interesting things that happens when you are published regularly in a certain field is that it establishes your credibility in that field, even when you have no formal education or degrees. As I mentioned earlier, I was published regularly in every Christian education publication over several years before I wrote my first Christian education book (I eventually wrote seven in that field). I had twenty years experience and no C.E. degree, but because of my extensive publishing credits, no one ever questioned my qualifications. You can do the same thing in your area of interest. Don't feel you must limit yourself to only one area; the following plan will work in a few different areas at the same time.

Now, sit down with a large sheet of paper (or the Market Survey form from the *Marketing Plan for More Sales*, listed in appendix B) and make the following lists: 1.) Topics you most want to write about, i.e., marriage, health, relationships, family, etc. 2.) Types of writing you want to do, i.e., feature articles, interviews/profiles, poetry, devotionals, Bible studies, teen fiction, etc. 3.) Potential target audiences for your work—which audiences/age groups are you most qualified to write for, e.g., children, teens, women, pastors, singles, etc. Keep in mind that this is a work sheet; you will be perfecting it and expanding it as you invest more time defining your market.

Target audience

A word about the target audience. Often this is an overlooked part of the equation. Most publications are closely targeted to a particular audience, so if you have no defined audience when you write, chances are you will not hit anyone with your material. For example, "adults" is not a target audience. Within the Adult designation we have college students, singles, young marrieds, families with preschoolers, families with school-age children, empty-nest adults, senior citizens, etc. That means your material has to target a specific audience and use illustrations, anecdotes, and references that the members of that group can identify with. The added advantage of looking at a variety of target audiences is that you can take the same basic material and write it up with a different target audience in mind. So instead of one article on a topic, you could write two, four, six, or more, by simply changing the target audience.

❖

Once you have the above lists compiled, what you want to do is to begin putting a topic, type of writing, and audience together into a potential product. For example: a feature article on marriage for newlyweds or a teen short story on relationships. Come up with as many combinations as you can. Now that you have identified the product, you need to determine what publications will be interested in that particular product for that particular audience. What you want to do is name the product at the top of your sheet and under it start listing the potential markets for that kind of piece.

Identifying your markets

The question then is: How do we know what the best markets are for each list? This is where we turn to our market guide and follow these steps:

1. Turn first to the topical listings and look for your topic or type of writing and target audience. For example, if you have identified money management for teens, go to the topic, "Money Management," and then down to the list of teen publications.

2. Look up each market on that list in the Alphabetical Listings, and read the listing. Every market may not be a good one for you, so look for those that indicate they might be, and eliminate those that aren't. For example, you might eliminate those from denominations you aren't comfortable or familiar with, or those that accept material only from teens.

3. As you find possible markets, add them to the appropriate tentative list to be investigated further.

4. After reading a listing that looks promising, pull from your files or send for a sample copy and writers' guidelines. The listing will tell you how to order them (size of envelope and number of stamps). Note: See below for additional information on sample copies and writers' guidelines.

5. Carefully read the guidelines, highlighting anything that indicates this is—or isn't—a good market for you. Read the copy or copies cover-to-cover, again noting anything you like or dislike about the publication. Based on what you discover, either drop the publication from your list or keep it on for the next step.

6. The next step is to analyze the markets you are interested in. You will find an appropriate analysis sheet in the *Market Plan for More Sales* or the *Top 50 Christian Periodical Publishers' Packet* (see resource list at the end of this book). If no analysis sheet is available, answer the following questions about each market (this exercise can be more valuable if you can get together with other writers and analyze several different issues of each publication together). Look for answers to the following kinds of questions: What is the basic slant of this publication? Who is their target audience? What kind of articles do they seem to prefer? Are most long or short? Are most articles serious, factual, anecdotal, humorous? Do they seem to prefer first or third person? Do they ever use second person (addressing the reader as "you"). Do they use a lot of quotes from authorities, statistics, case studies, personal experiences, etc.? Do they prefer certain kinds of leads? Look at individual articles, paragraph by paragraph, and see what the author included. Simply ask yourself if your topic would fit in this publication, and whether you could write in a way to fit their style. If so, leave them on your list; if not, drop them.

7. At this point you should have a list of potential markets for that topic or type of writing. You will repeat the process for each different list. Often you will do this for each topic as you are ready to write something different (rather than trying to complete all the lists at the same time). You will also continue to add and delete markets as you become aware of new markets or discover some markets are closed or unsuitable.

8. Once each list is compiled, you may put it in any order you like, such as best paying, largest circulation, most freelance, payment on acceptance, length, or whatever your priority is for that particular piece. It will not be until you reach this point that you will be ready to start writing your article or story.

Market Plan for Books

If you are seeking a market for a book, you go through much the same process, except that you will study the book publishers. Make your list of possible book topics across the top of your work sheet.

1. Find the list of possible publishers under the appropriate topical list. Realize that in some cases you may have to cross-reference more than one topic if yours isn't listed. For example, if you are writing an adult novel dealing with homosexuality, you would look at both "Adult Fiction" and "Controversial Issues," and see which publishers are on both lists. Although "Controversial Issues" refers to nonfiction, you can usually assume that if a company is willing to deal with it in nonfiction they will in fiction as well.

2. After reading the Alphabetical Listing for each publisher, eliminate those that don't look like good prospects, based on any restrictions or problems you find there.

3. Pull from your files or send for their writers' guidelines and a current book catalog. Their book catalog will list new books they are releasing, as well as books still available on their backlist.

4. Carefully read the guidelines and highlight any information of particular interest, especially anything that indicates this might be a good publisher for your book project (or that it would not).

5. Next, study the book catalog, following these steps:

   - Get an overview of the whole catalog, noting what types of books they publish. Is there anything they publish you aren't in agreement with? Would you feel comfortable having your book included in this catalog? If so, go on, if not, cross this one off your list. (Note: In some cases you may want your book included where it can provide "salt and light" even when you are not in agreement with other books in the catalog.)

- Next, look for the section that would include your book. Say it's a book on marriage. Do they have more than one book or a whole section on marriage books? If so, do they have a book on the same aspect of marriage that you planned to cover? (Check both frontlist and backlist books—frontlist books are books currently being released, and backlist books are ones published previously.) You want them to have a good number of books in the same general area, but if they have a book on exactly the same aspect of the topic, chances are they will not consider yours. Publishers typically will not publish a new book that is in direct competition to another book in their line. What you are looking for is a publisher who has a gap you can fill; where your book will complement their current list. So, if they have a number of books in your interest area, but not one on exactly the same aspect, then leave them on your list.

- At this point, ask yourself honestly if your book would fit naturally into this catalog.

6. For the next step in your book marketing, go to your local Christian bookstore. Most authors overlook this important step in the marketing process. A bookstore can be one of your most important resources in finding a publisher for your book. While at the bookstore do the following:

   - Find the section where they sell your topic. See what is already on the shelf. Can you find a book the same or similar to yours? (If so, make a note of the title, author, publisher, and publication date.)

- While you're checking out the books, pay attention to the covers, bindings, typestyles, graphics, etc., for each publisher. Is there a publisher that is particularly impressive, or one you don't care for? Make note of which ones they are.

- Which publishers seem to have the most books in this section? Check to see if all the publishers you are considering have books in this section. If not, try to find out why not (ask the clerk, book buyer, or manager).

- If possible, speak with the book buyer. If it is a large store, you may need to make an appointment ahead of time. Tell them the book you are planning and ask which publisher(s) they would go to for such a book. Many authors do not realize that certain publishers are known for producing certain types of books—and those are the publishers a bookstore is most likely to go to when ordering that type of book. As an author it is to your advantage to be published by a publisher known for the type of book you want to do.

- Also ask them any other questions that have come to mind as you have checked out the book shelves. Ask if they get many requests for the type of book you are planning, and if so, what books do they recommend or sell the best in this area? (Make note of this information for the marketing section of your book proposal. These are also the books you should read if you haven't already.)

- The bookstore is also a good marketing resource when you have an unusual product or topic in mind that does not fit the usual channels, or one that you can't find in the topical lists. For example, I once had plans for a file of 3x5-inch index cards of ideas for teachers. Since it was not the typical product, I went to the bookstore to see if I could find any sets of index cards for sale. What I needed was a publisher who had worked in this format previously and would know how to handle the production end of the process. The same thing usually works with any unusual format or topic.

7. At this point you should have a fairly reliable list of potential publishers for your projected book project. However, I would also encourage you to ask yourself very honestly whether the world needs your book. If you are just rehashing the same old topic in the same old way, it probably doesn't. If you have read the competing books you have found, you need to be convinced—and be able to convince a publisher—that your book is different or better than what is already available. If it isn't, then move on to another topic.

❖

That concludes this preliminary plan for both periodicals and books. When you reach this point in either process, you will be ready to go to work on those articles, stories, or books. The following sections will take you on to the next steps in the various areas of publishing.

Sample Copies, Book Catalogs, and Writers' Guidelines

Sample copies or catalogs and guidelines are a crucial part of your marketing research, so begin collecting and filing as many as you can. (See chapter 4 for ideas on filing them.) One of the highlights of many writers' conferences is their tables of samples and guidelines available free to conferees. Anytime you have a chance to pick them up for free, don't pass it up. Sending for them by mail is expensive and time-consuming. Once you have them, spend some time getting acquainted with them before you file them away. This is comparable to chatting with customers in any other business. The better you know your customers, the better you can meet their needs. Your goal with the samples—like with your customers—is to be able to recognize and call them by name as soon as possible.

If you have guidelines and samples that are obviously not markets for you, there is no sense keeping them and cluttering up your files. Pass them on to a writer friend or simply discard them. If you move into that area of interest in the future, you will need to get current guidelines and samples anyway.

Another source for market information on these publishers is their websites. Most book publishers and many periodicals now have their own sites. Some have guidelines available on the site that you can simply print off for your file. Many give you background information on the sponsoring denomination or organization, as well as sample articles from their publication or a list of upcoming book titles they are publishing. This is fast becoming one of our most valuable marketing tools.

Foreign Marketing

Some writers are interested in selling material to foreign markets. That is an option, and the *Market Guide* does include a lot of Canadian markets and a few from other countries. However, there are some inherent problems with writing for other countries. You will find a clue to the first problem mentioned in a few of the Canadian listings. Some of those editors indicate that they do not want submissions from U.S. authors. That is not because they don't like people from the U.S., but because our culture is so much a part of what we write that it usually does not fit the Canadian reader. So before you send anything to a Canadian or other foreign market, you need to edit out any such references. With some articles that may be impossible because the culture (or an understanding of the culture) is such a large part of the content. For that reason, not every article is suitable for foreign travel, so you will have to carefully select articles that will travel well to other cultures. Of course, some subjects are of universal interest, and the Internet has added to a more global view of the world—bringing us closer together. Foreign Christian markets are interested in how people in different countries live out their spirituality.

In selecting foreign markets, you need to limit yourself to English-speaking countries (unless you are fluent in other languages). But even though they speak English in England, you need to recognize and honor the differences in spelling and terminology. Avoid American slang or jargon that shouts "America." You will also need to weed out any references to American history, organizations, statistics, etc.

Because you have likely only sold North-American serial rights to articles sold in the states, you are free to sell them in other countries (except Canada--which is still in North America). Also, if you are submitting the same article in several different countries, it is still not considered a simultaneous submission, because each query is going into a different market.

When mailing to foreign countries, find out the proper amount of postage and how long it will take for delivery—either by air mail or by surface. Figure those times into your calculations when determining how long you should wait before following up on a submission. Also keep in mind that foreign countries may have poor postal service or be subject to postal strikes which may slow down the process considerably. Never put U.S. postage on your S.A.S.E.

There may also be some problems with understanding pay rates and foreign exchange rates. For example, in selling to Canada, you may be told that they will pay you $100 for an article, but they will mean $100 Canadian, not U.S. currency. So with the exchange rate you may make about $75 U.S, or less. Some foreign markets will pay in U.S. dollars if you ask. Some U.S. banks charge to cash foreign checks and even charge you a fee if the money is wired to your bank here, so check out applicable fees at your bank and determine the best way to handle such payments.

One more consideration with foreign sales is the tax ramifications. Always claim the foreign income (in U.S. dollars), although the foreign publishers aren't likely to report it or send you any form verifying what they have paid you during the year. It will be a good idea to make a habit of keeping copies of everything, including checks, from foreign markets.

Theme Lists

When you are sending for sample copies, keep a look out for those publications that also offer a theme list. A good number of publications are theme-oriented, which means that each issue—or at least a good portion of it—is devoted to a specific theme. Possible themes might include, prayer, faith, missions, politics, money/finances, nature, etc. Because they want to be sure they receive appropriate material to fit those themes, once or twice a year they will put out a list of upcoming themes. Some give just the overall theme like I did in my examples above, while others will list specific article ideas they are looking for. In either case, it is to your advantage to get a copy of the theme list and send material to fit.

Some lists will give you a specific deadline for each issue, but many do not. You can often get a reasonable idea of lead time by checking the market guide for how far ahead they want holiday or seasonal material. In any case, it is best to send such theme-related material as far ahead of time as possible. Don't wait until the day of the deadline to get it there. Because they will be concerned about filling the issue, they usually don't want to wait until the last minute to fill all the slots.

Some editors want a query for theme-related material, while others prefer to see the complete manuscript. Determine which your favorite editors prefer and send them what they want. Keep in mind that your chances of selling to a theme-related periodical are almost nil if you ignore the themes. On the other hand, you increase your chances tenfold if you study the magazine to see how they treat their themes, follow the theme list, and get your submissions in in plenty of time. Also, when submitting material to fit a theme, include a cover letter identifying the theme issue you are targeting.

Trends

Before we conclude this section on marketing, I want to say something about trends. Writers often ask me what I consider the latest trends, and how important it is for them to know and follow the trends. My general feeling is that it is not very important at all. Spotting trends is a difficult endeavor at best, and nearly impossible for the average writer. When I'm asked about trends, it is often by writers or would-be writers who think if they can just catch the edge of the next trend, their book or article is a sure sell. If that were possible, more writers would be doing it.

The problem is that by the time we are able to recognize a trend, it is usually on its way out. This is especially true when you are talking about books. Because a book often takes a year or two from completion to finished product (to say nothing of the several months to a year or more to write it), most trends will be a distant memory by the time the book hits the market.

For that reason, I have always encouraged writers to pay less attention to trends and more attention to their own or their friends' needs or concerns and write to those instead. If God gives you a burden for a particular subject or audience, that is a greater indicator of direction than is some undefinable trend.

More important than topic trends are the industry trends. Reading writers' newsletters or magazines, belonging to a writers' email or Internet group, attending conferences, and talking regularly with other writers will help keep you informed on what is happening in the marketplace.

Chapter 8

On Writing for Periodicals

I always recommend that writers start by writing articles. Although some people start out with aspirations to write a book, I think that is usually a mistake. There is much about writing that you only learn by doing it, and writing articles helps you put the things you have learned into practice with a quicker chance for feedback. You learn much about structure, organization, and simply how to put the words on paper.

Article Types

There are many types of articles, and as a writer you need to recognize and understand the different types so as to not limit yourself to the obvious. When editors say they want a feature article or survey article, you will want to know what they are talking about without having to ask. Following is a list of different types of articles with a simple description or explanation for each. If any of them catch your interest, seek out some books that will give you more in-depth information on that type and watch for good examples in your reading. In this book, we do not have the room to give you the information you would need to actually learn how to do that kind of article, but many such resources are available elsewhere (check the Resources list at the end of this book). Because a certain type of article may be identified with more than one name, keep looking until you find the description you want, or check the index.

Business writing

One of the better paying markets is writing articles for newsletters or trade journals that focus on a particular type of business. You don't have to be associated with the business yourself, although it helps if you have some experience or at least some interest in the field. You search for topics that seem needed, gather the information, interview those who know the field, and write. Some people do business writing to supplement or support writing the things they enjoy.

CBA Marketplace and *Christian Retailing* are both trade journals for Christian booksellers and publishers. They use articles of interest to bookstore owners, including author profiles, book reviews, and industry news. They suggest that you interview bookstore owners to find out what topics interest them, and research possible solutions. The same would apply to any other trade journal—find out who the audience is and interview members of that audience to find out what sorts of articles would intrigue them. Business writing can also include writing such things as brochures, pamphlets, résumés, newsletters, and promotional materials.

Controversy

Some articles present a controversial topic and offer a balanced report showing both sides of the issue: for example, an article on whether illegal aliens are hurting or helping our country, a piece on whether women submitting to their husbands is biblical, or one on the pros and cons of the death penalty.

Other articles take a position on a controversial topic and present it (see "Essay or Opinion" below).

Drama-in-life or narrative

These narrative articles are based on a real-life event. *Guideposts* magazine prints a lot of stories like this: for example, the story of a man who dives into shark-infested waters to save a drowning child or the story of a woman who is kidnapped but escapes her attackers.

A *first-person* article is the narrative of a true story you write about your *own* experiences. Example: Your story of working with the homeless in New York City.

An *as-told-to* story is one you write based on *someone else's* personal experience (as told to you, but written as if the person who experienced it were telling it). This is similar to ghost-writing, but you share in the byline. Watch the newspaper for potential story ideas and develop good interviewing skills. Example: You writing the story of a homeless person in New York City.

Human interest stories use personal experience to reveal something positive about human nature in general. Use your best fiction techniques to develop the story of a likable protagonist who overcomes insurmountable odds to reach a happy, positive, or satisfactory conclusion. This type of article is most often used by women's or general-interest magazines, not by technical or how-to publications. Example: Story of a family that has adopted disabled children or of someone who trusted God through hard times.

Essay or opinion (also called "think piece")

An essay is a thoughtful, insightful article that expresses the writer's opinion on any given topic. Since opinions are a dime a dozen, yours must be well-written, entertaining, provocative, and interesting. Newspapers usually use opinion pieces, as do many magazines. Magazines will often carry them on the final page of the issue as an "In My Opinion" column. Most are 1,000 words or less and deal with only one topic. Queries do not work well for this type of article, so send the complete manuscript. Examples include articles on national topics such as abortion or doctor-assisted suicide, or on local topics, such as proposals for local gun control, new freeways, or the closing of a local health facility.

In a *prophetic viewpoint article,* the writer predicts the result or outcome of some pending event or situation as it relates to the prophetic portions of the Bible.

Exposé

Writing an exposé can be exciting. Such articles reveal documented facts that bring to light some wrongdoing, injustice, or foul play. These require careful investigative reporting, not hearsay or rumors, and must not be malicious. Your local news will include many examples of exposés, including reports of a local politician embezzling city funds, or a nonprofit organization soliciting funds under false pretenses. An exposé might also be written on a historical figure or event.

Feature article

A feature article tells the story behind the news, enlarging on or interpreting the news for the readers. This type of article calls for more in-depth research on a topic. Often it is the lead article in a magazine. Since these topics are often tied to current events, you must move quickly so your piece will be timely and someone else won't beat you to the punch. Topics for lead articles are as varied as the magazines that use them.

A feature article usually pays more because it requires research and is so timely. At most publications, the best pay rate is reserved for feature articles. Although feature articles generally deal with politics, ethics, science, social issues, economics, or art, it is best if you specialize and gain a reputation in one or two of those areas. Read as much as you can in your selected topic area, seek out and cultivate relationships with experts in the field, and keep up with what is happening in that area of interest. Always query before tackling a feature article. Be sure of the market and the appropriate slant.

Ideas for feature articles are everywhere, and once you start tuning in to those potential topics, you will have more ideas than you can ever follow through on. Simply look for things that interest you—first—and will then interest your readers as well. Some features are profiles that focus on an individual; others are stories about situations, organizations, or programs.

Feature articles are not the place to start your writing career. Learn to write well and add a number of credits to your résumé before you tackle your first feature. Learn all you can about this specialized type of article while you hone your research and interviewing skills. A feature article is written in short, declarative sentences with active verbs, few adjectives, and simple descriptions. Ultimately, let the story tell itself. Examples of feature articles include stories of a local celebrity in the news, the effect of welfare reform, or what one school is doing to curb teen violence.

How-to

Most publications print some how-to articles. However, not every writer is good at this kind of piece. How-to writers tend to be well-organized and logical thinkers. You need to be able to take what might be a long and confusing process for doing something and turn it into small, logical steps that will lead the reader to a successful conclusion. Most how-tos tend to be related to one (or more) of the basic human interests: self, money, health, family, leisure time, romance, job, or spirituality.

Some how-tos will be written in a step 1, step 2, step 3 format. Others simply describe the procedure in paragraph form. Check on the preference of the editor, and know what type your target publication prefers. A how-to can be a short tip for use in a tips column or as a filler, or it can be a full-length article. Again, the editor's preference or magazine's style prevails. A query is usually preferable with a longer article, but tips and fillers can be sent as complete manuscripts. Sidebars are often used with how-tos to give sources for supplies, tips for success, or other material that would be awkward in the body of the article. Some how-tos will require step-by-step photographs or sketches (find out what your target publication requires). Before submitting the piece, have someone unfamiliar with the process read the article and/or follow the steps to see if it makes sense or if you have left out critical information.

Unless writing for a specialized audience, always assume your readers are not familiar with the technical jargon associated with your topic and put all instructions in everyday terms.

When looking for ideas for how-to articles, focus on or write down all the things you know how to do. The list is likely to be long. Determine who might want to know how to do each thing—that will be your target audience. Then decide which publications will reach that audience—that will be your market. Examples of how-to articles include: how to get the most out of your Bible study, how to teach your child to pray, how to deal with the Medicare system, how to get a reluctant teen to attend church, or how to make a birdhouse.

Humor

Most Christian and general publishers are in the market for humor, but few people can write it well. Humor is currently the twelfth most popular topic or type of article in the Christian market (out of over 120 topics). Of course, in this market the humor must have a purpose (though making us laugh at ourselves is sometimes enough) and must be clean. Even people who can be very funny in person may have difficulty writing in a funny way—it takes very different skills because your words must be funny without depending on sight, sound, tone of voice, inflection, or any of the other techniques that aid humor when it is told live.

Usually it is best to stick to ordinary subjects everyone can relate to. Generally speaking, editors will want to see a complete manuscript rather than a query (unless they require a query, in which case you should include a few samples of your humor in the query letter). Humor articles need to be short—not full-length features—and on a single topic. Besides articles, there is a market for books, short humor in newspapers, fillers, scripts, greeting cards, cartoons, jokes, poetry, and even speeches. The examples of possible topics for humor are as broad as human experience itself, but parenting is often chosen: for example, an article comparing a two-year-old's and a teenager's first taste of independence.

Inspirational

Although most people think an inspirational article is on a Christian theme, it can also be on anything that has a spiritual or uplifting nature. Spirituality has found a new popularity even in general markets, so the market for this type of article is more open than ever. An inspirational article aims not so much to entertain as to enrich the reader's life with a story or idea that will make a difference in how they think or feel about life. This is not the place to preach or try to inflict your deep convictions on others. These articles will often be based on a personal experience that has given you some insight you can share with others. Sometimes inspirational pieces can be tied to holidays, such as Easter or Christmas, or can be devotionals, personality profiles, personal experiences, fillers, or character-building pieces for children. Accepting the loss of a loved one, re-evaluating life's priorities after a personal crisis, or finding inspiration in an everyday event are all examples of inspirational articles.

Interview

A good interview of a fascinating character draws loads of readers. Interview articles can be personality profiles, or they can deal with a particular organization, event, project, or program. Usually interviews are written in a format like a script, simply giving the interviewer's question followed by the subject's answer, but some are written in more of an essay format. If you want to submit interview articles to a periodical that has indicated an interest in them, you will need to study some sample copies to see what format they use. Most editors prefer one type or the other, while a few will consider either. Obviously this will not just be a transcript of the interview.

After the interview, it is the author's job to select from the full transcript of the interview those questions and answers that will create a finished product that reflects the intended purpose of the article. In some cases you will need to edit or shorten the subject's response, which is all right as long as you do not change the essence of what he or she said. What this type of interview article does is give the readers of the publication access to the knowledge or insight of a subject who would not have the time, writing ability, or inclination to write an article himself or herself. Select your subjects carefully, determining which ones will be of most interest to the readers of a particular publication; for example, you could interview a scientist about a new scientific or medical discovery (or someone who is living with a condition or disease), a politician about new legislation being introduced, or a new pastor about future plans for the church.

You'll need good interview techniques for a variety of types of articles, so no matter what kind of writing you want to do, you will need to learn how to conduct an effective interview. Your goal will be to get all the information you want or need in as short a time as possible. That can only be accomplished if you know what to ask and how to ask it. Here are a few key guidelines for effective interviewing:

- Interview the subject in person if possible. A lot of what you will learn will be visual—things you will miss if you don't actually see the subject.
- Decide on the best location for the interview—the subject's home? office? your office? a neutral location? Not a noisy restaurant. Pick a place where the subject will be most comfortable and where you will have the fewest distractions.
- If the interviewee is not available in person, the interview can be done by phone. Call ahead to make an appointment for the interview call. A last resort would be to send a list of questions for the subject to answer and return to you.
- Learn all you can about the subject ahead of time so you don't waste time asking questions whose answer you can easily find elsewhere.
- Allow plenty of time—thirty minutes to two hours for an article interview.
- Take a tape recorder (with extra tapes and batteries), and be sure you can operate it easily. However, don't depend on it exclusively; take notes, too. If recording a phone interview, ask the subject for permission to do so.
- Write out four to six main questions ahead of time and have related questions prepared. But don't get bogged down in your questions. *Listen* to what the interviewee has

to say and base your next question on the last answer or comment, not on what's next on your list.

- Pay attention to what you see in the room (if you're on the subject's turf), and break the ice by talking about that rather than jumping right into your questions. Try to put the subject at ease. If you are relaxed, it is more likely that he or she will be.
- Avoid disagreeing or arguing with interviewees. You are there to find out who they are and how they think or feel on the issues, whether you agree or not.
- Generally, you should move from the simple, non-threatening questions to the harder issues, but you need to be sensitive to where the subject wants to start and the direction he or she wants to go. Don't let the subject sabotage the interview by avoiding the questions or issues you came for. Interrupt and get him or her back on track if you need to.
- Use open-ended questions. Never ask questions that have yes or no answers as that may be all you will get in reply.
- Avoid asking direct questions that may upset the interviewee. Rephrase them in less threatening ways, such as, "How do you answer your critics when they say . . . ?" Your questions should nudge the subject in the direction you want to go—questions that reveal feelings, values, and a unique point of view.
- If you are having trouble getting a handle on who this person is, ask a question such as, "If I were to ask your boss (wife, children, pastor) to describe you in one sentence, what would he or she say?"
- Use your notebook to record your visual observations: locale description, appearance, mannerisms, gestures, body language, interaction with or relationship to any others in the room, etc.
- Before closing the interview, check your list to be sure you covered everything. Also ask permission to call with follow-up questions if you missed or lost anything of importance or need to verify facts.

- Write up the interview as soon as possible, while the things you didn't write down are fresh in your mind. It is usually not necessary to transcribe the entire tape, just those parts that have important quotes.
- Some interviewees will ask to see the finished article before it is published. It is best not to show them, as they will always want you to change something. Tell them that you have a policy not to do so but you will verify all technical information and direct quotes before it goes to press. Let them know when and where it will be published, and promise to send a copy.
- For many interview articles you will need photographs.

News

Lots of writers find an outlet by writing news stories for their local newspapers or a news magazine, or writing newsbreaks (short reports) on items of universal interest for Christian magazines. Some newspapers or magazines will pay an author for providing news tips that you don't actually have to write up. In news stories you present the information in order of importance, with the most important facts first, followed by the background information. That way, if the editor is limited for space, he or she can cut the article off at any point and still have enough information for a complete piece. I can think of many examples of news articles: a piece on a local church event, a description of a group that is providing a specialized service to the community (such as transitional housing for the homeless), or a tip on a brewing controversy that is likely to erupt during an upcoming denominational convention.

Nostalgia

Although we often think of nostalgia magazines when we think of nostalgia articles, many different kinds of magazines use nostalgia. These articles generally deal with looking back at a period of time or an event, with a comparison to the present. Keep in mind that all nostalgia is not based in your grandparents' time. Every generation has memories of the "good old days."

My adult children talk nostalgically about when they were children and could go to a carnival or corner store by themselves. You might write a nostalgia article about the Christmas you remember best; memories of a mother/father/aunt/uncle/grandparent who made some impact on your life; a look at World War II shortages.

Personality profile

Although some magazines are technically or how-to oriented, stories of people are at the heart of many others. People like to read about people—people they can identify with and people they can admire, empathize with, or be inspired by. Often we are looking for answers to our own problems by reading about how others have dealt with and overcome similar obstacles. When doing a personality profile, don't try to cover an entire life; zero in on achievements or philosophy and fill in background at the end. When you start this piece, put a small sign within eyesight that will remind you why you are writing this article for this particular publication. Look at it regularly to keep your focus.

I once wrote a profile on a married-with-children, Christian female singer who had written a book on fitness. When selecting a potential market, I could have focused on her singing (for a music magazine), juggling career and family (for a women's magazine), fitness philosophy or how-to (for a fitness magazine), Christian testimony (for a Christian magazine). Although this subject offered a number of different slants, when I picked a market I had to keep my emphasis on the appropriate slant for that publication. In other words, I would not write the same article for each of these different publications. But I could have written a different article for each one, emphasizing a different aspect of her life in each version.

A celebrity profile may focus on a person's childhood, early years, or tough times (rather than a profile of current fame); on an everyday person doing extraordinary things or making a difference in the lives of others; on a celebrity's Christian life and experience; or on an unusual aspect in the life of a historical figure.

Photo story or photo essay

A story that is essentially told through a series of photographs, with or without captions, is a photo essay. These can be funny, poignant, or merely interesting. Some start with a paragraph or two of introduction and then let the photos tell the story. For example, a photo essay might catch children involved in various activities, exciting sports events, or unusual events in nature.

Regional

Regional writing deals with material that is related to or of interest to people in a specific region of the country. For example, an article on the development of a new beach area, sports complex, or historical house being opened to the public would carry a lot of regional interest. Such pieces would be sold to local newspapers and magazines.

Report/explanation

Reports give readers needed information on topics of interest, either in the form of a description of a particular situation or an explanation of the facts on a given topic. For example, a lawyer might explain what your legal rights are in a restaurant if you find a fly in your soup or get food poisoning.

Roundup or survey

Interview several different people on the same topic and write an article telling the story from the different viewpoint of each, and you've written a roundup. In essence it is an informal survey, but not a research project, based on the opinions or experiences of a number of different people (typically three to five), not on scientific research. The key is to select people who are knowledgeable on your selected topic and able to express themselves in an interesting manner. Determine the slant of your article before you start asking questions, and focus on the questions that will support that slant. This type of article does demand a query, and often can include a sidebar. Examples would include the joys of first-time fatherhood, dealing with a death in the church from the viewpoint of several different pastors, or ways successful women balance work and family.

Service piece

Some articles give readers the information they need to make a decision about purchasing certain items, services, or facilities. This type of article usually focuses on one particular category and gives readers as much information as possible on several options so they can make the right choice. For example, a service piece on daycare providers in your area would include a description and comparison of the various ones available. This would sell to a local or regional magazine or newspaper, not a national one, because of the topic. Periodicals that use service articles tend to buy them from freelancers, rather than writing them themselves, because they are time-consuming. This type of piece can be boring, so study some good examples of how to make them both interesting and informative, and stick to areas where you have some personal experience. *Consumer Reports* magazine is an example of a periodical that is almost entirely service pieces. If you were looking for a topic for a local newspaper, you might compare family programs, youth groups, or singles' programs in local churches; examine the best athletic centers in your town; or profile the best emergency facilities.

Keep in mind that criticizing a person or organization can lead to legal claims if you are not very careful. It is safest to simply describe differences without putting a negative value on them (e.g., "The youth group at First Baptist is very large and active and meets three times a week, while the one at Second Presbyterian is small and intimate and meets once a week").

Travel piece

Travel articles give insights and information about specific destinations. If you want to write about your travels, you should avoid large tourist attractions or other frequently traveled areas. It is best to find a unique angle or out-of-the-way place that hasn't been covered hundreds of times. Also look for new and different types of destinations and approaches to travel, such as eco-tourism (traveling to locations where you view nature from the viewpoint of preservation). Travel articles almost always require photographs, so take your own quality shots (advisable if you plan to do a lot of travel articles) or see what is available through the area's public relations office, Chamber of Commerce, or tourist bureau. For example, a travel article would not deal with the Disney World theme park, but perhaps what happens underground and backstage with the Disney characters, who cares for the landscaping, or what it's like to work in the park. You can also cover a geographical area focusing on the diversity of food, a particular type of art, or the architecture.

Once you recognize the different types of articles and have come up with a list of target markets for your material, you are ready to go to work. The basic idea is that you not write anything until you know whom you are writing it for. Later on I will offer you another tool to help you collect, organize, and compile all your potential ideas.

Sidebars

If people were sidebars, then Dr. Watson would be a sidebar to Sherlock Holmes—he isn't always necessary but makes the story better for his presence. Likewise, a sidebar is a block of information that is generally run in a column next to the article and often set within a box. It contains information that compliments the article but that would not be appropriate within the body of the article itself. A sidebar might focus on statistics, additional resources on the topic, a list of affiliated organizations, quotes from others on the topic, a quiz on the topic, a glossary of terms used in the article, an anecdote or case study on the topic, historical background, differing points of view, etc. A sidebar is often the professional touch that will sell an article. It gives it that extra pizzazz.

Some publications use a lot of sidebars and either require them or consider them a plus. Others never or seldom use them.

The *Market Guide* will indicate who uses them, and studying a few sample copies will tell you very quickly how many and what kind they use most often. Not sending a sidebar to an editor who prefers them is as bad as sending them to an editor who never uses them.

Every time you write an article, make a list of possible sidebars. Some articles will support more than one sidebar, so don't limit yourself or the editor. In your query, offer more than one choice for sidebars.

Should you expect extra payment for a sidebar? It depends. If the sidebar is included in the total number of words you are being paid for—you promised and delivered a 2,000 word article, including sidebar—then no. If, however, you deliver a 2,000 word article without a sidebar, and they later ask for an additional sidebar, then, yes, you should expect and get extra payment. The amount of payment will depend on whether you already have the additional information in your notes, or if you are going to have to do new research.

When submitting a sidebar, type it on a separate page (or pages) identified at the top as "Sidebar to (name of article)," or "Sidebar #1 to (name of article)" if you have more than one, or "Statistical Sidebar to (name of article)," or "Case-Study Sidebar to (name of article)." Type each as a separate manuscript and use your common sense in identifying them.

Holiday/Seasonal Submissions

Many publications are open to stories, articles, poetry, or fillers that are tied to a specific holiday or season. In fact, those who do use such material are often desperate for material to meet that need. Most will have more than they can use for Christmas or Easter, but very little available for Valentine's or Mother's Day. So think seasons or minor holidays instead of the obvious ones.

Many writers make the mistake of submitting seasonal material too late. A market guide or their guidelines will usually indicate how far ahead they need to receive this material. For most, it will be six to eighteen months ahead. I've had more than one editor complain to me that writers will send a Christmas story in November and be upset because they can't put it in the Christmas issue that year.

Poetry Submissions

You should not just send a random selection of poems. Periodicals that use poetry generally use poems that fit their focus. For example, a family magazine will want family-oriented poetry, a senior citizens magazine will use poetry related to nostalgia or aging issues, etc. If you carefully match your poetry to the appropriate markets, your chances of selling are much greater.

Put each poem on a separate page so editors can select the poems they want and return the others. Also check the poetry sections to see what type of poetry an editor prefers. Some accept any type, while others may prefer rhymed or unrhymed. Send them what they want. Most periodicals pay little or nothing for poetry (although there are exceptions), but if you are a poet you want to get your poetry published everywhere you can whether you are paid or not. The good poets rise to the top eventually, but you will never be discovered unless you are published widely. It is the established poet who has the best opportunity of having a book of poetry accepted by a royalty publisher.

Poets often ask whether they should enter poetry contests or submit to poetry anthologies. Contests are a good way to get some recognition for your poetry as long as there are no, or low, entry fees. A poetry contest that charges high entry fees is likely in it for the money, not to discover promising poets. The same is true of anthologies. Some are legitimate; some are not. Never get involved with an anthology if you must buy one or more copies as a requirement for entering. Buying a copy should simply be an option, not a requirement. Also, try to find out if they accept everyone or if they select only the best poetry. There is no value in being included in an anthology that is filled with awful poetry.

Article Idea Form

Most writers I know are busy people who struggle to find time to write. They long for those free stretches of time when they can let the words flow. Unfortunately those times come all too infrequently, and often when they do you sit down and realize you don't have a clue where to start. Sure you have that folder full of ideas you've jotted on slips of paper, backs of envelopes, or old napkins, but for most of them you have "lost the vision" (or don't have any idea what you had in mind). Because that seems to be true of most writers, I have come up with a simple form to help.

The Article/Story Market Form (see figure 8-1) is a simple way to organize those ideas in a workable manner that will prepare you to start writing immediately. The idea is to fill out (or start filling out) this form for each new idea that strikes you, and keep the forms in a folder or loose-leaf notebook on your writing desk. They could be sorted by topic or type of material. Following are a few ideas to help you better understand and use this form:

1. Start with the name of the periodical, not with the name of the piece. This is a reminder that as soon as you have an idea you must ask yourself whom you should write it for (check your list).

2. On the form, indicate what type of writing it will be—article, short story, poem, or whatever. Decide at this point what form would work the best or even if it could take more than one form, such as a short story and a poem.

3. Note where it refers to Special Column/Section. One of the most overlooked segments of the periodical market is the columns, departments, or special sections that depend on freelance submissions. Many periodicals have them, and they are highlighted under "Columns/Departments" in the alphabetical listings for periodicals in the *Christian Writers'*

Market Guide. Those listings give the name of the column, the primary focus, length, amount paid, and whether you need to query or send a complete manuscript. These columns vary widely in topics, including such things as marriage, family, health, opinion, practical/how-to ideas, etc. Since these are established sections of the magazines that must be filled each issue, and most writers ignore them, editors are often desperate to find material to fill them. In studying the *Christian Writers' Market Guide,* highlight any of these that you feel qualified to write for. On your form, indicate if this piece could or should be written to fit one of those columns.

4. When noting the length required, check the publication's guidelines and be sure it is within their range. I am often asked how long a piece should be if the guidelines give a range, such as 1,000 to 2,000 words. In most magazines, if not all, the longest lengths would be reserved for the feature articles or articles dealing with the primary focus of that particular magazine. That means that everything else would be shorter. So ask yourself: How important is this piece to the overall content of the magazine? If it is extremely important, then offer it at 2,000 words (or maximum length). If it is of lesser importance, rate that importance and set a length accordingly.

5. Based on your market guide or publisher guidelines, indicate whether you need to query or send a complete manuscript. That way you will know exactly what you need to do first when you get to this idea.

6. Indicate the pay rate, and based on that and the projected length, estimate what the total payment would be.

7. Information regarding payment time, reporting time (how soon you should expect them to get back to you), and openness to freelance (what percentage of their material comes

from freelance writers) should be found in your market guide or in their guidelines.

8. Give the idea a working title or at least indicate the general subject.

9. Under Special needs/taboos, note anything you learned about this market in your initial research that you need to keep in mind, such as the following: must be written in first person, include lots of anecdotes, or go heavy on the how-to.

10. Include enough in your brief description that you will remember what you had in mind when you come back to this later.

11. As you have thought about this piece, what authorities, resources, or contacts have come to mind? It might be a professional or layman who would provide good quotes. It might be another article or book you saw recently on the topic. It might be a friend who has recently had a similar experience. Write here anything or anyone who might give credibility to your piece.

12. Finally, list a couple of other potential markets in case this one rejects it.

Query Letter vs. Complete Manuscript

As you get better acquainted with publications and editors, you will find a difference in preference as to how they want to be contacted by you with freelance submissions. Some publishers want to see only the completed manuscript, some want only a query letter, and others will take either. As your market guide will indicate, some publishers will also accept phone, fax, or email queries. Since publishers vary widely in their acceptance of such queries, never send a query by fax or email unless they say they will accept one, and be *especially* careful of phone calls

Figure 8-1

ARTICLE/STORY IDEA FORM

Name of periodical: ____________________

Address: ____________________

____

Editor's Name: ____________________

Article____ Short Story___ Filler____ Poem___ Book Review ___

Other ____________________

Special Column/Section: ____________________

Length:____________Words __________Lines (poetry)

Poetry: rhymed_____ unrhymed_____

Query:______ Complete manuscript:______ Either:______

Pay rate:________ Estimated pay for this piece:____________

Pays on acceptance_______ On publication_______

Reporting time:______________

Openness/Percentage freelance written: ____________________

Working title/subject: ____________________

Special needs/taboos: ____________________

____

Brief description of piece: ____________________

____

____

____

Authorities/Contact persons/Resources: ____________________

____

____

Other potential markets: ____________________

____

unless the topic is very timely or you already have a working relationship with the editor. It is important to know what each wants and abide by that preference.

If they want a completed manuscript, send them something that fits their publication as exactly as possible. That means it is the right length, the right style, an appropriate topic, and the right slant. A publisher will know immediately if you have done your homework and are sending them something that matches who they are—or if you have chosen them as a last resort. Realize, however, that even if you match the criteria exactly you may still get a rejection. There are a lot of reasons for rejections that you have no control over, such as the publisher being overstocked with unpublished articles, having recently published or accepted something similar, experiencing overdrawn budgets. But even rejected manuscripts will be noticed if they are particularly well done in the publication's format.

Writing a Query Letter

I'm sure many of you are asking what a query letter is and what should be included. Basically, it is a sales letter—like a job application. You are telling the editor what you have to offer and asking if he or she is interested in seeing it. Beyond that it is a sample of your writing, so don't take it lightly. It must showcase the best writing you can do. It is the editor's first indication of what kind of writer you are.

The biggest complaint I get from editors about query letters is that they are not specific enough, so keep in mind that you want to tell the editor everything he or she needs to know to make an informed decision about whether your article is going to meet the publication's needs.

Before we get into the query letter itself, I want to explain the value of a query letter. First, it saves you writing a manuscript for which there is no market. Second, it saves editors the time and trouble of reading manuscripts they have no need of. Third and most importantly, it gives the editor a chance to have some input into your project before you actually write it. For example, an editor might like the idea but ask you to drop one portion and expand another area, or perhaps ask you to approach it from a different angle. Getting that information before you write saves a lot of unnecessary rewriting. A query is especially helpful when an interview or extensive research is involved.

Following are some guidelines that will help you develop a query letter that will convince an editor you have something publishable to offer. There are all kinds of sample query letters available—even formula queries—but I don't recommend using them. The purpose of a query letter is to catch a busy editor's attention. You will never do that with a formula query with the blanks filled in.

1. Before sending a query, do your homework and know enough about a publication to prepare an offer that will meet their specific requirements. Keep in mind that anything you can say that reflects your knowledge of their publication and audience will get an editor's attention. With major publications, send for a copy of their latest demographic study. You can then pick up information from that study or their guidelines to use in your letter. For example: "Since your target audience is working women, ages twenty to forty-five, this feature article on balancing family and work will meet one of their primary needs."

2. The query letter itself is a standard, typed business letter with letterhead (if available) and single spacing. Most are one to two pages; one page is preferable. Address it to a specific editor (name spelled correctly) unless the publication has not provided one (that means there is no editor's name given in the market guide at their request). If this is the case, then address it to "Dear Editor."

3. It should be neat, professional, with no errors. Double-check spelling, punctuation, typos, grammar, etc. Keep the tone of the letter professional, upbeat, and enthusiastic without overselling your idea. At the same time, let the letter reflect

something of who you are and the overall tone of the article you are offering. For example, if you are offering a humorous piece, your query can reflect an ability to write humor (light touch only; don't overdo it). If it is a how-to piece, the letter should reflect the kind of clarity and organization needed for that kind of writing.

4. Your query letter should include the following elements:

   - *A grabber opening to catch the editor's attention.* Pick out the most compelling element of your article and use it to pull the editor in. If your article itself has such an opening, use it and then go on to say, "This is how I plan to start a 1,500 word article on ________." The opening needs to state the subject of the article in a nutshell, then elaborate. Give the subject in the first line, or at least the first paragraph. The opening should also indicate your slant and why the reader should care about the topic.

   - *Samples of what will go into the article.* Include anything that shows the editor that there is something more to support your ideas. That could include such things as statistics, quotes with attribution, a brief anecdote or story that supports your point of view, and authorities to show it's not just your idea. Never withhold a surprise ending. (Some writers build to a dramatic conclusion, then promise they can reveal what happens if the publisher asks for the article.) Give the editor all the pertinent information, but whet his or her appetite for the details.

   - *A sharp focus.* Your query, like your article, must be sharply focused on a specific aspect of your subject. For example, you can't write an article on marriage; it has to be on one clearly defined aspect of marriage. If an editor wanted to know everything there was to know on a subject, he or she could look it up in an encyclopedia. An editor once told me to use a rifle—not a shotgun.

- *Needed specifics.* Give pertinent data, such as how long the piece will be, when you can have it ready, and what pictures or illustrations are available, if any. Be sure the length you suggest is appropriate to the magazine and to your topic. In indicating when you can have it ready, allow yourself sufficient time to complete it, and specify that it will be that length of time after you get their go-ahead. Generally speaking, you won't send photos with your query (except, perhaps, for a composite sheet), but will let them know what you have available.

- *Never mention money* in a query letter unless it is a publication you write for regularly and you have to discuss necessary expenses to get the story. Don't say, "I will accept your regular rate of pay" (that's all you're going to get anyway) or "I'll take less than your normal rate of pay," or "I'll write it for free if you'll just publish it." Any one of those will mark you as an amateur.

- *Qualifications/Professional Experience.* Tell what qualifies you to write this particular piece, which usually is your experience, background, education, or simply that you are extremely interested. Give your writing experience if you have any. If you don't, say nothing. For example, you might say, "I have sold over a hundred articles in the evangelical market, one of the latest to *Moody.*" When mentioning a specific magazine like this, pick your best credit in the same general field as the one you are querying. So if it is a women's magazine, mention the best women's magazine you have sold to. If you have a special skill that qualifies you to write this piece, tell them that. If you have access to a unique source, person, or event of importance to this piece, mention that.

- *Viewpoint.* They will want to know how you are going to approach this subject, in other words, your viewpoint. It may be that you are enthusiastic about the topic, that you are indignantly opposed to it, that you are amused by it, or that you are setting out to write an objective, balanced report on it. Indicate whether it will be written in first or third person, and if you are writing it as an observer or a participant. For example, I once wrote an article about dyslexia (a learning disability in children). I was not an expert on dyslexia, I didn't have it myself, I didn't work with dyslexic students, but I was the mother of a dyslexic child, and the article on how parents can best help a dyslexic child was written from a mother's viewpoint.

- *Timeliness*. If applicable, mention anything that indicates this topic is timely, such as linking it to a current trend, news event, recent statistics, or any factors that indicate popularity.

- *Title*. A great title can almost sell any article, so work at making your title as good as it can be and mention it in the letter. Note that publications tend to be fairly consistent in the number of words they use in a title, so pay attention to that as part of your homework. I simply go to the contents page of the publication and figure out the average number of words in their titles. Typically, a scholarly journal will use more words (six to eight words), than a teen paper (one to two words).

- *Postscript*. Take advantage of the fact that everyone reads the P.S. at the end of a letter. Use it to convey something important to the editor. In the postscript say something like, "Any suggestions on slant or special emphasis to benefit your readers will be appreciated." That simple sentence is important because it tells the editor you are willing to work with him or her—to rewrite if necessary. An editor's worst nightmare is a writer who refuses to rewrite or who insists that the writing was somehow so inspired that it would be sacrilegious to change a word.

➤ A few more points to keep in mind:

- If you haven't written for this publication before, you might want to include a résumé on a separate sheet, some tear sheets of previously published articles in this field, or the first four pages of this manuscript, so they have a sample of your writing.
- Realize that a go-ahead from an editor on a query does not mean he or she is buying it—only that he or she has agreed to look at it. Your letter should indicate that you are offering it "on speculation, of course."
- Some top markets will give a firm assignment, especially if you have written for them before or are well known in the field. If it is definitely an assignment, and they subsequently decide not to use it, some will pay what we call a "kill fee," which means they will pay you a fee *not* to publish it (to "kill" the piece). That fee is usually 10–50 percent of the regular payment. Your market guide should indicate which publishers pay a kill fee and what percentage. After you have been paid a kill fee you are free to sell the article elsewhere.
- When you submit an article as the result of a go-ahead from an editor on a query, mention that fact in the cover letter that goes with your completed article. Say something like, "Here is the article you asked to see in your letter of May 3rd." You could also include a photocopy of the editor's previous letter, and write "Requested Manuscript" on the outside of your envelope.
- Include a self-addressed, stamped envelope with every query.
- You will usually send a query to one publication at a time, unless it is a timely topic or a seasonal one. If you are submitting it simultaneously for those reasons, include that information in your query: "Because of the timeliness of this topic, I am sending simultaneous queries but will submit the article to only one publi-

cation at a time." You may send simultaneous queries to any publications that indicate in your market guide that they will accept simultaneous submissions.

- If a publisher accepts queries only, it usually means you must send a query even for poetry, fillers, and fiction. Some publishers, however, require a query for feature or major articles and a complete manuscript for everything else. Their guidelines will usually clarify exactly what they want.

Sending a Complete Manuscript

Just as some publishers require a query, others are adamant about accepting only complete manuscripts. That is especially true of publishers who publish mostly short pieces, material for children, humor, fiction, etc. They feel that it is easier to read a short manuscript than try to judge it by a query.

When sending a complete manuscript, you simply put your completed manuscript in an envelope with or without a cover letter. When determining whether or not to include a cover letter, check their listing in your market guide first to see if they ask for one. If so, include one that simply introduces you and your subject. If they don't ask for one, you will still include one if there is something specific you need to tell them, such as your qualifications for writing the piece (if the piece requires certain qualifications or experience), your reasons for using a pen name (if applicable), problems with permissions, or anything else it is important for them to know. (See "Cover Letter" in chapter 2.)

Dealing with Photos and Illustrations

Some of the articles you write will call for accompanying photographs and some will not. If your article is a personality profile or story about a particular place or event, most publishers will expect you to provide appropriate photos. You can take such photos yourself if you are a professional photographer or at least have a good camera and know how to take quality shots.

If not, you can hire someone to go along with you, or if the subject is a celebrity, his or her publicity department can often provide photos. Inquire about the availability of photos, or ask permission to take photos when you set up the interview. If the assignment and the publication are major enough, the publication may send out a photographer. For example, I once did an article about communicating with teenagers (using my family as an example), and to my surprise the magazine I wrote it for sent a professional photographer to my home to take photos of the family.

If a publication expects photographs, you will need to know exactly what they expect you to provide. Some want color transparencies, while others want black and white photos of a particular size (usually 8x10 inches). You can get this information from your market guide, their guidelines, or the editor. If possible, send a contact sheet or several photos for the editor to choose from. All photos need to be sharp and clear unless they are old photos included for historical purposes.

The question of payment for photos is not easy to answer. Some publishers consider the photos as part of the price and do not pay extra for them. Others consider them as a separate entity and pay accordingly. You will want to clarify this ahead of time, especially if you are paying a photographer to take the necessary photos. Keep in mind that you are actually leasing the photos, not selling them outright, so the photos and rights should be returned to you after use. Anytime you have questions about who is to provide photos or illustrations, ask the editor what is expected of you and what they can do to help.

Generally, the author is not expected to provide illustrations for an article. The periodical provides the regular illustrations. An exception might be things like charts or graphs needed to illustrate your piece. Even in those cases, however, if you provide a copy of the chart or graph they will have it professionally designed to appear in the magazine. Normally you won't be paid extra for these types of graphics.

Often writers ask if they need *model releases* for pictures they send with articles. Generally speaking you will not, unless the publication specifically asks for them. The exception is if the photo is going to be used on the cover. The key here is that the photos in no way reflect negatively on the subject. For example, you wouldn't do an article on drug addicts and use a photo of innocent bystanders to illustrate it—giving the impression that they were addicts.

Typically, model releases are required if the subject is recognizable and the photo is going to be used for commercial purposes, such as in an advertisement or for public relations. You can make up and print your own model release on a partial sheet of paper. Include blank lines for the release number, date the picture was taken, name of the subject, and a brief description of the scene. In the center of the slip, have a statement similar to this: "I *(name of subject or parent)* hereby give *(your name)* permission to reproduce and sell photographs that include me or my children, for editorial, advertising, or other lawful purposes." At the bottom have one or two lines for signatures and a date. A pad of photo release forms can also be found at local photography stores.

If you are also a photographer and wish to sell *stock photos* to magazines, that may be another form of income. The *Market Guide* indicates which periodicals buy photos. Study samples of the book publishers or periodicals you want to sell to and match their format: horizontal or vertical shots? color or black and white? prints or slides? people or nature? Stamp your name on each photo along with a copyright notice. Send slides in plastic sleeves and store in loose-leaf notebooks.

Article Contracts

Although we typically think of publishing contracts in conjunction with book publishing, some periodicals also offer contracts. Such contracts are usually short—about a page—and simply identify the article by name, indicate what rights are being purchased, the amount of payment, scheduled date of publication, etc. I'm only aware of a few Christian publications that use them, but there is no reason to feel nervous about such a contract as long as it spells out the terms exactly as you expected them to be. If it differs from your understanding of the agreement, ask for an explanation or necessary changes in the contract. Do not sign it unless you agree with the terms.

Realize, too, that you are not obligated to sign a contract just because they offer it. You always have the option of not selling the manuscript if you would be giving up too many rights or not being paid a fair amount. You need to be as careful about signing a publishing contract as you would be about signing a contract in any other area of business.

Once you've got yourself established as a writer of articles, then you might think about writing a book.

Chapter 9

On the Writing of Books

For most new writers, the thought of writing an entire book is overwhelming. It needn't be, as long as you select a subject broad enough to fill a book. If you can write, you can probably write a book. Think of it as stringing several articles together. The number of words and the time involved are not the critical deterrents to writing a book. It is the lack of careful planning and logical organization that is most likely to thwart would-be book writers. Beyond that, it is simply important to determine if your idea has a potential market.

For many writers, the problem is taking the vast array of information and organizing it, condensing it, and fitting it into a readable format. In this section I will take you step-by-step through the writing process, from selecting the topic, to creating a proposal for the publisher, to completing the final product. Since this book focuses on the business of being a writer more than on how to write, I will deal here with the function and the process, not how to get the words on paper.

Nonfiction Books: How to Begin

Every book and book proposal starts with an idea. As soon as that idea emerges clearly enough to be identified, I take a file folder and label the file accordingly. That folder finds a prominent place on or near my desk and becomes a receptacle for all the related ideas or resources that come along in the following months: articles on the subject, books on the topic (and their location), names of resource people, helpful websites, and other ideas that may eventually become part of the book.

When that folder becomes too fat, I sit down on the floor and start sorting out the contents into piles that represent the different aspects of the topics. When I am finished, I usually have a pile for each potential chapter. I make a new file folder for each stack, labeling it with the subject or with the possible title of that chapter. You may or may not be able to put the chapters in chronological order at this point, but that isn't important yet. (Alphabetize them for now.) Put the stack of folders near your desk again, and continue adding ideas and material to the appropriate folders as they come to you.

Now is the time to look at the list of chapters you have folders for and try to determine if you have missed anything. Often reading other books or articles on the topic will suggest additional chapters. If so, add folders for those chapters.

Start reading everything you can on the topic. Some writers say they never read other books on their potential topic because they don't want to inadvertently pick up other people's ideas; most experienced writers, however, find that everything they read adds to a wealth of knowledge on a topic and, after being assimilated with their own background, comes out with a unique perspective. You need to read everything you can so you know what is already out there and can ask yourself honestly if the world needs your book. If you do not have something new or better to offer than what has already been published, the world probably doesn't need it.

As you are reading other people's material, keep notes on where you got the book (public library, church library, from a friend), so you can find it again if you need it. If you find quotes you might want to use, keep a record of where you found them so you can ask permission later if needed. Also keep an eye out for sources of statistics, authorities to give quotes, case studies, or anything that will add to the content of your book. By this time, your chapter folders should be filling up.

When you reach this point, start reviewing the contents of each chapter folder, with an eye to achieving some balance. If one folder is too full, it may mean that part of the topic is too broad and you'll want to break it into two or three chapters.

Some of the other folders may have almost nothing in them. If that is the case, you'll need to decide if that folder's topic is too narrow to support a whole chapter, or if it is a necessary chapter that simply requires more research. Work with the folders until the chapters seem evenly balanced.

As you complete this step, you will also want to put the folders/chapters in logical order and type up a preliminary table of contents. You will find the table of contents changes as you get into the writing, but it's helpful to have a starting point.

During this time start working on your *thesis statement.* An important element in your book proposal, the thesis statement simply tells in one succinct sentence what your book is about. In essence it completes the sentence, "This is a book about . . . " (although you might not want to use those words). Until you have refined and defined your focus enough to put it into a sentence, you are not ready to start writing.

Preliminary questions

Before you start writing your book or your book proposal, work at answering the following questions. When you have answered them, you can either move on with your book project, decide you aren't ready to move on yet, or realize that this may not be a viable project.

1. What is your book about?
2. Who is the audience for this book?
3. What is your working title?
4. How long will this book be? Number of chapters? Number of pages?
5. Why is this book timely?
6. What qualifies you to write this book?
7. What other books have been written on this topic?
8. How is your book different or better than the others?
9. Who will you contact or interview for your book?
10. What other research will you need to do (gather statistics, circulate questionnaires, background reading)?

Time to start writing

After completing any additional research, you should be ready to start writing. You will want to start with an introduction and first chapter. After that you could work on what you think will be your best or favorite chapter, and at least one other chapter. Some books will need to be written chronologically, while you can skip around in others. At this point you will be ready to work on your proposal.

Nonfiction Book Proposal*

Most publishers prefer to get a book *proposal* initially rather than an entire manuscript. They also want to see your table of contents and one to three *sample chapters*. From your point of view, it is beneficial to approach a publisher at this stage of your writing because it gives the editor a chance to have some input into the project before you have actually written it. It also may save you writing a whole book that no one wants to buy. However, if this is your first book, you may feel more comfortable completing your first draft before attempting a proposal (then basing the proposal on what you have written). Note that some publishers prefer to see the completed manuscript, or only a query letter, first, but we will discuss those options below.

What the proposal should accomplish

A book proposal has a specific purpose and should accomplish certain objectives. Plan to:

- ➤ Highlight what you think are the most important aspects of the book
- ➤ Indicate how this book is different from others on the market and what specific need it will fill

*Though some aspects of the book proposal have been briefly referred to in chapter 2, this section will give you more information regarding the details of the proposal.

- Identify a specific audience and why they are likely to buy the book

- Establish why you should be the one to write this book

- Tell why they are the best publisher to publish it.

To complete the proposal, include the sample chapters to let them see how you write.

Once you determine who those potential publishers are (covered in chapter 7, "Market Plan for Books"), you will want to send them exactly what they want. That means you need to get a copy of their guidelines and follow those religiously. If the first publisher rejects the proposal, you may need to make some changes in the proposal before submitting it to the next publisher. Following you will find general information on preparing a book proposal, in case some publishers' guidelines are not specific.

Cover letter

Your proposal will start with a *cover letter.* Since most of the information the publisher needs to make a decision is contained in the proposal itself, the cover letter is used simply to introduce yourself and your book idea to the publisher. Use it to catch editors' interest so they'll read on. Highlight what you feel are the most important aspects of the book, tell why you are writing the book, and what qualifies you to do so. Keep this brief; you'll be going into more detail in the proposal. This letter should be personalized to the publisher as much as possible so they will believe you have selected them specifically. This is also the place to mention any legal concerns or problems you anticipate with things like permissions or finding photographs. Keep the letter to a page or two.

As you go on to prepare the rest of the proposal, don't try to conserve space by squeezing everything together. Leave as much white space as possible, so the proposal gives the impression of being easy to read.

Each of the following sections should begin on a separate page (unless they are very short).

First page

- Put your name, address, phone number, fax number, email address, and Social Security number in the upper left-hand corner.

- Center the working title at the top. Include a subtitle if it is needed to indicate what the book is about. If you don't have a firm title, but several possibilities, list the alternatives as well.

- Under the title and subtitle, put your thesis statement, telling in one sentence what the book is about.

- Follow that with a thesis paragraph that expands your thesis statement, focusing on the major points you will cover.

Table of contents

On the second page of your proposal, list the table of contents. Include the titles only, or expand the titles to include the main topics covered in each chapter. This may take more than a page. (Note that this is not the place to give a *full* description of the chapter, just an expansion on the title if appropriate.)

Chapter-by-chapter synopsis

On the next page, center the chapter number and title (i.e., "Chapter 1: In the Beginning") followed by a paragraph description of specifically what is included in that chapter. The *synopsis* is a blueprint for the editor to study to determine the exact development of the book, so don't be vague in these descriptions. Instead of saying, "This chapter will cover the five keys to good communication," tell what those five keys are. Editors often complain that chapter synopses are not specific enough. Keep in mind that this is all the editor has to go on to determine what you have to say and if there is a market for it.

At the same time, try to limit the descriptions to a few sentences. Editors should be able to read through this synopsis quickly and know exactly how you are developing your topic and how substantial your content is. The synopsis should whet their appetite for more detail but not leave them with a lot of questions about where the book is going.

You should be able to get two or three chapters to a page, leaving some white space between. When you have completed this, have someone read it who knows little or nothing about your book to see if it is clear.

Potential market

In this section you will tell the editor who the potential readers are. Be specific. The publisher wants to know who will buy this book. This becomes a balancing act between making the market specific enough to be identifiable, and broad enough to make the publishing of this book worthwhile. You will be in trouble right away if you indicate "All Christians." That is not a potential market, it is an overstatement and the easy way out. Think this through carefully and identify the best possible market segment: parents of preschoolers, new pastors, young Christians learning to study the Bible, working women, or stay-at-home moms with school-aged children, for instance. If your topic is very specialized, include any statistics available on how many people are affected by or involved with the subject.

Next, indicate what the competition is for this book. List at least two or three other titles on the topic (including author's name, publisher, and year published). Then tell how your book differs from each of them. In essence, you are justifying why there is a need for your book when there are other books on the topic available. Do not say there are no other books like it on the market unless you have checked and know that for a fact. Occasionally there will be no other books to name, but that is not necessarily in your favor. Rather than indicating there is a crying need, it may mean there is no market for such a book.

List any groups or organizations (especially groups in which you are personally involved or known) that may be associated with this topic and may be interested in advertising or distributing the book to their members.

Author's credentials

In this section focus on those credentials that qualify you to write this book, such as education and related life experience, and writing credits that give you credibility. This doesn't need to be a full résumé or life history.

Also tell the publisher if you will be available to help promote the book and to what extent. If you are unable to help at all, you need to tell them that too. Obviously it will be to your advantage if you can promote it, but they will probably not reject the book simply because you can't. However, if a book is on the line as far as being publishable, the extent to which an author can help in the promotion will often tip the balance in favor of publication.

If you know any people who are prominent or recognized in the field who might write a forward or endorse the book for pre-publication publicity, include that information.

Proposed format

This section will give the publisher important information as to the size and set-up of the book. Include the following information, realizing that much of it will have to be a "guess-timate" based on what you have written so far.

➤ *Number of pages.* Base this on the average number of manuscript pages in the chapters you have written, times the number of chapters. Most paperback books will have at least 125 typed pages, with most falling between 150 and 350 pages. Market guide listings will tell you the preferred length for most publishers. Some don't have a preference, as long as the book is an appropriate length for the topic and for the type of book it is.

➤ *Number of chapters.* This will be evident from your table of contents, but include it here for quick reference. The number of chapters will vary depending on the kind of book, but the average book has fifteen chapters (with an acceptable range of ten to twenty). Chapters average ten to fifteen pages, although some are shorter, and others are up to twenty pages. Books for a popular audience tend to have shorter chapters.

➤ *Number of words.* Again, you will have to base this estimate on the average number of words in the chapters you have written, times the number of chapters. Most books range from thirty thousand to sixty thousand words. It is important that your estimates for book length come as close as possible to the final product, because if the book is accepted, the publisher may plan the size and price of the book based on your estimate.

➤ *Graphics materials.* If the book will include any appendixes, photographs, charts, graphs, or illustrations, include a list and description of those.

Delivery of manuscript

The publisher will want to know how long it will be before the manuscript is completed. Calculate how long you think it will take to finish writing it, and then add about a month (it always takes longer than you anticipate). Give yourself a reasonable amount of time based on your schedule, the amount of research required, and other factors specific to the book. Obviously it is best to complete the book in a timely manner, but a publisher is not going to expect you to complete it in thirty days. An estimate of a year or more is not unreasonable if the intensity of the manuscript demands it.

On the bottom half of the same page, list any ideas you have for expansions or additions to the book, such as making it a series, preparing a leader's guide for group study, making the material available on audio or video tape, developing an accompanying workbook or related merchandise. Make these suggestions practical and suitable given the nature of the original book. They are only suggestions at this point.

Sample chapters

Send all the above material with one to three sample chapters to the publisher you have selected. Some publishers prefer to see everything you have finished at this point, but this is rare. Refer to the market guide you are using or to a copy of the publisher's guidelines and send only what the publisher recommends.

If a publisher only asks for a sampling, it's best to send the first chapter (so they can see how you get into the topic); whatever you think is the best chapter or the one with the most compelling information; and then another chapter of your choice, perhaps the most "risky" chapter—the one that includes any controversial ideas. Some publishers prefer two or three consecutive chapters. If a publisher wants only the proposal and no sample chapters, you might include the author's preface at the end of the proposal. Since the preface usually focuses on why you have written the book, it will give the publisher that information as well as providing a sample of how you write.

Because most publishers will take three or four months (often longer) to respond to your proposal, some authors prefer to send out their proposal simultaneously to save time. Some publishers accept simultaneous submissions, but others are offended by them, so check a market guide first to see which ones are open to them. Rewrite and slant your cover letter for each different publisher, and always tell them that it is a simultaneous submission, while assuring them that you will send the *complete* manuscript to only one publisher at a time.

The proposal can be sent loose in a manila envelope or slipped into a professional-looking folder. Some writers even have it professionally printed and bound in a regular or spiral binding, but this is usually an unnecessary cost since most publishers don't mind (and might prefer) an unbound proposal. To make the best impression it should be prepared on a computer and printed on a laser-quality printer. (Some editors have a negative initial reaction to a manuscript that has obviously been typed on a typewriter.) Always include a self-addressed stamped envelope with enough postage to return the proposal, or include a self-addressed #10 business-sized envelope with a first-class stamp for a response and tell the editor the proposal can be discarded if it is rejected.

Fiction Book: How to Begin

Preparing to write a novel will be somewhat different from preparing to write the nonfiction book. You might begin with the single folder, but will put into it the various elements of the story as they come to you, including characters, names, settings, events, plot twists. When I'm ready to start writing, I find it helpful to write all such information in a mid-size loose-leaf notebook for quick reference. One of the biggest problems with fiction is keeping all the details straight; having them listed in a notebook is very helpful. You could also keep this information in a computer file if you are comfortable with that.

Divide your notebook or computer file into the different elements of the novel, such as: the plot (general plot outline, plot twists and ideas as they come); characters (names, backgrounds, descriptions, tics, relationships); settings (names or descriptions of towns and streets, maps of houses, towns, neighborhoods); dialogue (snatches of dialogue as you think of them, pet expressions for characters, words used for dialect); history (family or period history that affects the plot or characters); changes/corrections (reminders of things you want to change or correct later). Add others as you find you need them. In the front of this notebook I also keep a record of dates when I started and completed the development of various aspects of the book.

As soon as you have your plot, characters, and setting well

established in your mind, you will be ready to start writing. Until you become established as a fiction writer, publishers will usually want to see a completed manuscript before offering you a contract. For that reason, you can either complete the book before contacting a publisher, or write three or four chapters and send with a query or proposal to see if you can interest a publisher. Even if you find an interested publisher, they will likely ask you to send the completed manuscript when it is finished before making their decision.

Fiction Book Proposal*

Even if the manuscript is completed, you will have to prepare a proposal for those who ask for one. Many of the elements of your proposal will be the same as for a nonfiction book, or can easily be adapted to fiction.

Cover letter

The cover letter will simply introduce the plot and overall theme of the story, tell how you came to write it, and give the editor some indication of your future plans for writing. Publishers who do fiction are generally looking for writers who have more than one book to offer. They are looking for and need writers who can continue to put out books at a fairly regular pace in the future. Although most publishers started out looking for series of books in fiction, many are now open to stand-alone novels.

First page

Set up the page the same way as described for a nonfiction book, but instead of the thesis statement and paragraph, give the genre of the novel, the basic theme, and a paragraph summary of the plot.

*Though some aspects of the book proposal have been briefly referred to in chapter 2, this section will give you more information regarding the details of the proposal.

Character sketches

Include the table of contents only if there are chapter titles. You will, however, need a list of at least the major characters, including brief sketches of each and information on the relationships between them. For example, John might be Michael's brother whom he hasn't spoken to in ten years, or Susan is Michael's sister whom he adores.

Synopsis/summary

If your book is already written, you may follow the format for chapter-by-chapter summaries used with nonfiction. If it is not written, it is easier to summarize it than to break it down by chapters.

In your summary simply tell what happens in the story, including as much suspense and intrigue as appropriate to keep the editor reading. Use present tense and simply tell the story as you would tell it to a friend who asks what it is about. Open with a hook to draw the editor in and to introduce the setting and the main characters. Give only as much description and background on the main characters as necessary to set the scene and make the characters interesting. (Minor characters don't need to be mentioned at all unless they play an important part in the plot). In popular fiction, the scene should be set for the reader as soon as possible. Reveal the main character's problem and indicate how it is going to be resolved. The rest of the synopsis will be devoted to telling about the action and how the plot develops to a satisfactory conclusion. Focus only on the major scenes and make sure the motivation is clear and logical. Don't withhold any endings or crucial details. From reading this the editor should be able to tell exactly how the plot unfolds.

The summary should be only two to eight pages unless the publisher's guidelines specify otherwise. You can offer to send an expanded plot summary if the publisher would like to see one, but at first keep the summary brief. Editors want to read as little as possible to learn as much as they need to know. They are looking for whether or not you can tell a good story and how well you write. This is not something that can be dashed off quickly. Spend some time working on it and polishing it to make it as clear, succinct, and compelling as possible. Sending a poorly written and disorganized summary is the best way to get a "no thank you" from a busy editor.

❖

The rest of the proposal—including the potential market, author credentials, proposed format, and delivery—will be much the same as described for nonfiction. Use your common sense in adapting it to fit your fiction project. If you have little information for these sections, it could be included in the cover letter instead. As with nonfiction, include one to three sample chapters.

Book Manuscript Preparation

A book manuscript has a very specific form. The general information should go on a *title page* (see figure 9-1), rather than in the upper corners as in a periodical manuscript. The rest of the manuscript should follow these basic guidelines.

- Number pages first to last rather than separately by chapter. The first chapter should begin on page 1. This means that the front matter should have a different numbering system. To easily identify the front matter, I suggest running heads: Contents - 1, Contents - 2, etc.; Introduction - 1, Introduction - 2, etc.

- Start each chapter on a new page, starting about one third of the way down the page.

- In the upper left-hand corner of each page, put your last name and a key word from the title. Put the page number in the upper right-hand corner.

Figure 9-1

TITLE

By

Ready Writer
Address
City, State, Zip

Phone Number
Fax Number (if applicable)
Email Address (if applicable)

Social Security Number

A Teen Novel

About 50,000 words

© 2003 Ready Writer

Do I Need an Agent?

Many new writers assume that if they are going to sell a book they will need an *agent*. Although that may be true in the general market, in the Christian/religious market it is not. Actually, agents are quite new on the scene in this market. Ten years ago you would have been hard pressed to find agents who handled religious material and even harder pressed to find a publisher who would willingly deal with one. That is changing, but slowly.

Today, most (but not all) publishers will accept book manuscripts through an agent. The *Christian Writers' Market Guide* indicates which will not. The number of Christian agents is beginning to grow. I've found that this year the number of Christian agents jumped from twenty-eight to about eighty. That's a significant increase, but many of those are general market agents who are now representing (or are willing to represent) Christian authors. Most of those who are strictly Christian agents are working primarily with top authors who make them enough money to make it worth their while. Only time will tell how successful this new batch of agents will be—and how well they will be accepted by Christian publishers.

The good news is that you don't need an agent to sell in this market. Most publishers still prefer to work directly with an author, for a variety of reasons. For some it is financial (agents tend to negotiate a better deal for their clients); but for many others it is because Christian publishers care about who the author is and that their life is consistent with their message—and an agent can get in the way of that.

How to find an agent

If you have sold a number of books and have more in the works, you may want to look for an agent. Even first-time authors might look for an agent if they have a project that is destined to be a bestseller (not just your mother's opinion).

The best way to get an agent is to talk with other writers who have them. If they are satisfied with their agent, ask if they will recommend you to the agent. More and more writers' conferences are bringing in agents as part of the conference staff, and that is another good way to meet and evaluate a potential agent. If you have no such contacts, look at the list of agents in the *Christian Writers' Market Guide*. Each listing tells you what kind of material they handle (more of them handle nonfiction than fiction).

Once you pick out the agents that look like good prospects for you, you can send a simultaneous query to each of the agents. Tell them who you are, highlight your writing experience, and give them a brief summary of the book or books you have in progress. Sell them on you as a writer and on the potential for your book. Generally they will want to see at least one completed manuscript, so don't approach them until you have one to send.

Indicate in the letter that you are sending this letter simultaneously to several agents but will select only one to work with. There is potential to have a good response with this approach, even if you are relatively unknown in the market. However, you need to move cautiously here. You may not want every agent who wants you. Ask for a list of books and authors they have represented. (If they are reluctant or refuse to provide such a list, look for a different agent.) Then talk to some of those authors, if possible. (You should be able to write them in care of their publishers.)

The problem with agents is that they don't have to have any particular training or credentials to call themselves an agent. What you need is an agent who knows the market well, is well known and well respected among the various publishers, and who can negotiate a better contract for you than you could do yourself. Publishers judge an agent by how appropriate the projects are that he or she brings to them. Agents with a poor publishing history who don't know what they are doing can hurt more than help. An unknown in the field is not likely to be any more effective than you will be on your own. Even if you don't have an agent, you can find people (including me) under editorial services in the *Christian Writers' Market Guide* who will evaluate a book contract for you. You'll have to do your own negotiating, but at least you'll know what to ask for.

How an agent works

Agents used to work under a "gentleman's agreement," but these days most of them have you sign a contract that says you will stay with them for one to three years and spells out the other terms of your agreement. Be as careful about signing one of these contracts as you would be with a publisher. In the past, most agents received 10 percent of the royalties you earn on your book. This has now gone to 15 percent for most agents, with 20 to 25 percent for foreign deals.

Typically, the publisher's contract specifies that royalties go to the agent, who takes out a percentage and mails you a check for the rest. That is one reason you need to have confidence in the agent. Some agents also charge for office expenses such as postage, phone calls, and photocopying manuscripts. A few will refund such payments when a manuscript sells. Avoid agents who ask for large fees up front or charge monthly fees to represent you. Many of them make their money on those fees, not on selling books.

Agents vary a great deal in what they do for the writer. Some will simply wait for you to send them a proposal and then start submitting it for you. Others will suggest ideas, help you develop future projects, and keep prodding you on. You should expect an agent to send you monthly (or at least quarterly) reports on who he or she has submitted the manuscript to, along with copies of the rejection letters. You need to voice such expectations; don't assume every agent will do that automatically.

It is also possible to have more than one agent if you are working in more than one field. For example, you may be writing both fiction and nonfiction, or writing in both the religious and general markets. Some agents might work with you in both areas, but if they don't, your contract should indicate that. For example, when I was writing general western novels, my contract excluded anything I wrote for the religious market. Some things that you write can be exempted from the contract as well, such as your articles and stories (which most agents won't handle anyway), or perhaps your children's books if you already have a publisher for those.

Do I need an agent if I already have a publisher?

Obviously if you already have a publisher, an agent is more likely to be willing to represent you, but do you still need one?

It depends. Approaching an agent at this point does give you leverage for catching their interest, and you will then have one for future projects. A good agent is able to negotiate a better contract than you can yourself. If you are not familiar with a publisher's contract, an agent can help you avoid common pitfalls. You will have to pay the agent a percentage, but some writers find that the higher percentage their agent has negotiated in the contract has paid the agent's 15 percent cut. An agent also watches for discrepancies in your royalty statement and confronts the publisher when necessary.

What if I'm dissatisfied with my agent?

Work at cultivating an honest, open relationship with your agent. If there are problems, or potential problems, ask questions immediately. Don't wait until the problem escalates. Many problems are based on a misunderstanding, so ask for clarification if needed. If the problems continue to grow, you might write or call the agent with a list of the difficulties you see. If the agent doesn't agree with you, or refuses to deal with the problems, then it may be time to end the relationship. If you reach that point of "unreconcilable differences," your contract should stipulate that either party can end the relationship with a thirty day written notice (or something similar). Know and understand what the contract says.

There are times when the agent ends the relationship. Sometimes this is because the client (you) demands too much time or attention. More often it is because the agent feels he or she cannot find a publisher for your book, or that you will not make him or her enough money to make it worth their time.

Even if you end your relationship with your agent, if you have contracts in force on which he or she is listed, the agent will get a percentage from that contract until the book goes out-of-print and all licensing agreements have expired. Some contracts also give (or an agent will request) sixty days in which to make any sales or close any deals that are pending when you terminate. You may, however, go ahead and start looking for a new agent immediately.

Collaboration

Collaborating with someone on a writing project is not something you want to get into without a lot of forethought. It is a lot like choosing a mate: you have to live with your partners (in a literary sense), you have to tolerate their foibles and they yours, you will spend a lot of time together, and it helps if you like them and are comfortable working with them. There are some very good reasons to seek a collaborator, but don't do so unless the circumstances justify the risks. Many writers agree that in most cases, collaboration produces more agony than ecstasy.

In general, you don't need a collaborator if you are capable and qualified to write the book yourself. However, some of the following may be reasons you need one:

- You don't have the education or experience necessary to give the book credibility.

- You are the expert and need someone to put the material in a layperson's language.

- Your experience is too limited and you need someone with experience in a different aspect of the problem to broaden the scope of the book.

- You are writing fiction as a man and need the female perspective, or vise versa.

- You are weak in one or more aspects of writing and need someone who can handle those parts.

- You need someone good at doing research or interviews, if that's not your strong suit.

- You have a story (or information) to share, but you are not a writer. (Also see the section on ghostwriting below.)

What you need in a collaborator is someone to do the parts of the writing that you cannot. Each writer must bring different talents to the table. If you and your potential collaborator both love interviewing, but you both hate research, it will not be a good match. Determine who wants to do (and is qualified to do) what. If your combined talents don't cover all the bases, then the match may not be right.

From my experience, the other crucial element in this relationship is mutual respect. Not only do you need different talents and abilities, you each need to respect the other person and what he or she is able to bring to the project. The minute that mutual respect is gone, the project is doomed. For example, I once worked with a psychologist putting his psycholog-ese into language the layperson could understand. At that point I had eleven published books, was good at the rewrites, and got him a contract with a major publisher with a six thousand dollar advance (before the book—his first—was completed), but as soon as he found out I didn't have a college degree, he made it obvious he had little respect for me or what I could do for his book. We ended up terminating the relationship before the book was finished. Although the relationship appeared to be a perfect fit in every other way, the lack of respect destroyed it.

Never agree to collaborate with someone you know only slightly or have never met. Plan several meetings to discuss the project before making any commitments. Talk about all the aspects of the project and any potential problems. Check out the other person's credentials and read some of his or her writing (books or articles). Determine how committed he or she would be to the project. If it is his or her first priority and your last, or the other way around, there could be a problem. Someone has described the perfect collaborator as "a writer who is flexible, can take criticism, overcome his or her ego, and work on a regular basis." Not an easy role to fill.

The collaborating process

The actual process of collaboration is also handled in a variety of ways, and you will need to decide which method will work best for this particular project. In some cases, one writer will write the rough draft and the other will rewrite and polish. This works well if one is the storyteller (in fiction) or knows the material (in nonfiction) and the other is the writer. Some fiction writers will plot a book together and then write alternate chapters, each editing the other's work and agreeing on any changes. One person could do all the writing, while the other does all the research and interviews. Although you will each do what you're best qualified to do, there will be some jobs neither of you particularly wants to do but that must be divided between you anyway.

Collaboration contract

Once you find a well-matched collaborator, it is time to draw up a *collaboration contract* between the two of you before you do anything else. It doesn't have to be a long, complicated document, just an agreement indicating what each of you will bring to the project; which name or names will be on the cover and in what order (or whether it will be "As told to" or "With"); how the money will be divided (50/50, 60/40, 40/60, or whatever), both advances and royalties; and under what circumstances the collaboration can be terminated, and how.*

Some of you may protest that the collaborator is your best friend, sister, pastor, even mother, and you won't need such a contract. Believe me, it is those kinds of close relationships that tend to most often end in grief. Any time money can become an issue, even the closest relationship can become difficult.

Effect on book contract

When you have a collaboration agreement, you will ask the publisher to copyright the book in both of your names. The publisher will record what percentage of the royalties go directly to which author, how the names are to go on the cover,

*For those interested in a sample collaboration contract, see the list of resources in appendix B.

and other similar issues. It doesn't matter to the publisher; you just need to let them know what you have agreed on.

Ghostwriting

There is a difference between collaboration and *ghostwriting*. In collaboration, usually both names are on the cover of the book. In ghostwriting, the person who provides the information or story may be listed on the cover as the author. The ghostwriter may or may not be acknowledged for "editorial contributions" in the front of the book. This often becomes an ethical question that each writer must settle. While some feel ghostwriting misleads the reading public, other writers find it a good way to help someone get a story out while giving the writer an opportunity to write before he has his own stories to tell.

If you decide to take on a ghostwriting project, you will also need a contract between you and the other person, similar to the collaboration contract. There are no cut-and-dried rules for how a ghostwriter is to be paid. Some are paid an outright fee for the project, usually negotiated ahead of time. Some get a share of the royalties and the advance. If the two of you came together looking for a mutually beneficial arrangement, you could split the money 50/50. If the subject has a publisher and then finds a writer, the split might be 60/40 in favor of the subject. But if the writer finds an interested publisher and approaches the subject about writing his or her story, the split could be 60/40 in favor of the writer. A lot will depend on how the writer is to get the material for the book—from writing notes, from a tape or video presentation, from a rough draft, from interviews, or in another form. The more work the writer must do, the higher the percentage the writer receives.

It is usually the promise of good fees that lure writers into ghostwriting since they don't get a byline. Some writers have a special talent for writing other people's stories and do that exclusively. Others do it as a sideline that pays the bills, but they continue to do their own writing and may eventually get out of the ghostwriting as their own career flourishes.

Indexing

Many nonfiction books need an *index.* Although authors may be unaware of this, most publishers hold the author responsible for supplying an index if one is needed. Authors can either do it themselves or pay a professional to prepare it. If you feel your book needs an index, talk to your editor about that possibility and ask how it should be handled. If you and the editor disagree on the need for an index, be prepared to fight for it, if necessary.

Most people are not trained to do indexes, but if you are detail-oriented and are willing to follow your publisher's chosen style manual (such as *The Chicago Manual of Style) exactly,* then do the index yourself. One advantage to doing the index yourself is that you are most familiar with the content of the book, the potential reader, the words and terms the reader is most likely to look up, and how the reader is likely to use the index.

Computer programs with indexing capabilities are now available, but don't rely solely on your computer; *always consult the style manual.* The important thing is that you prepare the list of words that will be included in the index, based on your intimate knowledge of the subject. The better your index, the better your book will be, so give some careful thought to planning and preparing an index that will enhance the book's usefulness. Subheadings may provide a starting point as to what should be indexed.

There may also be times when a book needs more than one index. For example, a craft book I wrote had three indexes: one that listed the projects alphabetically by name, one that listed the projects by type (such as painting, paper maché, gifts, nature crafts), and one organized by what supplies the projects called for (such as paper cups, craft sticks, plastic bottles). The three indexes made this a much more usable book, but the editor would never have known that if I hadn't come up with the idea.

An index must be prepared from the page proofs (usually very close to going to press), so you have the appropriate page numbers, but in some cases you can come up with the words or phrases that will be included at the time you complete the book, and add the page numbers later. Check with your editor to see how he or she wants you to handle this.

If your contract indicates that the author is responsible for the index and you choose to use a professional indexer, the publisher will hire someone to do it and charge you for that cost (usually charged against your royalty account). If, when you ask about an index, the publisher offers to take care of it, find out if that means they will pay for it or if you will be charged for it.

Book Contracts

One of the major highlights of most writers' careers is receiving that first *book contract*. Once the initial euphoria wears off, however, you are left with a major legal document full of confusing mumbo-jumbo. Most people's first reaction is that they need to find a good lawyer to protect their rights. The reality is that unless you have access to a lawyer who specializes in publishing contracts (and few authors could afford one of those on what we get paid!) a lawyer is of little use here.

Of much more value is a published author who is knowledgeable about the industry and about publishing contracts. Although you may not want to impose on a writing friend to provide such advice, some authors (such as those listed under "Editorial Services" in the *Christian Writers' Market Guide)* will provide such a service for a price. I have an old one-page contract in my files, but today some contracts are over twenty pages. Even experienced authors find contract evaluations an intimidating process and appreciate help keeping up with the inevitable changes in the industry.

Unfortunately, many writers don't know what to look for or who to turn to for help; they just sign whatever the publisher sends and hope for the best. The best is rarely what they get. It is not that publishers are out to get you, but in publishing (like everywhere else), a contract is always written to the maximum benefit of the one who writes it. Everything may be perfectly legal and aboveboard, but some authors end up with a contract that leaves them with few rights intact and even less money to show for their work.

Those more knowledgeable can steer you toward a contract that is fair to all involved. Realize, too, that your editor owes you a clear answer and/or explanation for every question you have concerning your contract, although you need to do your homework ahead of time and approach him or her with specific questions you were not able to find answers to elsewhere. An editor who is impatient or reluctant to answer such questions should send up an immediate red flag.

Despite these considerations, you don't need to approach the negotiating process as adversarial. It is best to go into it with the idea that you can work together toward a contract that is of mutual benefit. If you seem suspicious or combative from the start, the changes you want may be harder to get. Some writers have approached their editor with a list of changes they wanted and got them all just by asking.

Since evaluating your own contract can be like doing your own root canal, I will not try to take the time and space here to take you through all the various clauses you might come across. Realize that even a short, straightforward contract may be lacking some clauses that are crucial to protecting your rights. If you are concerned about the contract process, seek professional advice. A professional will not just explain the terminology, but the consequences as well.

Marketing Form

Along with your contract, a publisher will usually send you an *author's marketing form* to fill out and return. Some authors ignore this questionnaire, but this to their disadvantage. The questionnaire is one of the best ways for you to help your publisher sell your book, so take as much time as needed to fill it out thoughtfully and carefully, giving the publisher every bit of information they need to make your book successful.

These forms vary somewhat, but they generally ask for detailed information regarding the book. Most publicity and marketing personnel don't have time to read every book they promote, so it's important to highlight your book's key selling points, what organizations you belong to that are associated with the topic (and might help advertise or sell it), who you know in the field that might write a foreword or endorse the book for pre-publication publicity or back cover copy, and a list of people who should get review copies (people who might help promote it, not your friends or relatives). Give them every bit of information they ask for, plus anything else you can think of that would be helpful for promoting it.

Sometime you will have to take the initiative yourself and supply the publisher with such information whether they send you a questionnaire or not. If they send a form, but do not leave enough room to answer the questions adequately, feel free to type up your answers on a separate sheet. If they don't send a form, send as much of this type of information as you can. Some of the information you put on your marketing form will be the same as you included in your proposal. Do not assume that the people who are going to promote your book have all the information you sent your editor in the proposal.

Often when someone who is not as familiar with the content writes publicity material, they miss the most important selling points. In order to help market the book effectively, you can also write the back cover copy, catalog description, or a promotional blurb for your book. You know the book and what is most compelling about it, so provide these blurbs for marketers to use as references, even if they have to be rewritten. You will have at least given the marketers the information they need to include.

Promoting Your Book

Some authors assume that once they have a contract and the manuscript is delivered, their work is done and they can sit back and wait for the royalties to roll in. The successful authors know that publication is when the real work begins. Unfortunately royalties don't roll unless the book sells and sells well, and that takes the efforts of both the publisher and the author.

The problem for most authors, however, is that they are neither experienced nor comfortable with tooting their own horns. If your book is going to have any kind of chance at success, you need to set aside those feelings. You have poured your lifeblood into that book you just sold, and if you do not believe in it enough to toot that horn, how can you expect anyone else to? The books that are most successful in the marketplace are those that are promoted with a horn duet—not a solo by a publisher who may not know the right tune as well as you do.

So—how do you promote your book? Start by completing the marketing form as indicated earlier in this section. Allow at least a full day to complete that task, so you give the publisher something to work with.

Offer to provide your own *promotional copy,* such as the blurb for the back cover, catalog entry, press releases, and advertising copy for publicists to use for reference. Push to get good review comments to go on the back cover. To get those comments, the publisher needs to send copies of the page proofs to prominent people in the field who can read the book and provide positive comments about it. You will need to supply the publisher with a list of people you know who might consent to do so. Keep in mind that the endorsers need to be associated with the topic and are well known within the topic circles and—even better—recognized by the general public. I was once asked to endorse a children's missionary book for a particular denomination. However, since I was associated with neither missions nor the denomination, I declined. My comments would have been of no value in that particular market. You need to come up with people whose opinion makes a difference in the market you are targeting.

One of the best ways to promote your books is through a *speaking ministry.* If you speak to groups on the topic of your book, people are anxious to buy your book and learn even more. If you already have such a speaking ministry, now is the time to start expanding it.

If you have no speaking experience but would like to, you have several options. Join a local Toastmaster Group to hone your skills. Develop two or three different talks on various aspects of your topic, and try them out on anyone who will listen. You may need to start by giving talks for free at local churches or civic groups, but if you do well, ask for a letter of reference. Once you have polished your talk and have some good recommendations, you can expand the speaking into a paying ministry.

Following are a few promotional ideas you can begin working on:

- Have business cards printed up (or do them yourself on your computer) with the standard information about you on the front and the name of your book and the publisher on the back.

- When speaking, ask if you can bring books to sell. Take a spouse or friend along to sell them or ask if someone will be available to handle the book sales for you. Some groups will ask for 10 to 25 percent of the proceeds from book sales; others let you keep it all.

- Whether you are selling books at the end of the meeting or not, provide an order form so the book can be ordered later (someone always forgets their checkbook or needs to wait until payday).

- Send a copy of your book (or bring a copy by) to local newspapers, or editors of book review sections, within a fifty- to one-hundred mile radius. They are always looking for local people with success stories. Don't worry if they don't give your personal contact information regarding your book. Those interested will contact your publisher or bookstore directly and can be put in touch with you that way.

- Contact radio and television talk show producers in your local area or in those areas where you will be visiting. (Look in the yellow pages under Radio Broadcasting and Television Broadcasting.) Most writers assume that such talk shows are hard to get into, but the truth is that many shows are desperate for interesting guests, especially those who are local or are involved in a local event. Simply send them a copy of your book with a *press kit* (publicity materials), letting them know when you will be in town or available locally, and why their listeners would be interested in hearing you. This is most successful if you have a book on a current or controversial issue. Make friends with local talk show hosts and let them know you are available on short notice if they need someone to fill in. Even if you are homebound, you can now do radio interviews by phone.

➤ Contact local bookstores and let them know you are a local author. Tell them about your book(s), offer to autograph the copies they have in the store, do an autograph party, or participate in other special events they have planned. Make friends with local bookstore owners or buyers. When visiting in other areas, visit local bookstores, introduce yourself and offer to autograph copies of your book in the store. Bookstores are more likely to buy your book if they have met you, and they love to offer autographed books to their customers, using them for premiums and promotions.

➤ Anytime you have a speaking engagement or talk show appearance scheduled, let your publisher know to contact bookstores in the area so they are sure to have books available when customers come looking for them. If your publisher typically does not follow through on such requests, you can contact the stores yourself.

➤ Your publisher should send copies of your book for review to appropriate magazines. If they don't, either send copies yourself, or have a writing friend write reviews to send to those magazine that accept freelance book reviews.

- Stay in close communication with your publisher's publicist or public relations person. Find out what they are planning and let them know what you are doing. Anytime you are planning to be in other areas, let them know. They can often set up local radio or TV talk show appearances for you, and see that your books are in the local stores.

- If there are organizations or groups involved with the topic of your book, get involved and recognized within the group. Often they will review the book or offer free or inexpensive advertising in their newsletter. You may also be asked to speak to the group and be given the opportunity to sell books afterward.

- If yours is a how-to book with a clearly defined audience, you might consider selling it by direct mail. You can either solicit and fulfill orders yourself or hire a fulfillment company to do it for you. If you need a mailing list, there are companies that will rent you one in your specific target area.

- If your publisher does not have an 800 number for phone orders, consider setting up one for yourself that can be mentioned during interviews or in reviews or articles.

- Doing your first talk show interview can be scary, but it helps if you go prepared. Take with you a list of about ten typed questions that you think the host should ask you. Some shows actually ask you to supply such questions, so have them just in case. Rehearse your answers to all of those questions; not memorized responses, but well-thought-out, succinct, compelling answers that will interest people in what more you have to say in your book.

- Don't expect your publisher to send you on a whirlwind book-signing tour. This rarely happens unless you are able and willing to pay for it yourself.

- Keep in mind that you do not want to compete with your local bookseller; in fact, your book contract will probably prevent it. If you do sell directly to the public you need to sell your books at the retail price.

- If significant chapters in your book will stand alone, they can be offered as magazine articles, with a reference to your book in the author blurb at the end. Or certain parts of the book can be excerpted or rewritten as articles with a reference to the book.

When Your Book Goes Out-of-Print

Once a published book has been on the market for awhile, you can start worrying about what to do when it goes *out-of-print*. This eventuality should be covered in every book contract. Generally, you will be informed of the publisher's intent not to reprint it, and will be given the opportunity to buy the leftover books and plates or camera-ready copy (that the book is printed from).

At that point you will have about thirty days to decide if you want to exercise that option. This is, of course, assuming that the book goes out of print as a result of the publisher's decision. Some books go out of print because the publisher is sold or goes out of business. Both situations should be covered in your contract. Make sure you know what your contract says about these possible situations. When you get such a notice, respond immediately. If you do not respond within the time limit, you may be out of luck. The publisher will destroy the plates and sell the remaining inventory to a remainder house.

When given the choice to buy the leftover books and plates, your decision will need to be based on your particular situation. If you are able to sell books yourself, when you speak for example, then you will probably want to buy at least some of the stock. Realize, however, that sometimes there is little or no stock left at this point. For that reason, it is a good idea to put away a dozen copies of your book for future marketing. (We'll address what to do with those books below.)

As an author, it is sometimes helpful or even necessary to

watch for clues that your book may be going out-of-print—such things as not seeing it in the current catalog or having trouble getting copies. Also keep up with the latest industry news on your publishing company. Rumors of financial problems and late or nonexistent royalty payments could forecast their eminent demise.

If you feel that your book still has a market and you plan to get another publisher to pick it up and reprint it, you may want to buy the plates. That decision will be based on whether or not you want to make any changes to the book. If you do need to make changes, the plates will not be useable, so don't buy them. If the book can be reprinted as is, you might consider buying the plates. Although it is rare, a publisher may be more open to reprinting a book if they can skip the typesetting stage.

A note about buying the plates and leftover stock: Your contract probably indicates that you can buy these at the publisher's cost. Be aware that by the time the book goes out of print, the publisher may have no idea what the cost was, so you may have to negotiate. I have also heard from authors whose publishers have insisted they buy the plates for a certain amount as a condition of returning the rights to the author. If this happens to you and that stipulation was not written into the contract, stand firm and let the publisher know you expect the terms of the contract to be honored.

If you have decided to look for a publisher to reprint the book, look for those publishers with an *R* after their names in the appropriate topical listing of the *Christian Writer's Market Guide*. Go through the same basic marketing process as you did the first time. Make the proposal similar, but include the marketing history for the original version. Tell how many books sold, how it was marketed, if you have the plates, and why you think it still has a market. Include a chapter-by-chapter synopsis and a copy of the original published book (this is where you'll need the dozen copies you set aside).

If Your Publisher Goes Out of Business

In today's unpredictable book market, we never know when

one of the publishers will downsize, be sold, merge with another company, or go out of business all together. With the advent of desktop publishing, it is now easier for companies to start without adequate backing—and to go out of business just as quickly. However, even going with an older, established company can sometimes be risky. The important thing is to know what to do should you find yourself and one of your books as victims in such a downfall.

Your contract will control some of what happens, so check that first. The contract should say something to the effect that if the company goes bankrupt or out of business, the rights to your book will revert to you automatically (this is preferred) or within a specified length of time. If the contract does not specify what is to happen in such a case, then getting your rights back may be difficult, but usually not impossible.

It is best not to assume that this will happen automatically. You will need to follow through yourself. Whether or not your contract specifies what will happen, if the company goes out of business, write the publisher a letter asking that your book rights revert to you. If your contract does have a reversion clause, state this in the letter. In this letter you could also address the issue of buying leftover stock and the camera-ready copy for the book if you want to find another publisher elsewhere.

If the company has gone bankrupt or is quitting business, they may ask you to pay to get back the rights to your book. Before doing so, reread your contract so you know what provision, if any, it makes for this situation. If there are no set guidelines, you may need to start negotiating. Don't assume that you have to accept the publisher's initial offer. They will likely start out asking more than they expect to receive. If they need the money, they will take what they can get. Before going into this type of negotiation, decide how important this book is to you and what you are willing to pay to get the rights back. An older book with little future life might not be worth what it will cost to get the rights back. If it is a book crucial to your work or ministry, or one to which you have a strong emotional attachment, you may have little choice but to pay for it. If it is, indeed, a book with a future, you may be able to get this payment back in the way of an advance or royalties on a new edition with another publisher.

As far as the remaining books are concerned, again you will need to determine if you will be able to sell them easily. If you have a ready market for them—such as through speaking or direct mail—then go ahead and buy them at the best price you can negotiate. If they will end up sitting in your garage, let them go.

You also have some options concerning the plates or camera-ready copy. If the publisher is asking too high a price, then pass on buying them. Printers can work from the printed copy of the book as a master (you'll need two clean copies), or the book can be scanned into a computer, if necessary.

The key in all of these negotiations is to act quickly and decisively while you still have options and some bargaining power and before the company's assets are frozen and your book gets frozen with them.

Chapter 10

On Writing for Specialty Markets

Writers often think of writing only articles or books, but there are many other types of writing one can submit for publication. It is important to explore the breadth and scope of the publishing market and in doing so perhaps find your own special niche.

Beyond Articles: Other Opportunities for Writers

Below is an alphabetical list of some of the areas (other than articles) in which you might use your writing skills. If you have an interest in one of the areas, seek out other books that will give you more information. The resource list in appendix B will tell you which resources will provide additional help in these areas.

1. *Bible Studies.* The *Christian Writers' Market Guide* indicates which publishers do short Bible studies for use in periodicals. Get sample copies of those publications and determine which ones you might like to write for. It is usually best to query the editor with your ideas, send a sample Bible study adapted to the publisher's format, and let them know you will be happy to write on assignment for them or to query them with other ideas.

2. *Book/Music/Movie/Video/Software Reviews.* If you are interested in doing any kind of review, it is best to approach the periodicals and let them know you would be interested in an assignment. Use a market guide that tells you which publications are open to reviews. You could do a simulta-

neous letter to several publications telling them you are interested, indicating what topics or types of material you feel qualified to review, and enclosing one or two sample reviews to show them what you can do. It helps if you can review material in one or more specialized areas that they may need. Even though you may be using a similar cover letter, write the reviews to match the style and length of each publication you are approaching.

Some publications pay for reviews, usually minimal amounts, but many do not, except for letting you keep the book or product reviewed. Writing reviews, however, is a good way to get experience and exposure and may work into other assignments.

3. *Writing for Children.* Writing for children can include short stories, articles, poetry, crafts, puzzles, and games, as well as books. There are a number of good books on the market that will take you step-by-step through the process of writing any kind of children's book.

   If you want to write a children's book, you will have to make some important decisions before you write the first word. Decide first what age group you are going to write for. You cannot write a book "for children"; it must have a very specific target audience. Publishers vary somewhat on how they divide children into age groups, but it is roughly infant–two, three–five, six–eight, nine–eleven, twelve–fourteen, and fifteen–eighteen.

   After you decide the age range you are writing for, you must decide what type of book it will be. Depending on the intended audience, the book might be a board book, picture book, easy-reader, first chapter book, or novel. If you are not familiar with the different types of children's books, spend some time at the library or bookstore until you readily recognize the differences.

   If you want to write short pieces for magazines or Sunday school take-home papers (one of the best markets), you need to become very familiar with those publications.

There are other criteria for writing for children. You first need to understand that writing for children is not easier than writing for adults. In many ways it is much harder. If you do not have children of the age you are writing for or are not involved with them on a regular basis, do not even consider writing for them. Even rearing several children some time in the past does not qualify you to write for today's child or teen.

When you are with children, pay close attention to how they talk, dress, and interact with parents, teachers, other adults, siblings, and their peers. Use a notebook to write down everything that will be useful later.

Many people want to write children's picture books, but they are among the hardest to write and sell. Because they are usually four-color, they are expensive to produce. If you want to write picture books, you need to read at least a hundred of them before you start writing, paying close attention to the vocabulary and rhythm.

You may not be writing the book in rhyme, but picture books—because they are typically read aloud—should have a rhythm that makes them delightful reading. A picture book also has to fit the established picture-book format. Most are thirty-two pages, but they may vary from twenty-four to sixty-four pages (always multiples of eight pages because of the printing process). There are books available that will help you fit your book to that format and make it more appealing to prospective publishers.

3. *Christian Education How-to.* Most Christian-education magazines include how-to articles or tips for their readers. The articles can deal with almost any topic of interest to church school teachers or leaders. These can be full-length articles on topics such as discipline, promoting missions in class, or improving student participation. Or they can be short, individual ideas for such things as bulletin boards, crafts, and refreshments. These publications are particularly open to fresh, creative ideas.

4. *Columns.* Many magazines and newspapers are open to freelance columns, but they usually expect you to come to them with the idea, rather than seek you out. For that reason, read every magazine or paper with an eye toward what is missing or what you could offer them. My first column came just that way. I was very much involved in Christian education back then and was frustrated that my denominational leaders' magazine offered nothing for Sunday school teachers. I wrote and offered to do a how-to column for teachers and the magazine jumped at the chance. The editor said they knew they needed one, but didn't have anyone who could write it.

   If you have an idea for a column (it will need a specific slant and target audience), write up three sample columns that reflect the focus you have in mind and send them to the editor, along with your proposal. If the publication already has other columns, check them for length and plan yours accordingly. If the publication is local, send the material and follow-up with a phone call, or make an appointment to meet with the editor to discuss it.

   Magazines (if paying markets) usually pay for such columns; newspapers may not—at least initially. I recommend doing it for nothing if you have to. It is good discipline, gives you good writing credits, and helps get your name out there. If the column is a big success, you can often get the publication to pay you later (you'll usually have to ask). If you give the newspaper only one-time rights you can sell the same columns to another paper or magazine (see "Syndicates" below). All the columns I wrote for the Christian education magazine were later sold (some several times) as short articles to other magazines.

   Writing columns is not easy, as it takes an ongoing flow of ideas in the particular target area, requires the discipline of meeting guidelines, and must be tightly written. Every column needs to be interesting, make a point, and reflect your personal style or personality. It is more often about the ordinary than about the extraordinary.

If you plan to syndicate or sell reprints to your columns, you need to pay particular attention to what rights you sell. Your first choice would be to sell one-time rights. If you do, you may offer the columns to other publications (in a different area of the country or with a different reading audience) without waiting until it is published by the first publisher. On the other hand, if the publication insists on first rights, you won't be able to sell reprint rights until after the column is published.

It is also important to know whether the periodical is copyrighted. If the newspaper you write for, for instance, goes into public domain twenty-four hours after publication, you need to protect your copyright. If the column is in a copyrighted magazine, there is no problem. If, however, it is published in a newspaper, ask the editor to publish your copyright notice at the end of each column.

5. *Contests*. Contests are often a good way for a writer to get started. They are one of the primary outlets for some poets. Writing material to fit a theme and meeting a deadline are usually good discipline, and the prizes are a good incentive. You will, however, soon discover that there are contests and there are contests. Some will charge entry fees, some will not. If the contest is sponsored by a small group with few resources, the fee generally covers the cost of running the contest and the prizes. You will need to decide for yourself if the fee seems reasonable. However, there are a number of poetry contests around in which you are expected to buy a copy of the book they produce if your poem is accepted. The book is usually quite expensive ($40 to $50 or more) and the sponsor seems to accept a poem from anyone willing to buy the book. When confronted by such an "opportunity" you might want to check with your local librarian to see if the organization and book are something the library considers legitimate.

Generally speaking, any contest sponsored by an active writers' group, a writing conference, a publication for writers, or a publication looking for writers will give you an opportunity to have your writing evaluated and a chance for a prize and recognition. Some groups/organizations run annual conferences and you will soon begin to recognize those. The *Christian Writers' Market Guide* includes a list of contests in the topical lists for periodicals.

6. *Curriculum.* If you are a teacher at heart, are a good how-to writer, and enjoy writing within a specific structure, you may want to look into writing curriculum. This usually involves writing the weekly lesson plans for Sunday school teachers. There are opportunities to write for all ages, preschool through adult. It helps if you have a background in teaching Bible lessons or Sunday school, as experience seems to be more important than college degrees here.

   You don't pick the lesson topics. The publishers, mostly denominational, provide the basic lesson outline and you write the material based on that basic plan. It's like building a house to someone else's specifications. The publisher provides you with printed sheets that limit you to so many characters and so many lines per page. Usually you will be assigned a unit of thirteen lessons (enough for one quarter of the year), with a price quoted for the entire unit. Some writers like this kind of work since they get one substantial payment, rather than a lot of smaller ones as they would with articles. Other writers try curriculum but find they can't stand having their creativity stifled by the restrictions of this medium.

   One of the benefits of writing curriculum is that your material is circulated all over this country and sometimes beyond. It gives you the opportunity to use a wide variety of writing skills, such as fiction, puzzles, activities, dialogue, poetry, cartooning, theology, games, and tests. And you can establish yourself as a qualified writer for a certain target audience, such as preschoolers or teens.

   If you would like to write curriculum, go to your local Christian bookstore and buy samples of material from different companies for the age group (or groups) you want to write for. Study those carefully and then write a sample lesson for each company you are interested in based on the format of the example. Send your sample with a cover letter to each company, letting them know you would be interested in trying a short assignment on speculation. Tell them you know they can't use the enclosed sample, but you wanted them to see what you could do. If they are interested, they may send you a small assignment, or put your name in their files until they need you.

Sometimes publishers break in new writers by having them do curriculum revisions. If an activity in a particular lesson doesn't work well in class they might ask you to come up with a new idea to replace it.

7. *Devotionals.* Although some regular magazines or papers use devotions, usually "devotionals" refers to the small daily devotional booklets. These are listed in a separate section of the *Christian Writers' Market Guide.* Most of them follow a standard format: scripture verse, then a 150–300-word application or anecdote, followed by a brief prayer-thought for the day. A few of these publications, such as *The Upper Room,* are open to unsolicited submissions (as long as they fit their format), but most prefer to assign specific verses to fit their overall study. If you are interested in an assignment, write up a sample or two to fit a publisher's format and send it to them along with a request for a trial assignment. Some may respond with the assignment and, again, some may simply put you in their file until they need you.

   Some publications assign one or two verses (or a scripture passage from which you select a key verse), some may assign a group of seven verses for a consecutive week, and others assign the entire booklet for three months to one of their regular writers. Payment is per devotion, usually ranging from $5 to $20. Although this is a good "breaking in" place for new writers, some writers continue to write devotionals because they excel in this particular medium.

When writing devotions, start by meditating on the scripture and applying it to your own life. You might open your writing with a quotation, anecdote, or historical reference. Sometimes you will refer to the scripture and then apply it to a life situation, or you will share a life experience and relate that to the scripture. The closing prayer-thought will tie it all together. The best devotionals are those that can connect ordinary life to the divine.

8. *Fillers.* A filler is a short article or piece used to fill up any space left at the end of an article or between articles to maintain proper spacing. It can be as short as twenty-five to fifty words or as long as one thousand, although most are probably one hundred to eight hundred words. Fillers can cover almost any topic, but they need to fit the focus of the periodical and need to stick to a single theme.

   Once you start thinking fillers, you will find ideas everywhere: tidbits found in your research for other articles; that anecdote you couldn't use; interesting facts or statistics; a how-to; an inspiring quote or personal experience. You will be limited only by your imagination and sense of humor.

   Most publications use some fillers, but a few never do. A market guide will give you lists of those that do and what types of fillers they use. As you study each periodical, determine what types of fillers they tend to use most often and a typical length. Some publications have regular columns that use fillers.

   Filler manuscripts are prepared like any other submission and treated as a separate manuscript. Put the exact number of words in the upper right-hand corner, instead of an approximate count. A filler is usually selected because it is exactly the right length to fill that spot, so it is important that the editor know how many words there are in each filler available. If the filler does not have a title, include some kind of identification code in the upper right-hand corner. You may submit three to five fillers to one publication at one time. Payment is usually by the word for prose fillers, and a set fee for things such as cartoons or puzzles.

Following is a list of common types of fillers: devotional thoughts, personal experiences, little-known facts (science, nature, or history), editorials, problem-solution, figures of speech, brain teasers, poetry/light verse, epigrams/quips, definitions, signs, press typos, recipes, unusual photos, tips/how-tos/short-cuts, and opinions. Publications interested in puzzles are particularly open to new or original types of puzzles, not simply another crossword, word finder, or fill-in-the-blank. Some publications are always in the market for holiday or seasonal fillers.

9. *Greeting Cards.* The market for Christian greeting cards has grown considerably over the last few years. That market used to be dominated by conventional cards with pretty flowers and a scripture verse, but today Christian greeting cards are as delightful and creative as cards in the general market. If you want to write for the Christian card market, spend some time in Christian bookstores getting to know what the cards are like and determining which publishers produce the kind of cards you'd like to write. You do not have to provide the artwork, only the poem, sentiment or gag-line, and a description of the art, if needed.

   Type your ideas on 3x5 or 4x6 index cards, and submit them in batches of ten to fifteen, or as indicated in their market-guide listing. On the back of each card type your name and address and an identifying number. For example you could identify them by holiday, season or type, such as Val-1, Val-2, Val-3; or Chr-1, Chr-2, Chr-3; or GW-1, GW-2 (for get well). Pick codes that will be easily identifiable. That way you and the publisher can quickly determine which ideas they are accepting. Keep accurate record of all submissions and acceptances, or you will soon forget what you submitted where and what has sold.

   Payment varies widely ($5 to $200) and is usually made

on a per-idea basis. Poetry is often paid for by the line. A few publishers pay royalties, but most will buy an idea outright.

Some publishers are also open to ideas for new lines of cards. To present a new line, send a description of the line along with several samples. Publishers may be looking for artists or someone who can produce both the art and the sentiment. A camera-ready design, for example, pays $240 by one greeting card publisher.

10. *Letters to the Editor.* This is not a paying market but is a good place to polish your writing skills, learn to express yourself clearly and succinctly, see your name in print—and perhaps make an impact on society.

11. *Newsletters.* Some of the periodicals listed in the *Christian Writers' Market Guide* are newsletters. A few of them pay for submissions; most do not. However, they are open to submissions, and as a beginning writer you need to get your name in print as often as possible—payment or no payment. You may also find a good market in your own church newsletter or in newsletters of an organization you belong to.

12. *Online Publications.* Online publications are those that are available only on the Internet at a particular website—sometimes free to the public and sometimes by subscription. Sometimes they are a duplicate of a print publication, but more often are a separate entity. There are not a lot of online publications at this point, but we will see a lot more in the years to come.

    In some cases, if you sell a piece to the print edition of a publication, the publisher will also negotiate for electronic rights so the piece can be included in the online version. If their online version is entirely different—as it is with *Bible Advocate,* for example—the sales will be handled separately. At this point, many of the online publications do not pay. There are also unanswered questions about copyright protection. All of these issues will be addressed and dealt with as this new technology becomes more common.

The *Christian Writers' Market Guide* does give information on some of these online publications, so request the publishers' guidelines (usually available online) and study them carefully before submitting. Don't be afraid to ask questions, especially if they concern the protection of your rights.

13. *Pamphlets/Booklets.* A market guide will list those book publishers that also publish pamphlets or booklets. These can run anywhere from eight to ninety pages. If you have written something that falls into this range, go to your Christian bookstore and look for samples from each company, including publishers who may not be listed in your market guide. Check the samples to find those you like the best, as the quality and format varies from publisher to publisher. Also note the kinds of topics the publisher covers in this smaller format and the intended uses. Send for guidelines from publishers with samples you like, and follow the guidelines closely when you submit your ideas. Note that a pamphlet or booklet is more than a very short book. It must have a specific focus and a clearly defined audience. Think of it from a marketing standpoint. Who is going to buy it? How will it be marketed?

14. *Poetry.* Most people will tell you there is no market for poetry, but the *Christian Writers' Market Guide* lists 200 poetry markets (some that publish poetry exclusively) and over thirty-five book markets. It is probably a waste of time trying to start with a book of poetry, unless your poetry is exceptional or you are famous. I recommend that poets start by writing regularly for periodicals and establishing themselves as poets. Keep in mind that when you write for periodicals, typically the theme of the poetry has to be in line with the theme of the publication. For example, if it is a magazine for writers, the poetry must deal with

writing. Before submitting, study the poetry in each magazine you want to write for and note how the poetry relates to the theme of the publication. Then select or write poetry that relates in the same way. If it doesn't, then don't waste your time or the editors' time by sending it.

When submitting poetry, check a market guide or the publisher's guidelines and follow the specifications given there regarding type, length, and number of poems to send at one time. Some editors want only rhymed poetry, some want only unrhymed, and some will take either. Their listing may indicate that they accept poetry four to fifty lines or longer, so study their sample copies and see what length they typically use. If most of the poetry is short, then send short poems. If they tend to use full-page poems, send something of that length.

When preparing poetry to submit, handle each poem as a separate manuscript, no matter how short. That way, if you send more than one, the publication can select the ones they want and return the others. Center each poem on the page, top to bottom, and also center it across the page according to the longest line. Double-space it and leave three to four lines between stanzas. Rather than putting a word count in the upper right-hand corner as you would with other manuscripts, you will indicate the number of lines. If a poem does not have a title for identification, give it an identifying number in the upper right-hand corner as well.

Most publications make small payments for poetry, but some do pay up to $1/line. You will not make a fortune writing poetry for publications, but you can establish your name and reputation as a poet for possible future publication in books. Many poets opt to self-publish their poetry in book form, but the problem then becomes how to distribute the books and not have hundreds of them collecting dust in your garage. Make such a choice very carefully and only after exploring your options for distribution.

Ultimately, a writer cannot expect to make any significant money as a poet. A poet's motivation then becomes very different from most other writers. While others are seeking bylines and sales, the poet is seeking bylines and an audience. The ultimate success for a poet is an appreciative audience that recognizes and warms to their words—worth a lot more than $1 a line.

15. *Puzzles.** There is a wide market for puzzles in publications with target audiences ranging from young children to senior adults. In children's publications, puzzles often have to fit the theme or topic of the week's lesson. Theme-oriented publications most often want puzzles to match their themes. Study sample copies of a publication to get a better idea for the length and type of puzzles they use.

    Many of the children's papers or magazines are able to recycle puzzles as one batch of children moves into an older age group, and new ones move up. For that reason they buy a limited amount but are always open to new, creative types of puzzles. If you can create the professional artwork needed to present the puzzle it is a plus, but the publication does not expect you to. Simply send a copy of the puzzle, including any ideas for artwork, as well as the solution. You may send several (four to six) at the same time as long as they are prepared as separate manuscripts and all have titles or identification numbers.

16. *Scripts.* As Christian-oriented material is finding more of an audience in the media, there will be a growing need for Christian writers who can write scripts and meet the sophisticated demands of the entertainment industry while maintaining a Christian message. Look for books and computer programs to help you learn how to format and present scripts.

17. *Short stories.* Although the short-story market in magazines is somewhat limited, you will find a ready market for them

*Puzzle markets are listed in the *Christian Writers' Market Guide* under "Fillers: Word Puzzles."

in Sunday school take-home papers for all ages—two and three year olds through adults. If you want to write short stories for any age, send for guidelines and sample copies and read as many samples as you can for the age group or magazines you want to write for.

Carefully observe the required word length for each age group. Adult fiction may be as long as 1,500–3,500 words (occasionally longer) for magazines, but adult take-home papers typically want only 800–1,200 words. Teen magazines average about 1,000–2,200 words, and their take-home papers 700–1,200 words. Children's stories are usually quite short. The most open age for children's short stories is fourth through sixth graders (600–1,600 words), but there are also a few markets for first through third graders (400–1,000 words).

It takes special skills to write for very young children, and it is usually done on assignment. If you want to write for pre-schoolers, study several samples and then write two or three sample stories to send to publications for that age group and ask for an assignment.

18. *Specialty Products*. In the greeting card section of the *Christian Writers' Market Guide,* you will find a listing of needs for specialty products. Some greeting card companies are open to ideas or sayings for t-shirts, plaques, or coffee mugs. Other companies want ideas for board games or gift products. These markets are especially good for poets or for those who can write humor. Send for guidelines and study the products in your local Christian bookstore. Be creative.

19. *Sunday School Take-home Papers*. For those not familiar with the term, *take-home papers* are story leaflets that are given out to children, teens, and adults after Sunday school. This is one of the best and most open markets for freelancers. Most denominations have their own papers, and because the papers are given out weekly, they include a lot of free-

lance material, especially short stories. In fact, take-home papers are one of the best markets for short fiction. In addition to fiction, many use short nonfiction pieces (often their greatest need), and such things as puzzles, crafts, Bible studies, and nature pieces. The format varies a great deal from paper to paper, so study them carefully before submitting anything.*

20. *Syndicates.* If you are doing a regular column in a newspaper, you might want to consider getting the column into syndication. That means that the same column would be printed simultaneously in a number of newspapers around the country. There are syndicates that handle this process, if they believe your column is something of universal interest, or you can self-syndicate. That means instead of the syndicate finding papers to carry your column, you would contact them yourself. You should be able to find a list of syndicates or a list of possible newspapers at your local library or on the Internet.

    After you have had a column running successfully in at least one paper, start offering it to nearby weekly papers (sending samples from the first paper), then to other papers in your state, and then in other states. Keep in mind that a syndicated column must be of broad interest. You may need to offer to write the column for free for a trial period, but after the trial period you could ask for a nominal fee per column.

21. *Tracts.* If evangelism and outreach are your passions, there are still companies who produce tracts. You will find a list of those companies in the *Market Guide* under topical listings for books. Send for their guidelines and some sample tracts to study before submitting to them. Publishers have specific topic guidelines and length requirements.

*For a listing of take-home papers, see the topical listings for periodicals in the *Christian Writers' Market Guide.*

Chapter 11

On Writing 101

Though this book is about the business of writing rather than the writing process, there are a few elements of writing that everybody submitting a manuscript for publication needs to know. Listed below in alphabetical order (rather than in order of importance) are skills that any publisher expects to see you demonstrate in your writing.

Anecdotes

The first article I ever wrote came back from the first publisher I sent it to with this note written at the bottom: "We prefer the anecdotal approach." Of course, I was so new to writing, I didn't have a clue as to what they meant. I had to look it up in the dictionary. That was my first lesson in writing, and one that was well worth remembering. The truth is, most magazine and book publishers prefer you to illustrate your points with anecdotes.

What is an *anecdote?* In writing, an anecdote is an interesting, funny, or poignant story that helps the reader understand and remember your key points. Everyone likes a good story. That's why in writing, stories are central to explaining ideas. Often an article or a book that is too dry can be salvaged by adding anecdotes that bring the concepts to life. As you reread your material, looking at key ideas, consider adding an experience of your own or of someone you know that illustrates the point.

Anecdotes can be any length, but short is usually best. If you are writing an article, check on the typical length of anecdotes in the magazine you want to write for, and then write your article to fit the established pattern. It's often valuable to use a *split anecdote* in which you present half the story (basically setting the scene), go on to make a point, and then finish the story to drive home your point. Using split anecdotes can also be a helpful strategy for book chapters.

First-Person Narration

Many people enjoy writing stories or articles in the first person because it is natural and intimate. However, beginning writers are often advised against trying it because even though it comes easiest it is the most difficult point of view to execute well. *First-person narrative* can be effective at times but keep in mind that it can be hard to keep an objective perspective when writing in first-person. Because of that, don't write in first-person unless you're writing specifically to the needs of those who want or require it. Some publications, such as *Guideposts*, require the use of first-person, but the majority of publications prefer third-person, and some *never* use first-person. So remember that writing in first-person can limit your market.

Writing fiction in first-person may restrict your plotting possibilites since everything that happens has to be told from one person's point of view. When writing fiction it is best to think through the plot line and determine if it can be told in first-person before you start. Rewriting anything from first-person to third-person is a daunting task, so make that choice wisely.

One of the drawbacks to first-person point of view is the natural tendency to tell the reader more than he or she needs to know about what you or your character are thinking. You will not share every thought, any more than you would share every action. One of the advantages, however, of writing fiction in first-person is that you are not as likely to let the viewpoint wander from character to character—often a problem for beginning writers.

Probably the biggest problem for the writer is learning how to write in first-person without starting every sentence with "I." When you find a good first-person article or book, go through it and circle every "I" in the article or book chapter and then study what techniques the author used to avoid the word.

Leads

A *lead* is much more than how you begin an article or book. It is what usually determines whether the editor—and ultimately the reader—stays with you long enough to read on. A lead must excite or intrigue the reader as well as set the direction for the writer. Through it, an author sets a path and encourages the reader to follow. A reader wants to know two things when reading your book or article: "What do you have to offer?" and "What will it cost me?" If you can at least allude to answers to those questions in your lead, your reader will be hooked.

You will likely spend more time on your lead than on any other part of your article. For some articles and for some writers the lead practically writes itself. In other cases you must work for it. It is often difficulty in getting the lead right, or getting the lead at all, that keeps us from getting started. If it is a struggle for you, you might skip the lead, get right into the article, and then come back and write your lead later.

A lead must create interest by appealing to the reader's basic human needs or emotions and giving the reader a vested interest in reading on. Make it compelling but don't promise more than you are able to deliver.

There are many different types of leads. Often simply reviewing the options is enough to spark an idea. Following are a number of such options (in your reading, look for examples of these and other types of leads):

1. *Anecdotal Lead.* Use the story of a person or group that best illustrates the point of your introductory chapter or article—and introduces your main topic. It should be a compelling story that the reader can identify with. In a split anecdotal lead, you use the first half of the anecdote as your lead, and the conclusion of the anecdote in the middle or at the end of the article or book chapter. The anecdote you

use might also be a news event (a *news peg lead).*

2. *Case History Lead.* The case histories of one or more people can set up a problem that the article goes on to address.

3. *Comparison/Contrast Lead.* Compare or contrast two locations, opinions, things, or situations to create interest in your topic.

4. *Description Lead.* Could be the description of a character in fiction, of a location for a travel piece, or of an event for a news report.

5. *Dialogue Lead.* A dialogue between two characters in fiction or two people involved in a nonfiction piece can set the scene, reveal something about each person, and introduce or at least hint at the problem or situation to come.

6. *Direct Address.* Speaks directly to readers, drawing them into the text and giving them a stake in the action.

7. *Narrative or Fact.* A presentation of factual information in an interesting manner.

8. *Poetic Lead.* Uses poetry or flowery prose to create a certain mood for the reader. Should be used sparingly (if at all) and usually only if the same mood is going to be maintained throughout the piece.

9. *Question Lead.* Asks a question that the body of the article will answer.

10. *Quotation Lead.* This could be a scripture or a well-known quote that introduces the topic or sets the tone for the following piece or chapter. Scripture is not always the best choice for a lead, even for a religious publication. The use of other quotes are easy to overuse. Choose to use quota-

tions only if it best accomplishes your purpose. (Here's an example: "'You can't teach an old dog new tricks' took on new meaning when I switched on my first computer at age sixty-five.")

11. *Startling Statement Lead.* This is a statement that will shock readers and compel them to read on. (Here's an example: "Despite zero tolerance for weapons in most of this country's high schools, more than fifty teens will lose their lives in their own schools next year.")

12. *Survey Lead.* Similar to the case-history lead, this gives a series of case histories of people across the country or in different circumstances that shared the same problem or met the same fate. They need a common denominator.

Let me tell you what I am about to tell you is often the way beginning writers open an article or book, though not in those words. Instead of getting into something that will compel the reader to read on, many beginning writers mistakenly start with something like this: "I learned an important lesson about prayer the other day while I was caring for my elderly mother." Drop those introductory remarks and get right into the story about your mother.

A good lead will convince your readers that they need what you are about to say, that they will be able to identify with the problem presented, that you will give them insight or an insider's look at the problem, that you have some new information to share, or that they can simply look forward to being entertained. Your lead should reflect and introduce the overall tone of the article or book. For example, if it is a humorous piece, the lead should perhaps begin with a joke or funny anecdote. If it is a serious piece, the lead should never be funny.

If you have trouble writing your lead, try describing your article to someone who knows nothing about it. How do you introduce the subject to them? If you have a lead, but the article or story seems to be going nowhere, you may simply need to go back and rewrite your lead. You may have set yourself on the wrong path.

One of the best ways to learn how to write good leads is to read a lot of them. Every time you pick up a magazine, read each lead, identify what kind of lead it is, and determine how effective it is in getting you to read on. If you read a lead and then have no interest in completing the article, you will know the lead was ineffective. You might want to start a notebook of leads you especially like. Sometimes it helps to simply read through a number of good leads to get your own creative juices flowing.

Middles and Endings

After you catch your reader's attention with that all-important lead, it is time to look at the middle and end of your piece. Let's create a visual image that is easy to remember. If your lead were the cowcatcher at the front of a train used to clear the way, what would the rest of the train represent?

Locomotive. The cowcatcher or lead is attached to the locomotive that takes the train—or your writing—where it wants to go. At some point after the lead, you need to drop back and tell the reader where the piece is going. We have all read articles that rambled on and on but left the reader wondering where it was all going. Use your locomotive to give your reader that solid direction. Each time you read an article, look for that statement that gives the piece its direction.

Train Cars. Following the locomotive are any number of cars that you must fill with the substance of the article. One car might hold statistics, one an anecdote, one a quote from an authority, one a case study, one a personal experience, for instance. Give solid support to your premise by doing the kind of research that says this is more than just your idea. When the cars are filled, do one last check to be sure every car is going the same direction set by your locomotive. If you've gotten off on a tangent, that car will end up sitting on a side track.

Caboose. Once you have your cars in a proper order and all in a row, you will need a caboose to come along behind. Next to the lead, the ending is one of the most important features of your article. Since it is the last thing your reader will read, it is the thing they are most likely to remember. A good ending needs to wrap things up, give a feeling of satisfaction or finality, and leave your reader thinking, feeling, or even taking action.

A bad ending dilutes the point, preaches (hitting the reader over the head), tells the reader what to think (rather than letting him or her reach a conclusion), leaves too much unresolved, or ends on a different mood or makes a different point than the rest of the article.

Connectors. If the train is going to go anywhere, it needs two more things. First, the connectors that hold it all together. It is effective transitions that make a collection of cars a whole train. Some writers move smoothly and effortlessly from one point or part of their story to the next, while others struggle with every transition. If you are one who struggles with connectors, learn as much as you can about different types of transitions and how to make them. One way to do this is by reading a lot and noting how other writers do it. See the section below on transitions for more information on this.

Track. The last thing we need to make the train functional is the track. The track is connected to the first thing we need to consider—the slant or focus of our article. Actually the track is closely tied to your locomotive. Once you establish the locomotive you also lay down your track. That means that the locomotive, each car, and the caboose all must run on the same track and go in the same direction. If any one of them is off on a tangent—or side track—it will go nowhere. So when you have completed your piece, go back and test each segment to be sure it is on the right track. If not, drop it or rewrite it.

Point of View

Point of view is one of the most confusing and misunderstood aspects of fiction. Most of the first novels I critique have some problems with this area. It is not that the writer misunderstood how to do it—he or she simply was not aware it was something to be concerned about. The result is that the point of view typically shifts from character to character without following the rules.

Let's start with a clear definition of *point of view.* Essentially it refers to the central character (or characters) through whose eyes you see or experience the story. That means you see what is happening in the story from the viewpoint of a particular character (or characters), from the standpoint of the writer, or from an outside observer. As such, you know only what that character is thinking or feeling unless that character has special knowledge (e.g., if that character is an angel). Although it is not uncommon to see multiple points of view—even in best-selling fiction—usually the best fiction is written from a single viewpoint. (Short stories are nearly always told from one viewpoint). For example, if your story is about a young woman's struggle to gain independence from her mother, the story might be told from the young woman's perspective, and all we will know about her mother is what the daughter knows or sees or tells us, or what the action reveals. We won't get into the mother's head and see how she views the situation.

Some beginning writers complain that a single viewpoint prevents them and their readers from knowing what is happening inside the other characters, as indicated above, but the truth is we all live our lives from a single point of view—our own—and we manage quite well in discovering what those around us are feeling or thinking.

Many people write from the same point of view in all their fiction, but there are times another point of view might work better. The following information will clarify points of view and give you additional options:

First-person point of view. The story is told from a single viewpoint, but it is also told in first-person with one character narrating the story. For example: "I'm Irving, and this is the story of how I got to Montana." First-person works best for short stories. It helps the reader identify more closely with the character, but it may be difficult for the reader to maintain interest in one character for a whole novel.

Third-person point of view. This is the most commonly used viewpoint, in which you refer to the characters as "he" or "she." In essence, you as the writer tell the story but you tell it as if you were seeing it from one character's perspective at a time. For example, "Irving was still wondering how he got to Montana." If you are telling the story from the third-person viewpoint of one or two characters only, it is called *limited third-person.* In that case, for example, the story would be told either from Irving's viewpoint alone or from the viewpoint of Irving and his new girlfriend.

Another option is a *multiple third-person* where the viewpoint alternates between characters throughout the book or between characters and the writer. The trick here is not to change viewpoints within the same scene (which causes the reader confusion), but at the beginning of a new chapter or after a passage of time. For example, the first chapter might be from Irving's viewpoint, the second from his new neighbor's, the third from Irving's again, the fourth from his new girlfriend's, and so on.

Omniscient point of view. Here the story is told from the viewpoint of an all-seeing, all-knowing narrator—someone who knows what each character is thinking and feeling, what action is taking place, and what the results might be. For example: "This is the story of how Irving got to Montana." Although this point of view may seem to be the easiest to write since the writer can disclose what everyone is thinking and feeling, it also can keep the reader from establishing an intimate bond with any of the characters.

Developing skill in point of view. The beginning writer should learn how to write well from a single point of view before attempting multiple viewpoints. For practice, always identify (and critique) the point of view in the stories or novels you read. If you have already written a novel where the viewpoint was handled incorrectly, it may be very difficult, if not impossible, to change it now. Very often the plot you have established will not work if you shift to another viewpoint, so you will have to start over or put this novel aside until you understand viewpoint well enough to rewrite it correctly from another (or multiple) viewpoints.

It is wise to determine viewpoint by thinking through your story from a number of different viewpoints before you start. Choose one or more viewpoints based on what works best for this story. Generally, the viewpoint character must be the one who has the most to gain or lose in the story, the one most likely to be in every scene, and the most interesting. Occasionally the story is told from the viewpoint of a lesser character or even a bystander, but that is more difficult to do and won't work with every story.

If you are considering a first-person point of view, review the story carefully with a first-person perspective in mind and decide if it will work with your plot. Choose a multiple or omniscient point of view only if it is the only thing that will work. The key is to change viewpoint by choice—not by chance—and to change it only as often as absolutely necessary.

Referring to Scripture

Many of the new Christian writers who ask me to critique their manuscripts have a strong misconception about the use of Scripture verses in their writing. Most assume that since they are writing for a Christian market, they need to dot their writing liberally with Scripture. Actually the opposite is true. Most publishers prefer you to use only a *few* well-integrated verses, and some object to using any.

With formatting you have three possibilitites if you want to include the verse:

You are the salt of the earth (Matthew 5:13).

When Jesus tells his disciples that they are the salt of the earth . . .

or this:

> *Jesus tells his disciples, "You are the salt of the earth" (Matthew 5:13).*

or this:

> *In the fifth chapter of Matthew's gospel, Jesus tells his disciples they are "the salt of the earth."*

Choose the format style you feel is least obtrusive.

When referring to Scripture, never refer solely to book, chapter, and verse. Quote the Scripture text or refer to what it contains. Don't assume your readers—even your Christian readers—will know what the text is without looking it up. You also do not want to list a lot of references and assume your reader will be willing to look them up. Unless it is integrated into your writing (or you are writing a Bible study), most people will skip over both Scripture text and verse references.

For that reason, include a verse only if it is critical to the content of your article, and do not give in to the temptation to list six verses to make the same point. Choose the best verse you can find on the topic and include only that portion of the verse that is pertinent (being careful not to take it out of context).

One other problem I see regularly among would-be writers is writing a whole article expounding on what a certain passage means, without ever addressing how the passage applies to the reader's life. Without a strong application, your article will never see publication.

Research

Since I am covering Internet research elsewhere in this book, in this section I will concentrate on other research options. This is a topic that could fill a book of its own, so I will only try to give you some pointers here.

Libraries

➤ Seek out and get familiar with the biggest and best public, college/university, or Christian college libraries in your area.

➤ Ask for an information sheet and a tour.

➤ Get acquainted with the librarians, especially the research librarians.

➤ Spend free time in those sections of the library you will likely use the most.

➤ Learn how to use the new computerized cataloging system.

➤ Find out where to look for government pamphlets, newspapers, phone books, yearbooks/almanacs, encyclopedias, biographical dictionaries, books of facts, and other resources.

➤ Find out the library's capabilities and procedures for interlibrary loans on books or specialized resources.

➤ Check Christian colleges to determine if you are welcome to use their libraries, if they carry a large number of Christian periodicals you can review, and what Christian/religious resources they have that you won't find elsewhere.

Research by mail/email

Here are ways you can research by mail and email:

- Address your request for information to a specific resource person. (You'll get a better response if you treat the contact as an individual.)
- Be very specific about what information you need; tell why and when you need it (give them about ten days for a response).
- Keep letters informal and friendly. Always include an S.A.S.E. with any request if asking for information by mail.
- Most "experts" are happy to tell you what they know and

flattered that you asked them. When quoting them, give them credit, and if used in a book, include them in your acknowledgments.

- Since you may want to contact them again, maintain a good relationship with such sources. Send a note and a copy of the article or book as a thank-you for their help. (Or you might have your publisher send them a review copy of your book.)

Research by phone

Here are some helps to research by phone:

➤ If you want to call to ask for extensive information over the phone, it is best to write first to let the person know who you are and what information you want. Send a list of questions, if appropriate.

➤ In more informal situations you might call and ask if the person can answer a question or two at that time, or find out when you could call back at a more convenient time.

➤ Call the research department at local or out-of-town libraries to ask single questions.

➤ Call local colleges and ask who they have teaching there that is an "expert" in your area of need. Most will be happy to give you needed information or quotes.

Research locations

Visit local places of historical interest, specialized museums and libraries in the area, any interesting locations for fiction settings, or other places that might spark an idea. You might also send for needed information on geographical locations from an area's Chamber of Commerce or travel bureau.

Research newspapers, TV, and radio

Always be on the lookout for ideas for leads, interviews, personal interest stories, topics of public interest, trends, and religious news that might translate into article or story ideas.

Research your own library, files, and experience

- Develop a library of books and files on your topics of primary interest. This will provide one of your best resources for research in those areas.
- Search your own background for illustrations, anecdotes, and experiences you can use to add color to your writing.
- Brainstorm by yourself or with family and friends for original article, story, or book ideas.

❖

If you have access to the Internet, you can do most of the research mentioned above from your home office, so check out that information in chapter 4.

Self-Editing

The process of writing involves three main steps: Getting your thoughts and ideas down on paper; rereading and reworking the material to make your voice and tone consistent; checking for errors in spelling, punctuation, or grammar.

One of the greatest obstacles to being a successful writer is letting perfectionism get in the way of the writing process. When you write a *first draft,* simply get everything down on paper or screen without stopping to make every word and sentence perfect as you go. I find that once I have the essence of what I want to say into a tangible form, half of my work is done. I've completed the rough draft. Stopping to polish as you go disrupts the creative process and slows the production to such a point that you may never complete the work. So initially, be concerned only about getting it down.

Once you finish that first draft, go back and search for weakness in the tone, voice, or various areas of construction. If you are using a computer, some of the initial editing can be done on screen, but after the obvious corrections, print out a hard copy. Don't try to edit on the screen. Reading the text aloud helps you catch the sound and cadence of your writing and can be a valuable editing tool. As you read, make any corrections or notes in red pencil. If you know something is wrong but aren't sure how to correct it at that moment, simply make a note in the margin or attach a sticky note so you can come back and work on it later.

After an initial reading, it is often helpful to go through the manuscript checking on one element at a time. For example, for a fiction piece, go through and read all the dialogue, making sure it flows realistically. Then go back and read the words of one character at a time to be sure the dialogue is consistent with that character. If there is no significant difference in the way your characters talk, you may have to work to develop those distinctive differences. In fiction, you will also need to check on things such as time lines, personal description, scene descriptions, and being sure each plot thread is carried through to some conclusion.

In nonfiction, you will need to check organization. Do your thoughts follow a logical progression to the end? Are those thoughts clear? Do your transitions move your reader smoothly from one point or scene to another? Is there too much repetition of certain words or phrases? The more writing and rewriting you do, the easier it is to recognize those areas where you tend to have the most problems and where you need to concentrate your rewriting efforts.

In the third phase of your rewrite, you will concentrate on spelling, grammar, and punctuation. (If you are using a computer, don't depend on the spell check to catch all the spelling errors.) For some, this is the easy part. For others it may be the hardest, especially if your skills are weak in these areas. It may be helpful to have a friend, spouse, or teacher check for such errors.

When you discover the areas in which you have the most problems, look up the rules and study them until you feel confident that you know them. If possible, take a refresher course. A good spelling dictionary and thesaurus are essential, and a simple style manual, such as *The Elements of Style* (a classic by Strunk and White), will answer a lot of your questions. It may be helpful to develop a study notebook in which you write down your commonly misspelled words and grammar or punctuation errors so you can review them regularly. Eventually the rules will become second nature.

Cooling time

After completing the above steps, it will be time to let your manuscript "cool." Put it aside for two weeks to two months before you look at it again. At that point, edit it again, now with more objectivity. Work at eliminating any unnecessary words, tightening ideas and sentences up as much as possible and providing smooth transitions between thoughts. Work to either strengthen or eliminate weak points. Go through it sentence by sentence and ask, "Does this sentence say anything?" and "Does it say exactly what I want it to say?" You'll be surprised how often the answer to both of these questions is no. Your work in revising is to say yes to both these questions throughout your book or article. Make changes whenever you come across something that doesn't seem quite right. When you no longer catch any weaknesses as you read, it is nearly finished. Run the spell check again and print out a copy. After a final edit on the hard copy it is finished.

Checklist

Following is a list of some other possible self-editing steps. I would suggest that you develop your own self-editing checklist based on the steps mentioned above and below. You might personalize it by including those steps with which you need the most help and eliminating those you do automatically. It may also be helpful to have one checklist for fiction and another for nonfiction.

In addition to the steps already mentioned, you might add these to your checklist:

1. Consistent point of view?
2. Complete sentences (except where sentence fragments are used by choice)?
3. Eliminated jargon, clichés, Christian-ese (terms that the general audience may not know)?
4. Checked accuracy of all dates, quotes, Scripture references, figures, time lines?
5. Eliminated double negatives?
6. Any adjectives used as adverbs?
7. A new paragraph each time you started a new thought?
8. Do nouns and pronouns agree, either singular or plural?

Show, Don't Tell

In the world of writing, the adage "show, don't tell" is more than a well-worn cliché. That adage points to the heart of good, publishable writing. If a writer can understand this concept—and effectively practice it—his or her writing is more likely to leap from the rejection pile to the pile of those receiving acceptances and checks.

Much of the writing I have critiqued over the years has lacked this essential quality. Most writers tend to tell readers what to think and feel instead of setting up a situation and allowing them to draw *their own* conclusions. It is no wonder these writers are rejected repeatedly. Simply bombarding readers with your opinions will never change their minds. But by learning to present stories and information and detail that show and don't tell, we can change their lives.

What exactly do we mean by "Show, don't tell"? It is not all that difficult to understand. In your writing—whether fiction or nonfiction—avoid telling your reader any information that you can convey by example. I could leave the explanation right there and move on to another subject, but that means I would be guilty of "telling." I haven't shown you what I mean by all this. In essence, it is the difference between hearing a play read and seeing it in full production.

Let's start by identifying ways in which we "tell":

1. Simply stating or reciting facts or views.
2. Straight narrative; presenting a statement of what happened.
3. Preaching; telling your reader that this is the way it is.
4. In Christian writing, it is often presenting your views or interpretation of a Bible passage or scriptural concept without showing your readers how to apply it to their lives.

By contrast, following are some ways you can "show" in your writing:

1. Never call a tree a tree. Tell your reader that it is an oak tree, a towering redwood, or a weeping willow. By identifying the kind of tree—or bird, or house, or flower, or fence—you immediately create a visual image in the mind of your reader.

2. Cite examples. Use anecdotes, illustrations, personal experiences, or case histories to show your readers what you mean.

3. Support your facts with current statistics.

4. Use comparisons or contrasts to help your readers understand significance.

5. Quote authorities. A quote from an authority will often put your point into perspective or make it more applicable to the reader's needs.

6. Use historical references to put timing into perspective. For example, instead of saying, "Judy hadn't sat in on a college class for thirty years," say, "Judy hadn't sat in on a college class since Kennedy was in the White House."

7. Use geographical references in the same way. Example: "To Mark Little in Florida, the Spotted Owl controversy was a topic for his environmental group. But to John Harris from Oregon, it meant his kids might not go to college."

8. Point out the views of others on the topic or acknowledge any controversy surrounding the issue. If there is a strong voice in opposition to your views, then acknowledge that.

9. Use colorful descriptions of objects, places, actions, or reactions.

10. Use dialogue instead of narration or description to make a point or give background information.

❖

Anytime you are reading, watch for good examples of these and other techniques for "showing." You might want to start a notebook of good examples to refer to when your writing becomes stale or flat, or when you realize you are *telling* too much.

Titles

Many writers struggle with selecting the right title for their piece, and are frustrated if an editor changes it later. Some writers seem to be especially adept at picking the right title—an intriguing one that catches the reader's attention and draws him or her into the article or story—while others routinely come up blank.

We have all seen great titles that apparently were a strong selling point for the piece. If the book or article fulfills the promise of the title, we are satisfied, and the author has done the job well. If the title promises more than it delivers, we are frustrated and disappointed. Your readers will feel the same way. A good title will not only give a clue to what the article or book is going to be about, it will reflect some benefit for the reader, be entertaining, have relevance to the reader's life and needs, and be timely.

It's also important to take into account the length of the title. Although about six words is average, most publications have an individual preference for titles of a certain length. If you are writing an article, go to the table of contents of the magazine you wish to write for, count up the number of words in all the titles and calculate the average length. You will find that typically a more serious, theological magazine has longer titles—six to ten words—while in a teen publication titles are often one to three words (short and crisp). I advise that you determine the length the magazine tends to prefer and make yours fit that. It is not that you will be rejected because your title is too short or too long, but your title is one more way to show that you have done your homework and are writing this piece to fit that magazine's particular needs.

The same concept applies if you are writing a book. Look through the publisher's catalog and study the average length and tone of their titles. Try to match your proposed book title to their style of titling.

Your title should develop intrigue without telling too much. For example, if you were writing a story for children about a little girl's surprise birthday present, you would not name the story, "Mary's Surprise Horse." The title should intrigue and arouse interest in your reader, not answer a reader's questions or give away the plot before someone even starts reading.

If a title does not come naturally, here are a variety of tips and sources that might help: check a book of quotations (including twists on those quotations); use Bible quotes, proverbs, alliteration, or a quote from the book or article itself; ask a question that the article will answer; address the reader in the title with *You* or *Your*; use *How-To;* promise some reader benefit; indicate a number of steps involved *(Eight Ways to . . .);* or promise something "New." Though you may start out with a working title, it is best to wait until the piece is completed to make a final title decision.

Ultimately, the editor may change the title anyway. Some do

it as a matter of routine. In some cases the title is not right, in others it may not fit the overall tone of the magazine or publishing house or is too much like another they have used. There is no way you can know all those variables, but try to fit the title both to the piece and to the publisher.

About book titles: A book title needs to be easy for readers to remember and pronounce when they walk into a bookstore to request it. If your title is not easy to remember, you risk losing a sale—or lots of them. If you pick a cutesy or clever title that captures the reader's interest but fails to reflect the content of the book, add a subtitle that clearly identifies the contents (for example: *Near to the Heart of God: Daily Readings from the Spiritual Classics*). Ultimately what you want in a book title is one that will compel potential readers to pick up the book as soon as they read the title.

Writers often wonder if their title is original or if someone else has already used it. How will they know if they are stealing someone else's title? That is one thing you don't have to worry about. Because it would be impossible for the writer to know about all those other titles, titles cannot be copyrighted. Obviously you won't want to use a highly recognizable title, such as *Gone with the Wind* (which, by the way, the author originally named *Tomorrow is Another Day*) or other well-known titles almost considered trademarks. Be as creative and original as possible.

Transitions

One of the skills every writer needs to develop is smooth *transitions*—the ability to move from one subject to the next or one scene to the next without readers being aware that they have been moved. As a reader, you will often notice poor transitions. You have experienced one when all of a sudden the author changes subject or direction and leaves you behind wondering where the author is off to.

For some writers transitions come naturally, requiring little thought. Other writers find them an ongoing struggle and spend a good part of their rewriting making those transitions appear seamless. The truth is that the more experienced or better you are at writing, the more naturally those transitions will come. Often when a transition is particularly hard, it may be that you are getting too far from the slant of your piece and you shouldn't be trying to make such a leap.

Generally, transitions involve moving your reader in space, time, viewpoint, or emotion. Transitions of space must move the reader from one location to another; transitions of time move them from one time period to another; transitions of viewpoint from one point of information, belief or opinion to another; and transitions of emotion from being happy, to concerned, or angry, or depressed, or another emotion.

In nonfiction, if your piece is well organized, it is usually easy to move from one step or one point to the next. But in fiction, it is more difficult. You are constantly working with transitions—moving a character from one place to another, moving from one scene to another, covering lapses of time, using flashbacks and then returning to the present. All of these transitions take skill to be effective. You may run into the same kinds of problems if you are writing biography or autobiography. Will you tell the story chronologically or move from the present back to the person's birth, or skip around through his or her life?

There are a few tricks you can keep in mind to help you make those difficult transitions.

- Ask a question in one paragraph and answer it in the next. Example: Joe is standing on the curb with his camping gear wondering how he'll get to the church for the camp-out after his mother's car breaks down. In next paragraph, Uncle Harry rounds the corner in his new pick-up. Or, if you are relating a subject's accomplishments, you might want to transition to her background with a question like, "How did Jane Jones learn so much about wildlife habitat?" and then go on to answer that question.

- Repeat a word or phrase or main idea from a previous paragraph. This kind of link holds your piece together.

- Indicate time lapses. Time lapses can easily be indicated by starting those paragraphs with phrases, such as, "A few minutes later," "Two weeks after that," or "The next day."

- Establish Place. "Back at work," "Across town," or "In Allison's backyard."

- Use connecting words. If you are writing a how-to article, paragraphs are usually joined easily by such words as *first, next, then, finally*—words that show a step-by-step progression.

- Use bullets or similar devices to join related material in a list-type style as I have done in this section. This allows you to give a clear separation to each point.

Chapter 12

On Publishing Alternatives

Although every writer would like to have his or her book accepted by a royalty publisher and catapulted to the best-seller list, that is becoming less and less of a reality for the average writer. Although I still encourage writers to try for a royalty contract first, there are now more options available for those who have other resources. In this section I want to make you aware of some of them.

When I started in this business, and even up until the last few years, no one paid any attention to self-published books. Years ago, the only books done that way were through what we called vanity presses—a crude reference to people with unpublishable books who were so vain they paid to have them published. Over the years some people started publishing their own books through a local printer instead of paying the high prices demanded by the vanity houses. Although there seemed to be some acceptance of such books in general markets, they still were basically ignored in the Christian market.

However, over the last five years or so we have seen a dramatic turnaround in the feelings toward author-funded books in the Christian market. The primary reason for that change is that there are only so many royalty houses, many of whom have cut back on the number of titles they do per year, and they are unable to publish all of the good manuscripts that come across their desks. For that reason, those with resources and outlets for their books are turning to one of the author-funded alternatives.

Should You Pay for Your Book?

There are a number of reasons to consider author-funded publishing and reasons to avoid it. Here are some ideas for you to consider.

Why author-funded publishing can be beneficial

Money. If you have a good way to distribute the books yourself, such as a large direct-mail list or a speaking ministry where you can sell a lot of books, and if you have the resources to pay the production costs up front, then you could make a lot more money on your book than you would with a royalty. Direct selling is much more lucrative than going through a bookstore.

Control. Let's face it, another reason some authors self-publish is because they want to control all aspects of publication. When you sign a contract with a royalty house, you give them control over much of the production process. The publisher usually picks the cover and interior design, edits the book in their own style (though you also have a say in it), and sometimes even chooses a title without the author's input. While most reputable publishers make good choices and allow authors plenty of input, a few royalty publishers have treated authors so poorly that authors don't want to take the risk of relinquishing that much control.

Best alternative. There are certain types of books that it makes more sense to self-publish, such as poetry books, family histories, regional books, very timely topics (that can't wait on a royalty publisher), or those with a very specific and limited audience. Author-funded publishing will best fit your needs in these cases.

Possible contract offers. If your self-published book does well, you may then be able to interest a royalty publisher, or they might start approaching you with contract offers. But if it is selling that well, you may be making more profit than you would with a royalty contract, so calculate the cost before jumping at the offer. How often do you get a chance to reject a royalty publisher?

Why author-funding can be a disaster

Money. If you are successful at selling your book, you stand to gain by publishing on your own. But if you are unsuccessful at that, you could lose a great deal. A royalty publisher bears the cost of editing, printing, publicizing, and distributing your book, and therefore takes the loss if the book fails. Without a publisher, that loss is yours.

Quality Control. When you publish the book yourself, unless you can pay for professional editing, design, cover art, public relations and promotion, and distribution, you risk producing a book that looks and reads poorly and is not distributed to the major bookstore outlets. Most publishers are in business because they do something well—editing, producing, and distributing books. Most authors have few skills in these areas. That means that a book designed by its author is probably not going to look as good as a book designed by a professional cover designer, and it might not sell as well either.

Time and Space. When you publish a book yourself, you do a *lot* by yourself. The work of taking orders, collecting money, storing the books, and shipping is probably all going to be your job. Are you up for it? You must believe totally in your book and realize that it is going to take a commitment of not only money but time to deal with advertising, packing, and shipping books. Of course, if you have unlimited resources, you can hire people or companies to fill all these needs.

I've known authors who published their own books, spent hours and hours trying to sell it and thousands of dollars printing it, only to have it taking up space in the garage for years. The last thing you want as an author is to waste your time and money and precious living space on a book that isn't selling. Even if it does sell, you might have other things you'd like to do with your time and your basement. A royalty publisher carries all the responsibility of warehousing and shipping your book so that you can simply write.

Types of Author-Funded Publishing Ventures

If you wish to do your own publishing, you still have options. There are basically three types of publishing that authors can initiate themselves: self-publishing, subsidy publishing, and co-operative publishing.

Self-publishing

Self-publishing is when you take on the task of preparing your book for publication and then pay a printer to produce the books (printing covers, interiors, and binding). In other words, you act as the contractor and pay others as needed to perform the tasks. Thus, after you finish your manuscript, you will hire a copy-editor to proofread and make necessary corrections before it goes to the typesetter. You may pay someone to design a cover, and someone else to do the typesetting and layout. Then you pay the printer to produce the books. Self-publishing includes content and copy-editing, book and jacket design, layout, paste-up, typeface selection, paper selection, printing, binding, calculating press runs, pricing the book, obtaining an ISBN (International Standard Book Number) if you are selling to bookstores, applying for a copyright, publicizing, promoting, etc. You make all the decisions, have complete control over what is done and how, pay all the up-front costs, and also collect all the income from the sales.

The problem with taking this route is that until you have bids on all the services you will not know how much you can expect to pay per book, an important consideration in deciding whether to go this route. For those not wanting the responsibility of comparison shopping and making all these decisions alone, another option is a subsidy publisher.

Subsidy publishing

In subsidy publishing, you find a company that handles all the above steps for the writer and then charges the writer a set fee for the whole process, usually based on so much per copy. Generally speaking your cost will be higher per book than it would be if you self-published, but some of that is offset by the fact that the subsidy publisher already has qualified people to perform all the tasks needed and knows where to go to get the best service for the best price. As the need for subsidy publishers has grown, so has the quality of their work and the services they offer. Whereas vanity houses used to collect high prices and leave the author with a garage full of sometimes inferior-quality books, today's best subsidy publishers produce a first-quality product and offer some help with distribution. A few even offer a toll-free number and services to fill phone or mail orders. The cost for the publishing and extra services varies quite a bit, so you will want to do some comparison shopping. Subsidy publishers should be happy to give you an estimate.

One other difference in subsidy publishers is that some will publish any book you are willing to pay for, while others are almost as selective as a royalty publisher on the manuscripts they will accept.

Before signing a contract with a subsidy publisher, check out a number of the books they have published previously and ask for references of authors they have worked with. A reputable subsidy publisher will be happy to give you this information.

Although it used to be almost unheard of for a distributor or large chain to handle a subsidy-published book, today they are usually happy to carry them as long as they are well done, meet certain standards for size, and have a definable audience. In other words, if they think they can sell them. If your book has regional interest, stores in that region will usually be willing to carry it, even if it is not carried nationally. Internet stores, such as *Amazon.com* will also carry them for you, so you do not have to maintain your own website unless you want to.

Cooperative publishing

There is at least one other option for getting your book published, and that is what is usually called a cooperative publisher or a cooperative arrangement. This is a cross between a royalty publisher and a subsidy publisher. Publishers offer a variety of different cooperative options, but usually they produce the book and have you pay for the number of copies you want, but they pay for and sell the rest. For example, a cooperative publisher might agree to publish your book with a print run of 5,000. You agree to pay for 2,000 copies that you feel you will be able to sell yourself, and the publisher keeps, advertises, distributes, and sells the remaining 3,000. In some cases you will get a royalty on the books they sell, and sometimes not. Those details will be covered in your contract and must be considered carefully.

This arrangement can be an advantage to you over self-publishing or subsidy publishing because you have to pay only for the number of books you actually want, while getting the lower cost per book that comes with a bigger print run.

Conclusion

Because each of the above options offers both advantages and disadvantages to the writer looking for an alternative to the royalty publisher, you need to be very careful before entering into any agreement or committing to such a large project. Go in with your eyes open, seek as much help as you can find, do some comparison shopping, run the numbers, and know exactly what the costs will be to determine which, if any, of these options fits your needs (and pocketbook) the best.

The bottom line here is that this is not a decision that you can make lightly or based on emotion. It must be a sound business decision based on your resources and a realistic projection of salability. If you have a good book with an *easily* definable and reachable audience, then you will likely pay back your investment quickly and make some money besides. If it is a poor or mediocre book, you could be stuck with a big publishing bill and enough boxes of books to build your own fort. (See the "Resources" section at the end of this book for sources of more information.)

Appendix A

Glossary of Terms*

Advance. Amount of money a publisher pays an author, usually before a book is published. This money is deducted from the book's royalties after publication.

All rights. An outright sale of your material. By selling all rights, the author has no further control over the material sold.

Anecdote. A brief account or short story illustrating an idea or point.

Assignment. A piece commissioned by an editor or publisher at an agreed-upon price.

Avant-garde. Experimental and inventive.

Backlist. A list of a publisher's books that were published a year or more ago.

Bar code. Identification code and price on the back of a book, which is read by a scanner at check-out counters.

Bible version abbreviations. Some of the most frequently used Bible versions are, KJV: King James Version; NASV: New American Standard Version; NJB: New Jerusalem Bible; NIV: New International Version; NKJV: New King James Version; NRSV: New Revised Standard Version; RSV: Revised Standard Version.

Bimonthly. Every two months.

Biweekly. Every two weeks.

Bluelines. Printer's proofs. These are pre-press copies used to catch last-minute errors before a book is printed.

Book proposal. Submission of a book idea to an editor, usually includes a cover letter, thesis statement, chapter-by-chapter synopsis, market survey, and 1-3 sample chapters.

Byline. Author's name printed just below the title of a story or article.

Camera-ready copy. Text and/or artwork for a book that is ready for the press.

*For more information about any of these terms, see the index. For terms not listed here, go to this website: *www.writersdigest.com/newsletter/nsswm99glossary.html*

Circulation. The number of copies of each issue of a periodical sold or distributed.

Clips. See *Published clips.*

Column. A regularly appearing feature, section, or department in a periodical. Written by the same person or a different freelancer each time, but usually with the same title.

Contributor's copy. Copy of an issue of a periodical or of a book sent to the author who has written a work or contributed to it.

Copyright. Gives holder legal protection of a work.

Cover letter. An introductory letter that accompanies manuscript submissions.

Critique. An evaluation of a piece of writing.

Devotional. A short piece that attempts to provide spiritual discovery, inspiration, challenge, and/or encouragement.

Editorial guidelines. See *Writer's guidelines.*

Endorsements. Supportive comments regarding a book; usually printed on the back cover or in promotional material.

EPA/Evangelical Press Association. A professional trade organization for periodical publishers and associate members.

E-Proposals. Proposals sent via email.

E-Queries. Queries sent via email.

Essay. A composition, usually expressing the author's opinion on a specific subject.

Feature article. In-depth coverage of a subject, usually focusing on a person, event, process, organization, movement, trend, or issue; written to inform, explain, encourage, help, analyze, challenge, motivate, warn, or entertain.

Filler. A short item used to "fill" out the page of a periodical. For instance, it could be a news item, joke, anecdote, quote, light verse or short humor, puzzle or game.

First rights. A sale of your material for first use.

Foreign rights. Selling or giving permission to translate or reprint published material in a foreign country.

Foreword. Opening remarks in a book (by someone other than the author–often a well-known name) introducing the book and its author.

Freelance. As in "50 percent freelance": means that 50 percent of the material printed in the publication is supplied by freelance writers.

Freelancer or freelance writer. A writer who is not on salary, but sells his or her material to a number of different publishers.

Free verse. Poetry written without any clearly set structure.

Genre. Refers to type or classification, as in fiction or poetry. In fiction, such types as westerns, romances, mysteries, are referred to as *genre fiction.*

Glossy. A black-and-white photo with a shiny finish.

Go-ahead. When a publisher tells you to go ahead and write up or send your article idea.

Haiku. A Japanese poetry form limited to three lines and seventeen syllables.

Holiday/seasonal. A story, article, filler, or book that is related to a specific holiday or season.

Humor. Amusing or comical anecdotes that can add warmth and color to an article or story.

Interdenominational. Material distributed to a number of different church denominations.

International Postal Reply Coupon. See *IRC.*

Interview article. An article based on an interview with a person of interest to a specific readership.

IRC or IPRC. International Postal Reply Coupon for use with mailings to foreign publishers.

ISBN number. International Standard Book Number; the identification code needed for every book.

Journal. A periodical presenting news in a particular area.

Kill fee. A fee paid for a work done on assignment and subsequently not published.

Light verse. Simple, light-hearted poetry.

Mainstream fiction. Fiction that seeks to handle plot, character, and conflict on a deeper level than most genre fiction.

MS. Abbreviation for *manuscript.* (MSS is the plural.)

NASR. North American Serial Rights.

Newsbreak. A newsworthy item sent to a publisher.

Nondenominational. Not associated with a particular denomination.

Not copyrighted. Refers to a publication that does not register its copyright on each issue, or work on which an author has lost copyright protection.

On acceptance. Payment provided for a periodical article at the time of acceptance for publication.

On assignment. Writing something at the specific request of an editor or publisher.

On publication. Payment for an article at the time it is published.

On speculation. Writing for an editor or publisher based on the agreement that he or she will buy it only if he or she likes it.

One-time rights. Selling to any number of publications the right to publish a story for one time only (usually refers to publishing for a non-overlapping readership).

Over-run. Number of extra copies of a book printed during the initial print run.

Payment on acceptance. See *On acceptance.*

Payment on publication. See *On publication.*

Pen name. A name used for writing, in place of one's legal name.

Permissions. Requesting consent to use text or art from a copyrighted source.

Personal experience story. A story based on a real-life experience.

Personality profile. A feature article that highlights a specific person's life or accomplishments.

Photocopied submission. A photocopy submission of your manuscript sent to an editor (rather than an original manuscript).

Press kit. A compilation of promotional materials about a particular book or author, usually organized in a folder and used to publicize a book.

Pseudonym. See *Pen name.*

Published clips. Copies of actual articles a writer has had published.

Quarterly. Every three months.

Query letter. A letter sent to an editor presenting an article or book idea and asking if that editor has interest in the piece.

Reporting time. The number of weeks or months it takes an editor to get back to you about a query or manuscript you have sent in.

Reprint rights. Selling the right to republish an article or book that has already been published elsewhere.

Review copies. Books given to book reviewers, book buyers, radio or TV groups in order to promote that book.

Royalty. The percentage an author is paid by a publisher based on the price and sale of each copy of the author's book.

S.A.E. Self-addressed envelope (without stamps).

SAN. Standard Account Number, used to identify libraries, book dealers, or schools.

S.A.S.E. Self-addressed, stamped envelope. Always sent with a manuscript or query letter.

S.A.S.P. Self-addressed, stamped postcard. Sent with a manuscript submission, the S.A.S.P. is returned by publisher indicating the manuscript's arrival at the publishing house.

Satire. A type of humor, often sarcastic or skeptical, usually used to point out errors or misconceptions or question commonly-held beliefs.

Second serial rights. See *Reprint rights.*

Semiannual. Issued twice a year.

Serial. Refers to publication in a periodical.

Serialization. Breaking a story or article into two or more parts to run in successive issues of a periodical.

Series. A group of books or articles following the same topic or theme. May be written by the same or several different authors.

Sidebar. A short feature that accompanies an article, either elaborating on the piece, quoting from it, or giving additional information on the topic. It is often set apart, appearing within a box or a border.

Simultaneous rights. Rights for one piece sold or offered to several publishers at the same time.

Simultaneous submissions. The same manuscript sent to more than one publisher at the same time.

Slanting. Writing an article and gearing it toward the needs and interests of a particular market.

Speculation. See *On speculation.*

Staff-written material. Material written by the staff members of a publishing house.

Subsidiary rights. Rights—other than book rights—included in the book's contract and controlled by the book's publisher. This includes such things as paperback, book club, and movie rights.

Subsidy publisher. A book publisher who is paid by the author to publish the author's book (different from a royalty publisher, who pays the author).

Tabloid. A newspaper-format publication about half the size of a regular newspaper.

Take-home paper. A weekly or monthly periodical published for Sunday school students, children through adults.

Think piece. A magazine article taking an intellectual, philosophical, or provocative approach to a subject.

Transparencies. Positive color slides (not color prints).

Trade magazine. A magazine targeted to a particular trade or business.

Traditional verse. Poetry with one or more verses written with an established pattern that is repeated throughout.

Unsolicited manuscripts. A manuscript sent to an editor unrequested.

Vanity publisher. A publisher that will publish any book if production cost is paid by the author, and usually at a higher rate than charged by subsidy publishers.

Vita. An outline of one's work experience and personal history; a résumé.

Work-for-hire assignment. Writing commissioned by a publisher at an agreed-upon price, usually in a one-time payment that is not based upon a royalty. The writer gives the publisher full ownership and control of the material written as a work-for-hire assignment.

Writers' guidelines. An information sheet provided by a publisher that provides specific guidelines for writing or submitting material to that publisher.

Appendix B
Topical Index and Resources for Writers

Following you will find an alphabetical list of topics that are included in this book. Simply read through the list until you come to the topic you want and it will tell you on what page you will find it.

Topical Index

Resources for Writers

Finding the right resources to answer your questions on writing and selling can be frustrating. That is why I have written this book and set it up the way I have—to make it as easy as possible to find those answers. Over the years, I have also developed a variety of additional resources for writers, or found resources written by other Christian writers and teachers that cover areas I wasn't able to.

Below you will find a list of those resources, along with prices and ordering information. Those with an asterisk in front of them may be found at your local bookstore. The others can be purchased directly from me.

Ordering Information

Next to each of the following titles you will find the price, including postage. To order any of these, send your name, address, phone number, and e-mail address (if you have one), with a check or money order to: Sally Stuart, 1647 SW Pheasant Dr., Aloha, OR 97006; or order by credit card through Pay Pal from Website: www.stuartmarket.com. Credit card orders can only be accepted on the Website.

Fiction Resources

1. **The Complete Guide to Writing & Selling the Christian Novel,* Penelope Stokes (Cincinnati, OH; Writer's Digest Books, 1998) ISBN 0-89879-810-8.
2. **Getting Into Character,* Brandilyn Collins (New York, NY; John Wiley & Sons, 2002) ISBN 0-471-05894-7.
3. *How to Write and Sell a Christian Novel,* Gilbert Morris; $15 postpaid.
4. *The Professional Way to Create Characters,* Daniel E. Kline; $5 postpaid.
5. *The Professional Way to Write Dialogue,* Daniel E. Kline; $5 postpaid.

General Helps

1. *The Complete Guide to Christian Writing & Speaking,* edited by Susan Titus Osborn; $15 postpaid.

2. *A Complete Guide to Writing for Publication,* edited by Susan Titus Osborn; $18 postpaid.
3. **How to Write What You Love and Make a Living At It,* Dr. Dennis E. Hensley (Colorado Springs, CO; Shaw Books, 2000) ISBN 0-87788-174-X.
4. *Just Write!,* Susan Titus Osborn; $15 postpaid.

Internet Resources

1. *Electronic Research Sites & How to Use Them,* Deborah Page; $13 postpaid.
2. *Internet Directory of Christian Publishers.* Lists Websites or e-mail for all publishers who have them (over 100 not in the market guide); $9.50 postpaid.
3. **WriterSpeaker.com,* Carmen Leal (Colorado Springs, CO; Shaw Books, 2000) ISBN 0-87788-876-0.

Legal Concerns

1. *Copyright Law: What You Don't Know Can Cost You;* $18 postpaid.
2. *Permissions Packet.* Contains specific guidelines on how and when to ask permission to quote from other sources or Bible paraphrases; $6 postpaid.
3. *Totally Honest Tax Tips for Writers,* Sandy Cathcart; $10 postpaid.

Marketing Resources

1. *Agents: What You Need to Know,* Cecil Murphey; $5 postpaid.
2. **Christian Writers' Market Guide,* Sally E. Stuart (Colorado Springs, CO; Shaw Books) (Updated annually, released in January each year). ISBN changes annually.
3. *Christian Writers' Market Guide* on 3½" disk, ASCII, full text, not in a data base; $30 postpaid.
4. *Top 50 Magazine Marketing Packet.* Includes writers' guidelines and analysis sheets for the top 50 writer-friendly publications; $25 postpaid.
5. *A Marketing Plan for More Sales,* Sally Stuart; $5 postpaid.
6. *How to Submit an Article or Story to a Publisher,* Susan Titus Osborn; $5 postpaid.
7. *How to Submit a Book Proposal to a Publisher,* Susan Titus Osborn; $5 postpaid.
8. *Keeping Track of Your Periodical Manuscripts,* $5 postpaid.
9. *Keeping Track of Your Book Manuscripts,* $5 postpaid.

Nonfiction Resources

1. *The Art of Researching the Professional Way,* Kay Marshall Strom; $5 postpaid.
2. **Effective Magazine Writing,* Roger C. Palms (Colorado Springs, CO; Shaw Books, 2000) ISBN 0-87788-211-8.
3. *How to Write That Sure-Sell Magazine Article,* Susan Titus Osborn; $5 postpaid.
4. *How to Write the Personal Experience Article,* Susan Titus Osborn; $5 postpaid.

5. *Interviewing the Professional Way,* Kay Marshall Strom; $5 postpaid.
6. **Write on Target,* Dennis Hensley and Holly Miller, (Boston, MA; The Writer Inc., 1995) ISBN 0-87116-177-X.

Self-Promotion

1. *Savvy Approach to Book Sales,* Elaine Wright Colvin; $13 postpaid.
2. *You Can Market Your Book,* Carmen Leal; $18 postpaid.

Specialty Resources

1. *The Christian Poet,* Kristen Ingram; $13 postpaid.
2. *Getting the Most Out of Writing Conferences,* D.B. Zane; $6 postpaid.
3. *How to Develop a Professional Writers' Group,* Barbara J. Normandin; $5 postpaid.
4. *How to Write a Picture Book,* Susan Titus Osborn; $5 postpaid.
5. *How to Write Daily Devotionals That Inspire,* Susan Titus Osborn; $5 postpaid.
6. *Managing Stress as a Freelance Writer,* Dennis Hensley; $5 postpaid.
7. *Screenwriting for Christian Writers,* Barbara Nicolosi/Act One; $16 postpaid.
8. *Time Management for Writers,* Dennis Hensley; $5 postpaid.
9. *Writing and Selling Comedy and Humor,* Dennis Hensley; $5 postpaid.
10. *Writing for Young Adults the Professional Way,* Kay Marshall Strom; $5 postpaid.
11. *Writing Junior Books the Professional Way,* Kay Marshall Strom; $5 postpaid.

Spiritual Helps for Writers

1. **How to Keep a Spiritual Journal,* Ron Klug, (Minneapolis, MN; Augsburg, 2002) ISBN 0-8066-4357-9.
2. *100 Plus Motivational Moments for Christian Writers & Speakers,* compiled by Donna Goodrich, Mary Lou Klinger & Jan Potter; $13 postpaid.
3. *Write His Answer,* Marlene Bagnull; $14 postpaid.

Index

A

B

I

J

K

L

M

N

O

P

Q

R

S

T